Cusmanos

From Terrasini to Detroit

Volume I: The Cousinbook

by Lee Bothwell

ISBN: 1985820129
ISBN-13: 978-1985820128

Research never ends, but at some point you simply have to draw a line under it and report on your discoveries.

I started this project with two goals in mind: to learn more about our grandfather, and to discover if and how he was related to the other Cusmanos in Detroit. He died when Gary and I were 2, before the rest of his grandchildren were born, and we never got to hear his stories - we heard stories *about* him, but not the stories he carried inside himself, from the past. And because he, like other successful immigrants, moved away from the old neighborhood, we missed out on the communal stories too.

The documents I've found are no substitute for family stories, but they do provide a general sense of his place in the world. His family lived in the same area of Sicily for at least 500 years, and in the same little town [Terrasini] for 300. They seemed to be part of the professional class and they intermarried with families of that same class - the same handful of families, generation after generation. Some of our more distant relatives attained the status of "Don" - although I'm not sure whether that is a good or a bad thing. Our particular branch slipped a bit socially, into the artisan class (they were bakers). But they were never the poorest of the poor, and they still married into the same group of families. Our family - our grandfather - was part of an intimately and intricately connected network.

And then he was not.

Our great-grandfather was the restless spirit: first he moved halfway across Sicily, to Mazzara, and then halfway across the world, to Detroit. Our grandfather joined him there - whether he wanted to or not - when he was only 7 years old; the rest of the family arrived within a few years. And not only his immediate family - at least 15 of his first cousins came to Detroit as well. Some of the other Detroit Cusmanos were more distantly related, third and fifth cousins. And while I was correcting the proofs of this book, I discovered two earlier ancestors, so now our family not only extends back to the 1520s, it also extends horizontally to include some previously unconnected Detroiters, who are 8th or 9th cousins.

But although the network seemingly reconstituted itself in Detroit, in fact it did not. Many of the younger generation married non-Sicilians and moved to the suburbs and beyond. And the stories were lost.

I originally intended to put everything I discovered into one book, but it turned out to be too bulky, so this volume contains only information about our direct line and about Great-grandpa's first cousins. I think of it as "the cousinbook." If I can manage it, I intend to make a second volume with everything else - the rest of the Detroit Cusmanos for sure, and, if there is room, the collateral lines which remained in Sicily.

About the transcriptions of Sicilian church records:

These are available online for free from Family Search. (You might have to register, but that is a one-time deal, and is free.)
Go to search -> catalog -> Italy, Palermo, Terrasini Favarotta -> church records -> "registri ecclesastici . . ." -> the notes to this last entry say "available online, click here" - do so -> "browse through . . ." -> then you come to a list of towns, choose Terrasini Favarotta -> click on the parish "Maria Sanctissima delle Grazie" -> and - finally - you are at a list of all the films available. Phew.

I have not provided actual transcriptions, for a variety of reasons. What I have done is to extract names and dates, and I have made two editorial decisions:
1. If the record was in Latin, I used the nominative case for all the names (except sometimes when I forgot and used Italian).
2. I ignored the spelling of the last name, abbreviating it to C or G.

A baptism might appear like this:
 219 = 145 = 7 May 1644 - HOnofrio C - Salvatore & Rosolea.
The first number refers to the IMAGE number of the film, the second number is the page number of the actual volume that was filmed, then the date of baptism - then comes the name of the child, when born (if given - eg b today, yesterday, 3 days, the other day) - then the names of the parents - then in parentheses, the name of the godparent/s (if given). The marriages and deaths follow a similar format.

A proper footnote for a digital record is an incredibly bulky thing, so, since they all came from the same website, I have condensed them. [The Archives of the Archdiocese of Palermo is the ultimate source.] I think I have provided enough information for you to find the records - and if you are interested you should look them up yourself - mistakes are almost inevitable.

Good luck!

I. Introductory Material

A brief history of Sicily

Greeks

The history of Sicily starts with the Greeks. There were people there earlier, of course: there are cave paintings, and people known as Sicels and/or Siculs, and Thucydides mentions that some refugees from Troy settled there, but History, written down and remembered history, starts with the Greeks, in the 700s BCE. They established city-states, mostly on the southern and eastern sides of the island, and took part in the conflicts and cultural ferment of the Greek world.

> ". . . [T]hey gradually dislodged - without actually eliminating - the indigenous inhabitants, together with a number of Phoenician trading posts; they introduced the olive and the vine, and rapidly built up a flourishing community. This soon became one of the major cultural centers of the civilized world, the home of poets such as Stesichorus of Himera - he whom the gods struck blind for composing invectives against Helen of Troy - and philosophers such as the great Empedocles of Acragas [modern Agrigento], who did much valuable work on the transmigration of souls and, having already served a long and tedious apprenticeship as a shrub, suddenly relinquished his mortal clay for higher things one morning in 440 B.C., when another branch of scientific inquiry led him too far into the crater of Mt Etna." [1]

There are in Sicily, even today, some of the finest Greek temples in the world.

Carthaginians -> Rome

The Carthaginians became involved in some of the conflicts of the Greek Sicilians (there were also Greek settlements on the mainland of Italy which were mixed up in it all too). They had trading interests in the area, and were called on for help by one side or the other when the local rivalries flared up. Which - inevitably - brings us to Rome.

When Carthage was destroyed in 146 B.C., Sicily became a Roman province.

> "A few Greek cities managed to retain a measure of independence, but much of the island was taken over by the *latifundia*: those vast landed estates, owned by absentee Roman landlords, setting a pattern of land

---

[1] John Julius Norwich, *Sicily: an island at the crossroads of history* (New York: Random House, 2015), 4.

tenure which was to ruin Sicilian agriculture for the next 2,000 years. Liberty, meanwhile, was almost extinguished as the slave gangs toiled naked in the fields, sowing and harvesting grain for Rome."[2]

Although other provinces also sent grain to Rome, Sicily remained a major supplier. It was prosperous (the owners at least) and "quite astonishingly well-behaved."[3] There had been slave revolts in 139 and 104 B.C., but after they were put down - and after Augustus had punished the Sicilians for supporting Pompey - things calmed down. Little is known about Sicily for the rest of the Roman period.

Post-Rome -> Byzantine (Greeks)->Arabs -> Normans -> Spanish

Sicily was taken over briefly by the Vandals (468), and then the Byzantines arrived (535).

"Belisarius arrived in Sicily in 535, where he was almost universally welcomed. The exception was Palermo . . . ."[4]

Thus began the Byzantine rule of Sicily, which continued for 300 years or so. Then in 827, the local Byzantine governor revolted, and appealed to the Arabs for help. "They landed in strength, rapidly entrenched themselves, took little notice of Euphemius [the Byzantine] - who soon came to a violent end - and three years later stormed Palermo, making it their capital."[5]

Sicily did not suffer under Arab rule: they were civilized and tolerant; they brought in important crops (eggplant!) and agricultural practices (terracing, aqueducts), but they did quarrel among themselves. Because of their local rivalries, the Byzantines thought they might have a chance to retake the island, so they hired Norman mercenaries, which is, generally speaking, a bad move. In 1072, the Normans made their formal entry into Palermo - which had gone from being a "small port of secondary importance"[6] under the Byzantines to the capital of Arabic Sicily. It remained the capital under the Normans, who decided to rule for themselves rather than for the Byzantines.

If Sicily did not suffer under the Arabs, it positively flourished under the Normans. This was Sicily's golden age: it became a center of learning and culture. The Normans were tolerant, and managed to blend the different strains that made up Sicily: Arabs were in charge of the treasury, because they were the best mathematicians; a Greek was the head of the navy, because the Greeks were the best sailors. Unfortunately they ran out of

---

[2]Norwich, *Sicily*, 37.
[3]Norwich, *Sicily*, 51.
[4]Norwich, *Sicily*, 57.
[5]Norwich, *Sicily*, 58.
[6]Norwich, *Sicily*, 57.

legitimate male heirs, and after only a hundred years or so, Sicily became a football in international politics. The legal heir was Constance, who was married to Henry of Hohenstaufen: the Popes didn't like him and proclaimed Charles of Anjou the ruler of Sicily in 1266. The Sicilians revolted, were put down and punished until "by 1282, the Angevins had made themselves cordially detested throughout the Regno, both for the severity of their taxation and for the arrogance of their conduct. . . ."[7] This is when the "Sicilian Vespers" occurred. A Sicilian woman was propositioned by a French soldier, just outside of church, just as the bells were ringing for vespers; her husband killed him, a riot ensued, and by morning 2000 Frenchmen were dead.

Things were in an uproar for the next several years. The legal ruler (to the Sicilians) was Peter of Aragon, who was married to another woman of the Norman line, also named Constance. But the Popes remained set against them:

> The Papacy too had to look to its prestige, since Sicily and the Regno had been granted to Charles of Anjou by Pope Urban. That was why, immediately after the Vespers, Pope Martin IV - another Frenchman - had excommunicated Peter and laid the island under an interdict. Shortly afterward he went even further, declaring Peter deposed and deprived of his dominions, which he theoretically bestowed on King Phillip [France]'s younger son, the Count of Valois.[8]

It wasn't until 1301 that things were more or less settled, and the Spanish took over for good - for the next 400 years, during which, as Norwich says, nothing much happened. The Sicilians were given promises of a yearly parliament, and their consent was [supposed to be] necessary before war or peace was made - or new taxes imposed. On the other hand, the Spanish were not tolerant or cultured: they (eventually) expelled all the Jews and imported the Inquisition.

I think it was sometime between 1300 and 1600 that our people came to Sicily.

Once again there was a failure of heirs. After the War of the Spanish Succession (1701-1715?), Sicily again became a token on the board of international politics, and this time it wasn't the Popes who interfered so much as the "major powers:" Britain, France, Russia, Austria. Sicily was granted to Savoy, then Austria, then finally to Spain again - well, to the segment of the Spanish who ruled Naples. (It was part of the "Kingdom of the two Sicilies.") I'm not sure how happy anyone was, but things went

---

[7]Norwich, *Sicily* 125.
[8]Norwich, *Sicily*, 128-9.

swimmingly until Napoleon came on the scene.

Napoleon and the Bourbons

Napoleon made his brother-in-law, Joachim Murat, King of the two Sicilies. Whatever you might think of Napoleon as a tyrant, his government/s did in a way support the ideals of the French Revolution: liberty, equality, fraternity. In 1812, feudalism was outlawed in Sicily.

This came to an end in 1815, with the final defeat of Napoleon. The Great Powers turned Sicily back over to the reactionary Spanish Bourbons (the ones who had ruled before Napoleon). They were - did I mention this - reactionary, and rolled back all the liberal reforms passed by the Napoleons. This led to wide-spread discontent, and a revolt broke out in Spain in 1820, led by liberal military officers: the King capitulated more or less instantly. The Great Powers did not like this, but Spain was a long way away, so they let things slide. But when the revolt spread to Naples, well. That was too close to the Austrian territories in northern Italy, and the revolt was suppressed, mostly by Austria. Sicily had joined in the rebellion, but less in support of liberalism and more in protest of social conditions: "the people of Sicily wanted food, land, and freedom from oppressive taxation."[9]

There was a lot of unrest all during the 1800s. The revolt of 1820 was brutally repressed, and in 1837, the eastern cities of Catania and Siracusa had a try - also unsuccessful. In 1848, the year of revolution all over Europe, the insurgents actually won for a while: they proclaimed a provisional government in Palermo with a constitution and an elected parliament. This lasted only 18 months, and when it was put down the parliament was abolished and even more taxes were imposed. The people involved - and their families - were severely punished. A lot of them found it necessary to run for the hills and become bandits.

It was these bandits who were the backbone of Garibaldi's army in Sicily. They in fact had made another attempt to take Palermo in April of 1860 and this possibly helped convince Garibaldi that an invasion of Sicily might be possible.

Garibaldi landed in May, and by July the Bourbons were out.

Unification

Sicilians who had fought with Garibaldi naturally thought they would get to have some say in their government thereafter, and that things would

---

[9]What-When-How: In Depth Tutorials and Information, "Sicilian Revolutions of 1820 and 1848: women and the role women played by women in nineteenth-century revolutions in Sicily"
(http://what-when-how.com/women-and-war/sicilian-revolutions-of-1820-and-1848-women-and-the/ : accessed 1 June 2017).

improve. Alas, no. Garibaldi turned over the country to King Victor Emmanuele of Sardinia-Piedmont (also Duke of Savoy), and the Sicilians were once again ruled by outsiders. The Piedmontese had nothing in common with the Sicilians (including language) and considered them backward - northern Italians to this day tend to despise Sicilians. New taxes were imposed (people who had been too poor to be taxed by the Bourbons now found themselves having to pay), universal military service was required, and land reform turned out to be a joke: the land was not distributed to the peasants, but sold to the highest bidder(s), who worked to bring all local power into their own hands. Because the Piedmontese cared so little for Sicily, except as a source of revenue, they (the highest bidders) succeeded, and the Mafia was born. These locals (Mafiosi) blocked any liberal policies enacted by the national government (free education, for example) and in general made life even worse for everyone else.

And so people started leaving.

Between 1876 and 1924, seventeen million Italians emigrated abroad; Italy's entire population in 1900 was less than forty million. The vast majority of the emigrants, like my grandparents, were from the south. In the decade before 1910, the year my grandfather sailed from Palermo, two million Sicilians - over half of the island's population - abandoned their ancestral villages for the uncertainties of an immigrant's life.

Eighty-five percent of Sicilians were landless agricultural laborers in 1900, walking up to ten miles per day to work others' fields. Just under 90 percent of the island had passed into the hands of absentee landowners. The population density of the island was 438 people to the square mile, ten times that of the United States and greater than the population density of China or India.

Hence, the explosion, massive and unprecedented emigration, the cresting of one of the greatest human floods in history: nine million Italians to the Americas; seven and a half million to northern Europe; another five hundred thousand to Asia and Africa.[10]

Our people left with the 2 million other Sicilians, in the 1900-1910s.

---

[10]Frank Viviano, *Blood Washes Blood : a true story of love, murder, and redemption under the Sicilian Sun* (New York: Washington Square Press (published by Pocket Books), 2001), p. 46.

Timeline of Sicilian History

Prehistory
>   cave paintings
>   Tribes: Sican, Siculian, Ausonians, Elymians (refugees from Troy, according to Thucydides)
>   part of Mycenean trade network (~1400 BC-1200 BC)
>   later, part of Phoenecian trade network

Greeks
>   most important settlements in the east and south
>   landed at Acragas [Agrigento] 734 BC
>   - 1st permanent settlement Gela 688 BC
>   brought in Olives, Grapes
>   natives "dislodged" - as well as Phoenecian trading posts
>   took important part in wars, culture of Greek world

Carthaginians
>   became involved in local Sicilian rivalries
>   later, wars with Rome involved the Sicilians
>   destroyed by Rome 146 BC -> Sicily becomes Roman province

Romans
>   cut down forests to grow wheat (for export to Rome)
>   created latifundia - large estates - which became standard for Sicily (except in some eastern areas) *These large estates were a major contributing factor to the rise of the Mafia many years later.*
>   slave labor -> slave revolts -> repression
>   Sicilians, except for a few cities (including Palermo), were not made citizens

Barbarians
>   Rome invaded by barbarians who are not much interested in Sicily - except for Vandals who take it over for about 8 years

Byzantines (Greek)
>   Justinian expands Eastern Empire, Sicily becomes part of it (535 - General Belisarius)

Arabs
>   827, invited to help local Byzantine Governor in rebellion against Empire
>   ~830 - made Palermo their capital
>   religious tolerance, culture, trade
>   - terracing, aqueducts - cotton, papyrus, melon, pistachio, citrus, date palm, sugar-cane, eggplant
>   Favarotta is probably named from "fawar," Arabic for "fountain"

Normans

 local rivalries - civil war 1035 - Byzantines see chance to take back Sicily, use Norman mercenaries

 ~1059 - given dukedoms of Apulia, Calabria, Sicily by Pope (who did not own them)

 1072 - formal entry into Palermo

 religious tolerance, culture, trade

 This is Sicily's (second) golden age

Swabians (Hohenstaufen)

 Norman heiress (Constance) married to Henry of Hohenstaufen
  (s/o Frederick Barbarossa)

 Popes don't like them - give Sicily to Charles of Anjou 1266

French

 Sicilians revolt against Pope's decision (1267) -> brutal suppression, govt reorganized,   land confiscated ->

 Sicilian Vespers 1282 March 30 - massacre of 2000 Frenchmen

 1285 Charles of Anjou dies

Spanish

 Peter of Aragon (married to Norman/Hohenstaufen heiress) = de facto King of Sicily

 Popes refuse to recognize him and continue to try to give Sicily to Angevins - treaty 1295

 Sicilians refuse to accept it - finally treaty 1301 - Sicily to Aragon (provisionally)

 nothing much happens for the next 400 years[11]

 1347 - the Black Death

 1428 - King Alfonso V ordered Sicily's Jews to convert to Catholicism

 1492 - 100,000 Jews expelled from Sicily

 1516 - full scale popular uprising in Palermo -> ~1523 -> nothing

 1571 - Battle of Lepanto - Turkish fleet destroyed BUT piracy along the Barbary coast

  -> 2-3 major raids each year "no farmhouse within ten miles of the sea was safe"[12] - 1559, 1574 - raids on the outskirts of Palermo itself

1582 - Lorenzo di Cosimano, son of Antonio/Andrea, baptized in Carini
  [so probably they were there earlier]

---

[11]After 1292, Sicily "became a colony of Spain, and for the next four centuries or so *virtually nothing happened.* [italics in text] Viceroys came and went, the barons continued to exploit the peasantry, but there were so few important events that a detailed chronological account becomes impossible." John Julius Norwich, *Sicily: an island at the crossroads of history* (New York: Random House, 2015), xiv.

[12]Ibid., 132

1614-1648 - Thirty Years' War

1647 - crop failures, export of food, rising prices -> revolt -> nothing

1669 - Mt Etna erupted at least twice, killing 35,000

1674 - revolt in Messina - appeal to France

1674 - 1ˢᵗ mention of a Gusmano in church records of Cinisi

1694 - Mt Etna erupted

1701 - 1715? - War of the Spanish succession

1712 - Treaty of Utrecht -> Sicily to Victor Amadeus of Savoy
    1718 Spain again - v Austria

1720 - Treaty of London - Sicily part of HRE (Austria)
    Bourbons

1732 - our ancestor Giovanni married Anna Maria Purpura in Cinisi, but he was said to be "of Favarotta;" many of their children lived in Terrasini/Favarotta.

1735 - Spain again (Naples) - Spanish Bourbons
    at first Sicilians are happy enough with the Spanish, but
    eventually they come to hate them

1798 - King & Queen Palermo

1799 - French defeat K&Q -> riots -> lose

1806 - Brits effectively rule Sicily - King back

Napoleon and after

1808-1815 Joachim Murat (Napoleon's b-in-law) becomes king of
Naples & Sicily - liberal policies, "liberty, equality etc."

1812 - abolition of feudalism

1815 - Napolean defeated, reactionary policies restored
    Spanish Bourbons (Naples) again

1820 - rebellion -> put down by (mostly) Austria

1848 - Sicilians in Palermo proclaimed a Provisional Government
    - constitution, elected parliament - survived only 18 mo.
    -> brutal reprisals, parliament abolished, crippling food taxes ->
    banditry

1860 - Italian unification

April - attempt by locals to storm Palermo - cease fire April 17
    (Giuseppe Badalamenti, Cinisi)

May 11 - Garibaldi lands at Marsala

May 15 - peasants join Garibaldi and slaughter the Bourbon army

July 20 - Bourbons leave Sicily

Unification (1861->)

not self-rule, but rule from Piedmont - a place with entirely different
    history, problems

new taxes (some people too poor to pay taxes to Bourbons are now
    taxed), which mostly benefit northern Italy

requirement for national military service

land reform -> local barons sell out to highest bidders, who are not
    interested in implementing the (few) helpful measures from
    Piedmont (free education eg)
    -> under the Bourbons, local big-wigs had been kept somewhat
    in check by the national govt, but under Piedmont, the locals
    soon gain control of all local government, power

=> this is the beginning of the Mafia

HOWEVER - the new regime also established the constitutional right
    to travel whenever and wherever desired
    -> massive emigration (by 1870, politicians were beginning to
    worry about it)

1868 - Mt Etna erupted

1885-1909 - our family seemed to alternate between living in Mazzara and Terrasini

    1890s - national Italian govt wanted to become 1ˢᵗ class power ->
    enlarge army, navy -> more taxes (Italians were "the most taxed
    people in Europe"[13]) -> more emigration

1901 - Great Grandpa Giovanni emigrated[14]

1903 - Grandpa Jack emigrated[15]

1905 - Giovanni's daughters, Maria Assunta[16] and Rosalia[17] emigrated

    1904-1908 -series of earthquakes - (1908 -Messina - 70-100K people
    died)

    agricultural disasters - olives and grapes infested with parasites &
    decimated

---

[13]Jerre Mangione and Ben Morreale, *La Storia: five centuries of the Italian American experience* (New York: Harper Perennial, 1993), p. 72.

[14]Manifest, *Karamania*, 25 November 1901, page 205, line 16, Giovanni Gusmano, 41; images, "Passenger Lists, 1820-1957," *Ancestry.com* (http: ancestry.com: accessed 6 September 2016). The page had been taped, and the tape made the image quite difficult to read.

[15]Manifest, *Nord America*, 7 May 1903, page 33, line 14, Giovanni Gusmano, 7; images, "Passenger Lists, 1820-1957," *Ancestry.com* (http: ancestry.com: accessed 6 September 2016).

[16]*Statue of Liberty - Ellis Island Foundation*, database with images (http://www.ellisisland.org : accessed 3 September 2016), "Ship Manifest: Manifest for *Lombardia*," handwritten on form, entry for Maria Cusumano, age 22, arrived 21 April 1905.

[17]Manifest, *Neapolitan Prince*, 2 September 1905, p.51, line 17, Rosalia Cusumano, age 19; images, "New York Passenger Lists, 1820-1957," *Ancestry.com* (http://ancestry.com: accessed 27 August 2016).

1909 - Chris and Grandma Lena emigrated[18]
    1943 - Brits & Americans invade Sicily
    1944 - Americans turn over control to anti-fascists = Mafia

---

[18]Manifest, *Regina d'Italia*, 16 June 1909, page 168, line 9, Cristofaro Cusumano, 9; images, "Passenger Lists, 1820-1957," *Ancestry.com* (http: ancestry.com: accessed 6 September 2016).

Geography: Terrasini, Favarotta, Cinisi
and Carini

These are three closely related villages or hamlets about 19 miles west of Palermo, on the Gulf of Castellamare. Favarotta is right on the water, Terrasini is a little inland, and Cinisi is even further inland, on a hillside overlooking a fertile valley. The area was important in Roman times; there have been found some late-Roman docks, as well as pottery, and it is possible that it was known as Cetaria "the place where they catch tuna" - certainly tuna-fishing is of major importance today.

The Arabs (829-1072 - more or less) loved Cinisi for its excellent agricultural land and pastures, and made it a stronghold, which the Normans took only after a long siege. It survived the Normans, but was destroyed when the Swabians/Hohenstaufens took over - after another fierce resistance. After 1250 the area became "tcnimcnta terrarum" - without population or stable settlement structures. The land was owned by various baronial families, but not much use was made of it, until about 1610, although some resettlement of Cinisi was done in the 1300s, when it was donated to the Monastery of San Martino delle Scale.

Favarotta, named for the spring that rises nearby (from the Arabic "fawar," meaning "fountain"), was settled by fishermen. It was separated from Terrasini (which was a little agricultural settlement) by the Gifina river, which was later filled in and disappeared. The two towns were officially merged in 1836,[19] but the area was called Terrasini-Favarotta long before that. In fact, the whole area was apparently known as Terrasini as far back as the 1200s.

> ". . . [I]nvisible borders . . . separated the upper village of Terrasini from the fishing hamlet of Favarotta and the surrounding rural countryside. On a conventional map, the three districts were knitted into the illusion of a single community. In reality, they were distinct social worlds. They had their own dialects. They observed the feast days of their own saints. And they had married by those divisions,

---

[19] 1836 "The village of Favarotta ceases to belong to the town of Cinisi, remaining aggregate as far as the seashore to the town of Terrasini. The town of Cinisi preserves the entire its current territory." {"Collezione delle Leggi e de' decreti reali del Regno delle Due Sicilie" [" The Collection of Laws and of royal decrees of the Kingdom of the Two Sicilies], Naples, 1836: 85}.

until very recently, as though the Piazza Duomo and the municipal limits were unbreachable ramparts.

   Buggisi cu buggisi, viddanu cu viddanu, marinaru cu marinaru, the village code proclaimed. "Merchant with merchant, peasant with peasant, fisherman with fisherman."[20]

Cinisi seems to have been the largest of the three settlements in the 1600s, and the church there, Santa Fara Virgine, served all three. Church records for Santa Fara start in 1672. The main church in Terrasini, Maria Sanctissima delle Grazie, was built in - well, I've seen different dates, 1663, 1683, 1684 - but the church records there start only in 1736. Both Santa Fara and Mara SS delle Grazie were mother churches; there was also a daughter church, Santa Rosalia, which seems to have served mostly Favarotta - it is referred to as Santa Rosalia Favarotta, Santa Rosalia Cinisi, Santa Rosalia Suburbi (I *think* all those names refer to the same church). Santa Rosalia's records were sometimes copied to Maria SS delle Grazie, and when the church ceased to exist (? - it is not on the list of current Terrasini churches) the remaining records were stored there. Our ancestors appear in the records for all three churches.

And then there is Carini: our ancestors were there earlier, but I only found out about it later. It too is west of Palermo, not quite as far as Cinisi. It seems to have been always a named place, and has been identified as the ancient city of Hykkara (of the Sikals) which was conquered by the Athenians, and the inhabitants massacred or enslaved. Later, it was an important diocese of the Byzantines; later it was mentioned in Arab histories and geographies; later still, a Norman castle was built there. The mother church was built in the late 1400s (I assume this was Maria SS Assunta?) and completed in the late 1700s.[21] (Another source says it was created as a parish in 1523 - although I cannot now find that source, sigh.) Our ancestors appear in the records of Carini from 1556 as Cosimano, Cosmano, or di Cosimano. And occasionally, I have just [July 2018] discovered, Ambotta!

---

[20]Viviano, *Blood washes blood*, 53.
[21]http://www.italythisway.com/places/carini.php

About the Gusmano/Cusmanos

The name has been spelled in many different ways over the years. The earliest records I have found, in Carini, in the 1500s, spell it di Cosimano - and after a while it becomes Cosimano without the "di." In Cinisi and Terrasini, the name is most often spelled Cusmano, with Cusumano a common variant, and very occasionally Cusimano. In the mid-1800s the variant "Gusmano" became common. ALL these variants appear in the US records, as well as others - the name can be found with any vowel in any position in the name - including some that are just plain wrong (Cassamano, Casnav!). Over time, different branches of the family chose different variants to become standard for them. It was (according to our family lore) Grandma Ruth who decided to make the name into "Cusman," and supposedly it was because she didn't want her family to be confused with other, less law-abiding, Cusmanos.

After I found out that there was a Spanish name, Guzmán, I jumped to the conclusion that that must have been the original form of our name, and that our people had come to Sicily with the Spaniards in the late 1200s/early 1300s. I am no longer so sure of that: if that were the case, shouldn't the Gusmano variant be the earliest one? I have found no records to support or disprove this idea, so it remains just another possibility.

[The Spaniards arrived in the late 1200s, after the Sicilian Vespers (1282)[22] had made it clear that the French were not going to be acceptable to the Sicilians. They were in control (well, they were the official rulers) for the next 400 years, during which time, as one historian says, nothing much happened.]

Our people seem to have lived in Carini first (records from 1556) and then they moved to Cinisi (sometime before 1684) and then to Favarotta and Terrasini in the 1730s. It is entirely possible they lived in Carini for much longer, since it was an ancient place, or they could have lived somewhere

---

[22]The Sicilian Vespers (1282): this was during the time the Popes were heavily involved in European politics. They gave Sicily to Charles of Anjou in 1266 (although there was a perfectly good Norman heiress), the Sicilians rebelled, and were brutally suppressed (1267). The Angevins were cordially hated for their arrogance (and taxes), and when a French soldier insulted a Sicilian woman - right outside church, just as the bells were ringing for vespers - her husband killed him, a riot ensued, and then a massacre. The Popes continued to support the Angevins, but the Sicilians this time continued to resist, and eventually the Spaniards took over.

else first. This mobility of theirs is quite surprising to me, and makes me think they were probably not peasants tied to the land.

Other than that, I have no idea what they did for a living (until we get down to Great Grandpa Giovanni who was a baker). (And I think some of our cousins were fishermen.) I am guessing they were neither originally. I am hoping they were not among the exploiters of the peasantry, but it is possible - several of the early people were referred to as Magister/Maestro and while I am not certain exactly what that means, I suspect it implies some sort of managerial position. And "di Cosimano" has a vaguely gentrified sound to it.

[On the other hand, some of the money needed for the Thirty Years' War (1618-1648) was raised by selling titles: "the right to add the word 'Don' before a name could be bought for a hundred scudi; for more distinguished titles the prices rose astronomically."[23] So is it possible that LESS distinguished titles, like Magister/Maestro, were also bought and sold? It was right around this time that our people became Maestros.] [But on the third hand, this *would* mean that they were not as poor as peasants.]

Not all the younger sons retained - or bought - the title Maestro. Our great-grandfather was a baker (as I mentioned), and it seems that his grandfather might have been one too; but however lowly that occupation might seem, it was still a step up from being an absolute peasant.

Also it seems to have been a family tradition that at least one Gusmano/Cusmano in every generation became a priest. This is another mixed blessing. We think it an honorable calling, but "village priests were generally regarded as parasites, demanding money of the poor while being supported by the government. . . . 'If you want to be rich,' an adage advised, 'become a thief, a policeman, or a priest.' . . . Overriding all other criticism of the Italian clergy was the belief that the village priest almost invariably sided with the gentry. The animosity between priest and villagers was such that the priest rarely followed his parishioners to America."[24] In America, southern Italians "tended to equate the Church with the oppressive forces which they had fled Italy to escape. Italian-American men were especially hostile to the clergy, whose authority might sometimes come into conflict with their own patriarchal control of the family."[25]

---

[23]Ibid., 163-4.
[24]Jerre Mangione and Ben Morreale, *La Storia: five centuries of the Italian American experience* (New York: Harper Perennial, 1993), p. 327.
[25]Frances Malpezzi and William M. Clements, *Italian-American Folklore* (Little Rock, Ark.: August House, Inc., 1992), p. 113.

I am curious about all this because class is politics, and I wonder where our ancestors stood during the various (later) revolts and rebellions. Did they support the Palermo commune in 1848? Did they welcome Garibaldi in 1860? And I wonder what their lives were like. Did they suffer reprisals for their political stands? Were they (or their cousins) ever forced into banditry? Sometimes people disappear from the church records, and sometimes they reappear after several years: did they simply try life in a new town ("Before immigration fever struck in the 1890s, Sicilians seldom ventured more than a half day's walk from their birthplaces."[26]) or had they been hiding out in the mountains for a while like Viviano's own ancestor? Most of all, did their neighbors *like* them? Alas, our grandfather never left us any family stories.

About the women:

I know even less about the women than I do about the men. I assume they were kept on a tight leash while they were young, considering that Italian-American women - until quite recently - had to be chaperoned everywhere (and remembering the courtship of Apollonia by Michael Corleone).

The impression I got from looking at the church records is that a woman would get married, and then have a baby every year (or maybe every two years) for the next 20 years. And many of the babies - maybe even half of them - died. It seems to me a very sad life, and it doesn't seem to leave time for them to have done much else. Other than that, we just get glimpses of them. Some women were midwives - who sometimes took on the responsibility of baptizing some of the babies. The wives of agricultural laborers had to bring food out to their husbands in the fields - and presumably they had to prepare it first. And we know that Grandma Lena helped Grandpa Giovanni in the bakery. Beyond that, nothing.

[For an interesting article on the women in the 19th century revolutions, there is a website: What-When-How: In Depth Tutorials and Information, "Sicilian Revolutions of 1820 and 1848: women and the role women played by women in nineteenth-century revolutions in Sicily," (http://what-when-how.com/women-and-war/sicilian-revolutions-of-1820-and-1848-women-and-the/ : accessed 1 June 2017).]

---

[26]Frank Viviano, *Blood washes blood : a true story of love, murder, and redemption under the Sicilian Sun* (New York: Washington Square Press (published by Pocket Books), 2001) p. 33.

One surprising thing was the number of illegitimate babies in the church
records. They are listed as "of unknown parents" - and how could the parents
truly be unknown, in a small village? - or sometimes they are given their
mother's name with the father listed as unknown. Occasionally, especially
after unification, some couples got married in a civil ceremony a few years
before being married in the church.

At any rate, these babies were often brought to be baptized by the midwives
who had delivered them. As to what happened to them next, I'm not sure. I
don't think there was an orphanage. I found one death record where the
child-of-unknown-parents was listed as having been raised by X; I found one
marriage where the wife was of-unknown-parents.

Here is one more curious fact:
> Once King Charles had returned to Naples after his coronation in 1735,
> Sicily returned to its old ways. The Sicilians had never allowed
> themselves to become Austrianized, resisting all Austrian attempts to
> subvert them just as they had resisted those of Piedmont. After four
> centuries of Spanish occupation they remained essentially Spanish, and
> the fact that they were now ruled from Naples rather than from Madrid
> at first made remarkably little difference. The King, for all his
> Italianate ways, was by birth a Spaniard; large areas of Sicily remained
> in Spanish hands; the upper classes and those with any pretensions to
> gentility continued to speak Spanish as they had for generations . . . . [27]

Some of our ancestors surely had pretensions to gentility (what else is using
the title Maestro?) so they spoke Spanish?!!!

---

[27]Norwich, *Sicily*, 186.

The Early Ones
Antonio ~1562, Lorenzo 1582
Salvatore 1616

1. **Antonio? Andrea?** ~1562

The earliest Cusmano ancestor I have been able to find so far is
Antonio (I think) born sometime before 1562 (this is assuming he was at
least 20 when son Lorenzo was born). I have not found any records for him
specifically, just son Lorenzo's baptismal & marriage records. I am not even
entirely sure his name was Antonio - the name is abbreviated, the
handwriting is difficult to read - it could be an abbreviation for Andreas. His
wife could have been Girolama.

The baptismal record was from the church in Carini now known as
Maria Sanctissima Assunta (apparently there was an earlier church or
churches - the names Sacramento and Sebastian are mentioned) [Actually, SS
Sacramento is an Oratory.] It was formed as a parish in 1523, but the first
baptismal records available at Family search are from 1556, volume 4. It
doesn't really matter, because I can't read them (I found an entry in the index
for Antonio but when I went to the page indicated, I had no idea what it
said).

These early records spell the name Cosimano or di Cosimano (or
Cosmano).

Because of the difficulty reading the records, I have not attempted to
search further.

2. **Lorenzo** 1582

After this possibly apocryphal Antonio, comes Lorenzo (Laurenzo)
baptized 12 August 1582.[28]

99 = 56 = 12 Aug 1582 - Laurenzo s/o Anto? di C Carini gilorma? -
Another researcher says gilorma is a form of the name Gerolama
He married Antonia or Antonella, last name possibly d'Amato, in 1608.[29]

159 = 9 = 5 Oct 1608 - Laurenzo di C

- Antonino & Germa (Gerolama?) Carini

Antonia - Matteo & Catarina d'Amato?

---

[28]Maria Santissima Assunta, Carini, Palermo, Sicily, Italy, Baptismal register n. 7,
1579-1585, p. 56, Laurenzo di Cosimano baptism 1582; *Family Search.org*,
"Battesimi 1579-1616," image 99 of 588.
[29]Maria Santissima Assunta, Carini, Palermo, Sicily, Italy, Marriage register n. 7,
1607-1617, p. 9, Laurenzo di C marriage 1608; *Family Search.org*, "Matrimoni,
morti 1592-1676," image 159 of 675.

Their son Salvatore (our next ancestor) was born in 1616. Probably they had more children, both before and after Salvatore was born, but, as I mentioned, I have gotten discouraged and given up looking.

3. Salvatore - 1616-1665

Salvatore was born and baptized in Carini in 1616 NOT Cinisi, as I had earlier assumed. He seems to have lived and died in Carini, which is a town slightly to the east of Cinisi (which is slightly to the east of Terrasini). It was his sons (some of them) who moved on to Cinisi and points west.

He married a woman named Rosalia (it is spelled Rosolea in the records) Camminato; they had at least two children, Onofrio b 1644 and Giuseppe b 1646. She died sometime after that, and he was married again, in 1652, to our next ancestress Margarita Paci or di Paci. Their son Giacomo, named after her father, was born in 1654 - Giacomo was one of the sons who eventually moved to Cinisi. Next (actually, the next for whom I found a record) came daughter Melchiora (1657), and sons Francesco (1661) and Giovanni (1663). I have not been able to find baptismal records for the two other sons who moved to Cinisi, Benedetto and our next ancestor Angelo - but they are identified as sons of Salvatore & Margarita on their marriage and death records. I had estimated that they were born in about 1663 and 1664, but they would have had to be squeezed in quickly, given the birth-dates of the other sons.

Salvatore died in May 1665, and nine months later (Jan 1666), his final child, a daughter, Giuseppa, was born. Margarita lived on until 1672.

All of these births and deaths were registered in Carini. And as you can see, there are more records to be searched for.

Timeline Salvatore & Margarita

1616 Feb 20 - baptized, Carini[30]

     563 = 155 = 20 Feb 1616 - Salvatore di C - Lorenzo & Antonella

1643 June 7 - married Rosalia (Rosolea) Caminati[31]

     271 = 48 = 7 June 1643 - Salvatore di C bach - Lorenzo & Anta

          Rosolea Caminati - Michaele & Giovanna

---

[30]Maria Santissima Assunta, Carini, Palermo, Sicily, Italy, Baptismal register n. 9, 1608-1617, p. 155, Salvatore di C baptism 1616; *Family Search.org*, "Battesimi 1579-1616," image 563 of 588.

[31]Maria Santissima Assunta, Carini, Palermo, Sicily, Italy, Marriage register n. 8, 1638-1660, p. 48, Salvatore di C marriage 1643; *Family Search.org*, "Matrimoni, morti 1592-1676," image 271 of 675.

1644 May 7 - son Onofrio baptized[32]
    219 = 145 = 7 May 1644 - HOnofrio C - Salvatore & Rosolea
1646 March 17 - son Giuseppe baptized[33]
    325 = 7 = 17 March 1646 - Josephus C - Salvatore & Rosolia
1646-1652 - wife Rosalia died
1652 Feb 13 - married Margarita di Paci[34]
    363 = 141 = 13 Feb 1652 - Salvatore C wid
        - s/o late Laurenzo & Antonia
        Margarita di Paci - Jacobo & Vincenza?
1654 Oct 7 - son Giacomo baptized[35] - Maria SS Assunta, Carini
    65 = 29 = 7 Oct 1654 - Jacobus C - Salvatore & Margarita
        1674 m Catarina Zappa Cinisi
        1719 died Cinisi (age 65)
1657 Aug 22 - daughter Melchiora born[36]
    141 = 104 = 22 Aug 1657 tod - Melchiora C - Salvatore & Margarita
1661 Oct 11 - son Francesco born[37]
    306 = 90 = 11 Oct 1661 yest - Franciscus C - Salvatore & Margarita
1663 Dec 20 - son Giovanni born[38]
    373 = 157 = 20 Dec 1663 yest - Joannes C - Salvator & Margarita
~1663 - son Benedetto born
    1681 m Rosa Taormina Cinisi
    1733 died Cinisi (age ~70)

---

[32]Maria Santissima Assunta, Carini, Palermo, Sicily, Italy, Baptismal register n. 12, 1638-1646, p. 145, HOnofrio C baptism 1644; *Family Search.org*, "Battesimi 1638-1653," image 219 of 539.

[33]Maria Santissima Assunta, Carini, Palermo, Sicily, Italy, Baptismal register n. 13, 1646-1653, p. 7, Josephus C baptism 1646; *Family Search.org*, "Battesimi 1638-1653," image 325 of 539.

[34]Maria Santissima Assunta, Carini, Palermo, Sicily, Italy, Marriage register n. 8, 1638-1660, p. 141, Salvatore di C marriage 1652; *Family Search.org*, "Matrimoni, morti 1592-1676," image 363 of 675.

[35]Maria Santissima Assunta, Carini, Palermo, Sicily, Italy, Baptismal register n. 14, 1653-1658, p. 29, Jacobus C baptism 1654; *Family Search.org*, "Battesimi 1653-1677," image 65 of 778.

[36]Maria Santissima Assunta, Carini, Palermo, Sicily, Italy, Baptismal register n. 14, 1653-1658, p. 104, Melchiora C baptism 1657; *Family Search.org*, "Battesimi 1653-1677," image 141 of 778.

[37]Maria Santissima Assunta, Carini, Palermo, Sicily, Italy, Baptismal register n. 15, 1659-1663, p. 90, Franciscus C baptism 1661; *Family Search.org*, "Battesimi 1653-1677," image 306 of 778.

[38]Maria Santissima Assunta, Carini, Palermo, Sicily, Italy, Baptismal register n. 15, 1659-1663, p. 157, Joannes C baptism 1663; *Family Search.org*, "Battesimi 1653-1677," image 373 of 778.

~1664 - son Angelo born
    1684 son baptized Cinisi
    1689 m Francesca Cracchiolo Cinisi
    1722 died Cinisi (age 40???)
1665 May 1 - died[39]
    136 = 99 = 1 May 1665 - Salvator C ~45
    - s/o late Laurentius? & Antonina?
1666 Jan 10 - daughter Giuseppa born[40]
    466 = 52 = 10 Jan 1666 today- Josepha C - late Salvatore & Margarita
1672 Jan 20 - wife Margarita died[41]
    306 = 89 = 20 Jan 1672 - Margarita C ~40 - late Jacobo di Paci?

Salvatore's Children

4. Children of Salvatore & Rosolea Caminati
    5. Onofrio 1644
    5. Giuseppe 1666
  Children of Salvatore & Margarita di Paci
    5. Giacomo 1654-1719 + Catherina Zappa, Anna di Marco -> Cinisi
    5. Melchiora 1657
    5. Francesco 1661
    5. Benedicto ~1663 -1733+ Rosa Taormina -> Cinisi
    5. Giovanni 1663
    5. Angelo ~1664-1722 + Francesca Cracchiolo -> Cinisi
      - *our next ancestor*
    5. Giuseppa 1666

For the records I have gathered on the children of Salvatore & Margarita (other than Angelo), see Volume 2.

Giacomo married Catarina Zappa in 1674 and they had at least five children (Dorothea, Giovanna Margarita, Filippo, Pietro Giuseppe Albero, and Salvatore). Catarina died, and Giacomo married Anna di Marco in 1692; they had at least four children (Rosaria Anna, Genevesa, Angela Girolama, and Giovanni).

---

[39]Maria Santissima Assunta, Carini, Palermo, Sicily, Italy, Death register n. 8, 1658-1666, p. 99, Salvator C death 1665; *Family Search.org*, "Morti 1658-1692," image 136 of 623.

[40]Maria Santissima Assunta, Carini, Palermo, Sicily, Italy, Baptismal register n. 16, 1664-1670, p. 53, Joseph C baptism 1666; *Family Search.org*, "Battesimi 1653-1677," image 455 of 778.

[41]Maria Santissima Assunta, Carini, Palermo, Sicily, Italy, Death register n. 8, 1658-1666, p. 306, Margarita C death 1672; *Family Search.org*, "Morti 1658-1692," image 306 of 623.

Benedetto married Rosalia Taormina in 1681; their children, all girls (the ones I found records for), were Vincenza, Epifemia Angela, Anna Benedicta, Elisabetta, Francesca, Pietra, another Benedicta, and Cirena Antonia (born 1703).

Angelo married Francesca Cracchiolo in 1683, and their first child, Salvatore Alessandro, was born in 1684, Their other children were: Sebastiana, Francesca, Antonio, Giovanna, Francesco, Giovanni (our next ancestor, born 1694), Angela Melchiora, another Angela, another Francesco (with a middle name of Giacomo), Pietra Grazia, Filippa Giuseppa, and finally Vito Filippo. Angelo died in 1722, Francesca in 1732.

About Salvatore's final, posthumous child, Giuseppa, I know nothing.

I don't know what any of these folks did for a living, but some of them were given the title of Magistro (which I think of as equivalent to "Mr" but I might be wrong). I am also guessing that it indicates the person was a member of the middle class, possibly a professional of some kind or a manager? At any rate, they were not farm-workers (or fishermen). Salvatore is always referred to as just plain Salvatore, but Angelo is given the title in a couple of records, although not all.

Angelo and Francesca seem to have spent their lives in Cinisi, but many of their children, including our ancestor Giovanni, moved to the nearby village of Terrasini. It seems that Giacomo's descendants stayed in Cinisi. I don't know about Benedetto's because they were all girls (all the ones I found anyway).

Generation 2: Angelo & Francesca Cracchiolo

Note: Angelo is actually generation 4, but I found the earlier people by accident later in my searches, and I didn't want to go back and re-number everything - so I have continued to refer him as being of Generation 2.

Our next ancestor, Angelo, was one of three sons of Salvatore & Margarita Gusmano (or Cusmano) (or Cosimano or di Cosimano - depending on where the records were written) who appear in the records of Cinisi. Unfortunately he doesn't appear in the records of Carini, where he was probably born. What we know about him comes entirely from the church records in Cinisi and Terrasini: births, marriages, deaths. There wasn't even a lot of history going on at that time.

Angelo married his wife Francesca Cracchiolo on 26 July 1683 in Cinisi. The marriage record says Angelo was living in Terrasini at that time, but the children (they had nine more) were still baptized in Cinisi, so maybe it was only a brief sojourn in Terrasini - or maybe they preferred to continue in the church they were familiar with (the Terrasini church was being built, starting (maybe) in 1663 and (maybe) in 1684). Their first child, Salvatore Alessandro, named after Angelo's father, was born in 1684 and died when he was only six years old; daughter Sebastiana was born around the same time. Daughter Francesca (named after her mother?) survived her childhood, married Antonio Lo Vasco and died in 1751, at the ripe old age of 65. Then came Antonio Vincenzo (who also survived and propered) and the rest. Four of their thirteen children (probably) died young, five made it to adulthood; I don't know what happened to the last four (three of whom were female, so they might have disappeared behind a different name).

He was occasionally given the title of Magister/Maestro, which (as I have repeated several times) may mean he was part of the managerial class. All three of his sons who appear in the records (I don't know what happened to the youngest, Vito) were also given the title, but some of the grandsons were not. [The Chinese say it takes three generations to rise (to the mandarin class), and three generations to fall back from it.] His eldest surviving son stayed in Cinisi, but the other two, our ancestor Giovanni and his brother Francesco, eventually became residents of Terrasini.

He died in 1722, his wife in 1732, and I don't have anything more to say about him.

Timeline Angelo & Francesca
2. Angelo ~1664 - 1722 + Francesca Cracciolo (1689)

~1664 born (this is a total guess, based on the year his first child was born)
1683 July 26 - married Francesca Cracchiolo[42]

    52 = 39 = 26 July 1683 - Angelus C bach Cin lives Terr
       - Salvatore & Margarita
       Francesca Cracchiolo - Vito & Lucretia

1684 March 31 - son Salvatore Alessandro born[43] (died 1690)[44]

    103 = 139 = 31 March 1684 b today
       - Salvatore Alessandro C - Angelo & Francesca Cracchiolo
    death
    53 = 45 = 3 Apr 1690 - Salvator C 6 - Angelus

~1684 - daughter Sebastiana born (died 1744)[45]

    87 = 41 = 17 Apr 1744 - Sebastiana C 60y - Angelus & Francesca

~1686 - daughter Francesca born (died 1751) + Antonio LoVasco[46]

    106 = 64 = 16 June 1751 - Francisca C & LoVasco 65
       - wife liv Antionio LoVasco
       d/o late Mr Angelo & Francesca

1687 Feb 11 - son Antonio Vincenzo born[47]

    40 = 42 = 12 Feb 1687 b yest - Antonius Vincentius C
       - Angelo & Francesca

---

[42]Santa Fara Vergine, Cinisi, Palermo, Sicily, Italy, Marriage register 1672-1701, page 39, Angelus Cusmano, 1683; *FamilySearch.org*, "Matrimoni 1672-1701," image 52 of 100.

[43]Santa Fara Vergine, Cinisi, Palermo, Sicily, Italy, Baptismal register 1672-1684, page 139, Salvator Alessandro Cusmano, 1684; *FamilySearch.org*, "Battesimi 1672-1684," image 103 of 155.

[44]Santa Fara Vergine, Cinisi, Palermo, Sicily, Italy, Death register 1672-1697, page 45, Salvator Cusmano, 1690; *FamilySearch.org*, "Morti 1672-1697," image 53 of 68.

[45]Santa Fara Vergine, Cinisi, Palermo, Sicily, Italy, Death register 1734-1765, page 41, Sebastiana C death 1744; *FamilySearch.org*, "Morti 1734-1765," image 87 of 201.

[46]Santa Rosalia Favarotta (daughter church), Terrasini, Palermo, Sicily, Italy, Death register v. 1, 1736-1750, p. 64, Francisca Cusmano & LoVasco, 1751; *Family Search.org*, ""Morti 1736-1788," image 106 of 642.

[47]Santa Fara Vergine, Cinisi, Palermo, Sicily, Italy, Baptismal register 1684-1696, page 43, Antonius Vincentius Cusmano, 1687; *FamilySearch.org*, "Battesimi 1684-1696," image 40 of 99.

1690 Oct 6 - daughter Giovanna born[48] (died 9 Oct)[49]

    64 = 81 = 6 Oct 1690 b today - Joanna C - Angelo & Francesca

    death

    54 = 45 = 9 Oct 1690 - Joanna C - Angelus

1691 Aug 17 - son Francesco baptized[50]

    69 = 91 = 17 Aug 1691 - Francesco C - Angelo & Francesca

1694 Aug 28 - son Giovanni born[51]

    86 = 127 = 29 Aug 1694 b yest - Joannes C

        - Mr Angelus & Francisca

1696 Oct 9 - daughter Angela Melchiora born[52] (died 1698)[53]

    31 = 2 = 9 Oct 1696 - Angela Melchiora C b today

       - Angelo & Francesca

    death

    36 = 3 = 18 Jan 1698 - Melchiora C 2 - Angelo

1698 Oct 26 - daughter Angela baptized[54]

    55 = 21 = 26 Oct 1698 - Angela C - Angelo & Francesca

1700 June 3 - son Francesco Giacomo baptized[55] (died 1739)[56]

    72 = 36 = 3 June 1700 - Franciscus Joachim - Angelo & Francesca

    death

---

[48]Santa Fara Vergine, Cinisi, Palermo, Sicily, Italy, Baptismal register 1684-1696, page 81, Joanna Cusmano, 1690; *FamilySearch.org*, "Battesimi 1684-1696," image 64 of 99.

[49]Santa Fara Vergine, Cinisi, Palermo, Sicily, Italy, Death register 1672-1697, page 45, Joanna Cusmano, 1690; *FamilySearch.org*, "Morti 1672-1697," image 54 of 68.

[50]Santa Fara Vergine, Cinisi, Palermo, Sicily, Italy, Baptismal register 1684-1696, page 91, Franciscus Cusmano, 1691; *FamilySearch.org*, "Battesimi 1684-1696," image 69 of 99.

[51]Santa Fara Vergine, Cinisi, Palermo, Sicily, Italy, Baptismal register 1684-1696, page 127, Joannes Cusmano, 1694; *FamilySearch.org*, "Battesimi 1684-1696," image 86 of 99.

[52]Santa Fara Vergine, Cinisi, Palermo, Sicily, Italy, Baptismal register 1696-1709, page 2, Angela Melchiora, 1696; *FamilySearch.org*, "Battesimi 1696-1709," image 31 of 162.

[53]Santa Fara Vergine, Cinisi, Palermo, Sicily, Italy, Death register 1697-1722, page 3, Melchiora C death 1698; *FamilySearch.org*, "Morti 1697-1722," image 36 of 149.

[54]Santa Fara Vergine, Cinisi, Palermo, Sicily, Italy, Baptismal register 1696-1709, page 21, Angela Cusmano, 1698; *FamilySearch.org*, "Battesimi 1696-1709," image 55 of 162.

[55]Santa Fara Vergine, Cinisi, Palermo, Sicily, Italy, Baptismal register 1696-1709, page 36, Franciscus Joachim Cusmano, 1700; *FamilySearch.org*, "Battesimi 1696-1709," image 72 of 162.

[56]Santa Rosalia Favarotta (daughter church), Terrasini, Palermo, Sicily, Italy, Death register v. 1, 1736-1750, p. 17, Franciscus Cusmano, 1739; *Family Search.org*, ""Morti 1736-1788," image 54 of 642.

54 = 17 = 22 Apr 1739 - Franciscus C 35 - Mr Angelo & Francesca
1702 Oct 11 - daughter Pietra Grazia baptized[57] (died Dec)[58]
    101 = 62 = 11 Oct 1702 - Petra Grazia C - Mr Angelo & Francesca
    death
    53 = 18 = 22 Dec 1702 - Petra C 4 m - Mr Angelo & Francesca
1704 March 4 - daughter Filippa Giuseppa born[59]
    116 = 75 = 9 March 1704 (5) - Philippa Josepha C
        - Angelo & Francesca
1709 June 6 - son Vito Filippo born[60]
    157 = 114 = 7? June 1709 b yest - Vitus Philippus C
    - Angelo & Francesca
1722 Aug 31 - died[61]
    41 = 3 = 31 Aug 1722 - Mr Angelus C - Salvatore & Margarita
       age looks like 40, but that is obviously wrong. Could be 49, but
that is wrong too
1732 Feb 12 - wife Francesca died[62]
    117 = 74 = 12 Feb 1732 - Francisca C 75 - w/o Mr Angelus
        -Vito & Lucretia Cracchiolo

Children of Angelo & Francesca Cracchiolo

3. Salvatore Alessandro 1684-1690
3. Sebastiana ~1684-1744
3. Francesca ~1686-1751 + Antonio Lo Vasco
3. **Antonio** (Mr) Vincenzo 1687-1754 + Giovanna Maniaci (1715)
3. Giovanna 1690-1690
3. Francesco 1691

---

[57]Santa Fara Vergine, Cinisi, Palermo, Sicily, Italy, Baptismal register 1696-1709, page 62, Petra Gratia Cusmano, 1702; *FamilySearch.org*, "Battesimi 1696-1709," image 101 of 162.

[58]Santa Fara Vergine, Cinisi, Palermo, Sicily, Italy, Death register 1697-1722, page 18, Petra C death 1702; *FamilySearch.org*, "Morti 1697-1722," image 53 of 149.

[59]Santa Fara Vergine, Cinisi, Palermo, Sicily, Italy, Baptismal register 1696-1709, page 75, Philippa Josepha Cusmano, 1704; *FamilySearch.org*, "Battesimi 1696-1709," image 116 of 162.

[60]Santa Fara Vergine, Cinisi, Palermo, Sicily, Italy, Baptismal register 1696-1709, page 114, Vitus Philippus Cusmano, 1709; *FamilySearch.org*, "Battesimi 1696-1709," image 157 of 162.

[61]Santa Fara Vergine, Cinisi, Palermo, Sicily, Italy, Death register 1722-1734, page 3, Mr Angelus Cusmano, 1722; *FamilySearch.org*, "Morti 1722-1734," image 41 of 138.

[62]Santa Fara Vergine, Cinisi, Palermo, Sicily, Italy, Death register 1722-1734, page 74, Francisca Cusmano, 1732; *FamilySearch.org*, "Morti 1722-1734," image 117 of 138.

3. Giovanni (Mr) 1694-1761 + Anna Maria Purpura (1732)
3. Angela Melchiora 1696-1698
3. Angela 1698
3. **Francesco** (Mr) Giacomo 1700-1739 + Angela di Luca (1723)
3. Pietra Grazia 1702-1702
3. Filippa Giuseppa 1704
3. Vito Filippo 1709

All these children were baptized in Cinisi, at the church of Santa Fara Virgine.

Salvatore died age 6; Giovanna died a few days old; Angela Melchiora died aged 2; I am assuming Francesco (1691) died young, since there was another Francesco born to the couple.

I don't know what happened to the girls Angela (1698), Pietra Grazia (1702), Filippa Giuseppe (1704) or to the youngest son Vito Filippo (1709). Antonio and his sons stayed in Cinisi; some of his grandsons moved to Favarotta or Terrasini; some of his later descendants moved to Detroit.

Giovanni, our next ancestor, seems to have moved to Favarotta, and maybe into Terrasini itself; his children and grandchildren lived in Terrasini. Francesco - I am assuming the one in the records is the second named Francesco - also moved to Favarotta/Terrasini. Many of his descendants moved to Detroit.

Sister Francesca probably moved to Terrasini as well - her death record is from Santa Rosalia Favarotta. Sister Sebastiana lived to age 60 and died in Cinisi, but I have no more information about her.

For the records I have found on the other descendants of Angelo and Francesca, see Volume 2.

Generation 3: Giovanni & Anna Maria Purpura

Note: Giovanni is actually generation 5, but I found the earlier people by accident later in my searches, and I didn't want to go back and re-number everything - so I have continued to refer him as being of Generation 3.

He was born in 1694 to Angelo & Francesca Cracchiolo. He was the seventh of thirteen children, seven boys and six girls (some of them died young). His father was given the honorific title "Magister" (Latin) or "Maestro" (Italian). I am not entirely sure what this means, but I suspect it might have been used for the professional/managerial class. He, himself, was also given the title.

He was born in Cinisi, the town next to Terrasini, and baptized in the church of Santa Fara Virgine. He got married in that church in 1732, to Anna Maria Purpura. The marriage record says he was born in Cinisi, but was now living in Favarotta (which is where his wife was from). I am not entirely clear on the history of this, but it seems that Terrasini itself was a small agricultural settlement, and Favarotta was a fishing settlement nearby, which was connected to Cinisi itself. In 1836, Favarotta was detached from Cinisi and joined to Terrasini.

In 1733, Giovanni and Anna Maria's first son, named Michael Giuseppe, was born; he was baptized in Santa Fara. According to Sicilian tradition, he should have been named Angelo, after his grandfather, but he was not. Their first (and, it turns out, only) daughter, Francesca - named after his mother - was born in 1736, and also baptized in Santa Fara. The next son *was* named Angelo - Archangelo in fact; he was born in 1739, and baptized in the church of Santa Rosalia Favarotta, as were the next several children. [I can't tell if the final two were baptized in Santa Rosalia or in Maria SS delle Grazie - the records of Santa Rosalia seem to have been moved to the mother church and stored there.]

Giovanni and Anna Maria had at least 5 more children, all boys. They were: Giacomo Gaetano (1742), Pietro Vito (1745), Giovanni Liborio Calogero (1749), Carlo Francesco Paolo (1752- our next ancestor), and Antonio Giovanni Simone (1755). Giovanni was 61, Anna Maria 43 when their last son was born.

Their son Angelo became a priest - or at least he started down that path; he was made a sub-deacon in 1762, deacon in 1763, but I found no further records for him. The priesthood was definitely a calling for the family - there was at least one Gusmano/Cusmano priest in every generation - not all in our direct line! - most of them serving in the local diocese.

At some point, one member of the Gusmano/Cusmano family built a home near the center of Terrasini. "The family's ancestral home stood near the present site of Mike's salumeria. [just a few blocks from the Piazza Duomo]."[63]

Their older sons - Giuseppe, Gaetano - were given the honorific "Maestro," but the younger ones were not.

Giovanni died in 1761, Anna Maria in 1765.

Timeline Giovanni & Anna Maria Purpura
Giovanni b 1694 d 1761, Anna Maria b ~1712 d 1765

1694 Aug 28 - born[64] - Cinisi to Mr Angelo & Francesca,
    baptized Santa Fara Virgine, Cinisi
    86 = 127 = 29 Aug 1694 b yest - Joannes C
    - Mr Angelus & Francisca
1732 Nov 4 - married Anna Maria Purpura[65] - Santa Fara Virgine, Cinisi
    42 = 21 = 4 Nov 1732 - Mr Joannes C, Cin now Fav, unm
    - Angelo & Francesca
        Anna Maria Purpura, Fav, unm - Nicolo & Antonia
1733 Aug 1 - son Michael Giuseppe born[66] - baptized Santa Fara
    174 = 105 = 2 Aug 1733 b yest - Michael Joseph
    - Mr Joe C & Anna Maria Purpura
    married Giovanna Russo 1755 -> 7ch (Giovanna d 1768)
    married Petra Ferrara 1769 -> 1ch
    died 1795 (Petra d 1800)
1736 March 26 - daughter Francesca born[67] (died 1803)[68]
    - baptized Santa Fara
    55 = 5 = 27 March 1736 b yest - Francisca Caterina Vita
        - Mr Joannes & Anna Maria Purpura

---

[63]Viviano, *Blood washes blood*, 38-9.

[64]Santa Fara Vergine, Cinisi, Palermo, Sicily, Italy, Baptismal register 1684-1696, page 127, Joannes Cusmano, 1694; *FamilySearch.org*, "Battesimi 1684-1696," image 86 of 99.

[65]Santa Fara Vergine, Cinisi, Palermo, Sicily, Italy, Marriage register 1727-1744, page 21, Mr Joannes Cusmano, 1732; *FamilySearch.org*, "Matrimoni 1727-1744," image 42 of 98.

[66]Santa Fara Vergine, Cinisi, Palermo, Sicily, Italy, Baptismal register 1726-1735, page 105, Michael Joseph Cusmano, 1733; *FamilySearch.org*, "Battesimi 1726-1735," image 174 of 210.

[67]Santa Fara Vergine, Cinisi, Palermo, Sicily, Italy, Baptismal register 1735-1748, page 5, Francesca Catherina Cusmano, 1736; *FamilySearch.org*, "Battesimi 1735-1748," image 55 of 193.

[68]Maria Santissima delle Grazie (Chiesa Madre [Mother Church]), Terrasini, Palermo, Sicily, Italy, Death Register, v. 80 (1799-1835) p. 58, Francesca Gusmano & Leto, 1803; *Family Search.org*, "Morti 1782-1835," image 209 of 480.

17xx - married Francesco Leto
death
209 = 58 = 28 June 1803 - Francisca G & Leto 70
        - wid late Mr Franciscus
        d/o Mr Joannes & Anna Maria G
1739 Jan 24 - son Archangelo born[69] - baptized Santa Rosalia
        98 = 17 = 24 Jan 1739 b today - Archangelus C
        - Joanne C & Anna Maria Purpura (Santa Rosalia)
        53 = 24 = 24 Jan 1739 - Archangelo C
        - Joannes C & Anna Maria Purpura (Maria SS delle Grazie)
Angelo - subdeacon[70]
74 = 52 = 9 May 1762 - suddiacono d Angelo C
        - s/o Mr Giovanni & Anna Maria C
Angelo - deacon[71]
76 = 55 = 14 Mar 1763 - Angelo Cusmano 1st den deacon
        s/o Mr Giovanni & Anna Maria C
1742 June 12 - son Giacomo Gaetano born[72] - baptized Santa Rosalia
        171 = 10 = 12 Jun 1742 - Jacobus Cajetanus Cusimano
        - Mr Joannes & Anna Maria C
married Francesca Palazzolo 1766 -> 4ch
don't know what happened to him after 1781

---

[69]Santa Rosalia Favarotta (daughter church), Terrasini, Palermo, Sicily, Italy, Baptismal register v. 2, 1738-1740, p. 17, Archangelus Cusmano, baptism 1739; *Family Search.org*, "Battesimi, matrimoni, pubblicationi, morti 1736-1754," image 98 of 507. AND Maria Santissima delle Grazie (Chiesa Madre [Mother Church]), Terrasini, Palermo, Sicily, Italy, Baptismal register v. 7, 1736-1754, p. 24 Archangelo Cusmano, baptism 1739; *Family Search.org*, "Battesimi, matrimoni, pubblicationi, morti 1736-1760," image 53 of 475.

[70]Maria Santissima delle Grazie, Terrasini, Palermo, Sicily, Italy, "Liber Denunciandorum, 1749 . . . ," suddiacono d Angelo C, 1762; *Family Search.org*, "Documenti Matrimoniali 1749-1795," image 74 of 471.

[71]Maria Santissima delle Grazie, Terrasini, Palermo, Sicily, Italy, "Liber Denunciandorum, 1749 . . . ," Angelo C, 1763; *Family Search.org*, "Documenti Matrimoniali 1749-1795," image 76 of 471.

[72]Santa Rosalia Favarotta, Terrasini, Palermo, Sicily, Italy, Baptismal register v. 8, 1741-1743, p. 10, Jacobus Cajetanus Cusimano baptism, 1742; *Family Search.org*, "Battesimi, matrimoni, pubblicationi, morti 1736-1760," image 171 of 475.

1745 Feb 10 - son Pietro Vito born[73] - baptized Santa Rosalia
    439 = 20 = 10 Feb 1745 - Petrus Vitus C
        - Mr Joannes & Anna Maria C 20 (Santa Rosalia)
    91 = 63 = 10 Feb 1745 b today - Petrus Vitus G
        - Mr Joannes & Anna Maria C   (Maria SS delle Grazie)
married Stefania Brisciano 1766 -> 8ch (Stefania d 1799)
died 1803
1749 Feb 11 - son Giovanni Liborio Calogero born[74]
    340 = 14 = 12 Feb 1749 b yest - Joannes Liberius Calogerus C
        - Mr Joannes C & Anna Maria Purpura (Santa Rosalia)
    137 = 106 = 12 Feb 1749 - Joannes Liborius Calogerus G
        - Mr Joannes & Anna Maria Purpura (Maria SS delle Grazie)
married Catherina Aiello 1776 -> 8 children
don't know what happened to him after 1799
1752 Feb 2 - son Carlo Francesco Paolo born[75] - our next ancestor
    281= 26 = 2 Feb 1752 b today - Carolus Francesco Paolo C
        - Mr Joannes & Anna Maria
married Gaetana Palazzolo -> 11 children
died 1821
1755 Oct 27 - son Antonio Giovanni Simone born[76]
    323 = 65 = 28 Oct 1755 b yest - Antonius Joannes C
        - Mr Joannes & Anna Maria C

---

[73]Santa Rosalia Favarotta, Terrasini, Palermo, Sicily, Italy, Baptismal register v. 6, 1743-1746, p. 20, Petrus Vitus Cusmano baptism, 1745; *Family Search.org*, "Battesimi, matrimoni, pubblicationi, morti 1736-1754," image 439 of 507. AND Maria Santissima delle Grazie (Chiesa Madre [Mother Church]), Terrasini, Palermo, Sicily, Italy, Baptismal register v. 7, 1736-1754, p. 91, Petrus Vitus Gusmano, baptism 1745; *Family Search.org*, "Battesimi, matrimoni, pubblicationi, morti 1736-1760," image 63 of 475.

[74]Santa Rosalia Favarotta, Terrasini, Palermo, Sicily, Italy, Baptismal register v. 5 [sic], 1748-1754, p. 14, Joannes Liberius Calogerus Cusmano baptism, 1749; *Family Search.org*, "Battesimi, matrimoni, pubblicationi, morti 1736-1754," image 340 of 507. AND Maria Santissima delle Grazie (Chiesa Madre [Mother Church]), Terrasini, Palermo, Sicily, Italy, Baptismal register v. 7, 1736-1754, p. 106, Joannes Liberius Calogerus , baptism 1749; *Family Search.org*, "Battesimi, matrimoni, pubblicationi, morti 1736-1760," image 137 of 475.

[75]Maria Santissima delle Grazie, Terrasini, Palermo, Sicily, Italy, Baptismal register v. 9, 1749-1756, p. 26, Carolus Franciscus Paulus C baptism, 1752; *Family Search.org*, "Battesimi, matrimoni, pubblicationi, morti 1736-1760," image 281 of 475.

[76]Maria Santissima delle Grazie, Terrasini, Palermo, Sicily, Italy, Baptismal register v. 9, 1749-1756, p. 65, Antonius Joannes C baptism, 1755; *Fam Search.org*, "Battesimi, matrimoni, pubblicationi, morti 1736-1760," image 323 of 475.

married Antonia Mazzola
don't know what happened to him after his marriage in 1786
1761 July 2 - Giovanni died[77]
    361 = 14 = 2 July 1761 - Mr Joannes C 65
    - Mr Angelus & Francesca
1765 Aug 8 - Anna Maria Purpura Cusmano died[78]
    403 = 51 = 8 Aug 1765 - Anna Maria Cusmano 53
      - w/o Mr Joannes C
      d/o late Nicolaus & Antonia Purpura

Children of Giovanni and Anna Maria Purpura

4. Michael **Giuseppe** (Mr) 1733 - 1795 + Giovanna Russo (1755), +Pietra Ferrara (1769)
4. Francesca 1736 - 1803 + Francesco Leto
4. Archangelo 1739 - priest
4. Giacomo **Gaetano** 1742 - ? + Francesca Palazzolo (1766)
4. Pietro **Vito** 1745-1803 + Stefania Brisciano (1766)
4. Giovanni **Liborio** Caolgero 1749 - ?+ Caterina Aiello (1776)
4. Carlo **Francesco Paolo** 1752-1821 + Gaetana Palazzolo (1781)
4. Antonio Giovanni Simone 1755 - ? + Antonia Mazzola (1786)

The first two children were baptized in Cinisi (Santa Fara); the rest in Favarotta (Santa Rosalia) or maybe in Terrasini itself. All of them survived to adulthood. Angelo was on the way at least to becoming a priest - he was made a sub-deacon and then a deacon - but I found no records for him after that.

Gaetano disappeared after 1781 (age 39), Antonio Giovanni after his marriage in 1786 (age 31), Liborio after 1797 (age 48). Liborio probably and Giovanni possibly moved to Siccaria (Balestrate). Giuseppe, Francesca and Vito seem to have stayed in Terrasini (although I found one of Giuseppe's grandsons getting married in Cinisi).

And of course, our next ancestor Francesco Paolo also stayed in Terrasini.

For the records I have found on the other children of Giovanni & Anna Maria, see Volume 2.

---

[77]Maria Santissima delle Grazie, Terrasini, Palermo, Sicily, Italy, Death Register, v. 77, p. 14, Mr Joannes C, 1761; *Family Search.org*, "Morti 1736-1788," image 361 of 642.

[78]Maria Santissima delle Grazie, Terrasini, Palermo, Sicily Ital, Death Reg, v. 77, p. 51, Anna Maria C, 1765; *Fam Search.org*, "Morti 1736-1788," image 403 of 642.

Generation 4 : Francesco Paolo & Gaetana Palazzolo

*Note: Francesco Paolo is actually generation 6, but I found the earlier
people by accident later, and I didn't want to go back and re-number
everything - so I have continued to refer him as being of Generation 4.*

Carlo Francesco Paolo, known as Francesco or Francesco Paolo (that
seems to have been a compound name, like Mary Ann), was born in
Terrasini, and baptized at the mother church, Maria Santissima delle Grazie.
"The Cusmano name was one of the most common in Terrasini; two
nineteenth-century pastors of Maria Santissima delle Grazie had been
Cusmanos. The family's ancestral home stood . . . [just a few blocks from
the Piazza Duomo where the church was]"[79] I don't know that our people
lived in the "ancestral home," but it would not be out of the question.

He was the seventh (that we know of) child, sixth son, of Mr Giovanni
Cusumano/Cusmano/Gusmano and Anna Maria Purpura. Two of his older
brothers also carried the "Maestro" title, but the younger sons, including our
Francesco, did not. Francesco was only 9 when his father died, so that may
have had something to do with it - maybe he had had to be indentured out???
Although I have no idea what he did for a living.

He married Gaetana Palazzolo in 1781, and together they had 11
children: 8 girls, 3 boys. Five of the children (two of the boys) died in
infancy; our next ancestor, Giovanni Vito, was the only surviving son. Two
of the girls died when they were in their teens; one died unmarried at age 21;
I haven't traced the other two.

His wife, Gaetana Palazzolo, died in 1806 (two years after her last
child was born) at age 47. He lived another 15 years and died in 1821, at 69.
[His daughter Vita - the one I assumed was the caretaker - died in 1818, so I
don't know who, if anyone, took care of him for the last three years.]

---

[79]Frank Viviano, *Blood Washes Blood: a True Story of Love, Murder, and
Redemption under the Sicilian Sun* (New York: Washington Square Press, 2001), 38-
39.

Timeline Francesco Paolo and Gaetana Palazzolo
Francesco b 1752, died 1821; Gaetana b x, d 1806

1752 Feb 2 - born[80]
> 281= 26 = 2 Feb 1752 b today - Carolus Francesco Paolo C
> - Mr Joannes & Anna Maria C

1781 Feb 16 - married Gaetana Palazzolo[81]
> *banns*
> 161 = 129 = 27 Jan 1781 = 1st - Francesco Paolo C bach Terr
> - Mr Giovanni & Anna Maria
> Gaetana Palazzolo - Pietro & Rosa
>
> *marriage*
> 35 = 3 = 16 Feb 1781 - Francesco Paolo C, Terr - unm
> -- Mr Joannes & Anna Maria C
> Caetana Palazzolo - Petrus & Rosa

1781 December - daughter Anna Maria Giuseppa born[82]
> 104 = 46 = blot Dec 1781 b yest - Anna Maria Josepha C
> - Francesco & Gaetana C

1783 Feb 4 - daughter Rosa Francesca born[83] - m 1809[84] - died 1850[85]
> 124 = 65 = 5 Feb 1783 b yest - Rosa Francesca C
> - Francesco Paolo C & Cajetana

---

[80]Maria Santissima delle Grazie, Terrasini, Palermo, Sicily, Italy, Baptismal register v. 9, 1749-1756, p. 26, Carolus Franciscus Paulus C baptism, 1752; *Family Search.org*, "Battesimi, matrimoni, pubblicationi, morti 1736-1760," image 281 of 475.

[81]Maria Santissima delle Grazie (Chiesa Madre [Mother Church]), Terrasini, Palermo, Sicily, Italy, "Liber Denunciandorum, 1749 . . . ," p. 129, Francesco Paolo C, 1st banns 27 Jan 1781; *Family Search.org*, "Documenti Matrimoniali 1749-1795," image 161 of 471. AND Maria Santissima delle Grazie, Terrasini, Palermo, Sicily, Italy, Marriage register, v. ?, 1780-1807, p.3, Franciscus Paulus C, 1781; *Family Search.org*, "Matrimoni 1757-1835," image 35 of 580.

[82]Maria Santissima delle Grazie, Terrasini, Palermo, Sicily, Italy, Baptismal register, 1778-1789, v. 14, p. 46, Anna Maria Joseph C baptism 1781; *Family Search.org*, "Battesimi 1778-1801," image 104 of 437.

[83]Maria Santissima delle Grazie, Terrasini, Palermo, Sicily, Italy, Baptismal register, 1778-1789, v. 14, p. 65, Rosa Francesca C baptism 1783; *Family Search.org*, "Battesimi 1778-1801," image 124 of 437.

[84]Maria Santissima delle Grazie, Terrasini, Palermo, Sicily, Italy, Liber Denunciandorum, v. 70 1787 . . . , p. 114/5, Matteo Bommarito banns 1809; *Family Search.org*, "Documenti Matrimoniali 1787-1843," image 179 of 492.

[85]Maria Santissima delle Grazie, Terrasini, Palermo, Sicily, Italy, Death Register, v. 83, 1843-1859, p. 70, Rosa G death 1850; *Family Search.org*, "Morti 1818-1859," image 454 of 562.

marriage (banns)
> 179 = 114/5 = 28 May 1809 1st - Matteo Bommarito unm Terr
>> - Giovanni & Maria Anna Ventimiglia
>>> Rosa G unm Terr - Francesco Paolo & late Gaetana Palazzolo
>>> 2nd - 1 June - 3rd 4 June

death
> 454 = 70 = 12 Dec 1850 - Rosa G 70 - wid late Matteo Bommarito
>> d/o Francesco & Cajetana Palazzolo

1785 Jan 2 - daughter Antonia Alberta born[86] (died 1801, age 15)[87]
> 152 = 91 = 3 Jan 1785 b yest - Antonia Alberta C
>> - Francesco & Gaetana C

death
> 171 = 23 = 30 July 1801 - Antonia G 15
>> Francesco Paolo & Cajetana

1787 July 10 - son Giovanni Carlo born[88] (died 1788)[89]
> 187 = 124 = 11 July 1787 b yest - Joannes Carolus C
>> - Francesco Paolo & Cajetana C

death
> 639 = 82 = 20 May 1788 - Joannes C 10m?
>> - Francesco Paolo & Cajetana

1789 April 18 - daughter Grazia Giuseppa born[90]
> 210 = 143 = 19 Apr 1789 b yest - Gratia Josepha C
>> - Francesco Paolo & Cajetana C

---

[86]Maria Santissima delle Grazie, Terrasini, Palermo, Sicily, Italy, Baptismal register, 1778-1789, v. 14, p. 91, Antonia Alberta C baptism 1785; *Family Search.org*, "Battesimi 1778-1801," image 152 of 437.

[87]Maria Santissima delle Grazie (Chiesa Madre [Mother Church]), Terrasini, Palermo, Sicily, Italy, Death Register, v. 80 (1799-1835) p. 23, Antonia Gusmano, 1801; *Family Search.org*, "Morti 1782-1835," image 171 of 480.

[88]Maria Santissima delle Grazie, Terrasini, Palermo, Sicily, Italy, Baptismal register, 1778-1789, v. 14, p. 124, Joannes Carolus C baptism 1787; *Family Search.org*, "Battesimi 1778-1801," image 187 of 437.

[89]Maria Santissima delle Grazie, Terrasini, Palermo, Sicily, Italy, Death Register, v. 78, p. 82, Joannes C, 1788; *Family Search.org*, "Morti 1736-1788," image 639 of 642.

[90]Maria Santissima delle Grazie, Terrasini, Palermo, Sicily, Italy, Baptismal register, 1778-1789, v. 14, p. 143, Gratia Josepha C baptism 1789; *Family Search.org*, "Battesimi 1778-1801," image 210 of 437.

1791 March - daughter Giovanna Providenza born[91] (died September)[92]
    277 = 22 = – March 1791 b yest - Joanna Providentia G
     - Francesco Paolo & Cajetana C
    death
     23 = 102 = 18 Sept 1791 - Joanna G 7m - Francesco Paolo & Cajetana
1792 Aug 31 - daughter Giuseppa Nicolina born[93] (died 1808, age 16)[94]
    298 = 38 = 1 Sept 1792 b yest - Josepha Nicolina C
     - Francesco Paolo & Cajetana C
    death
    258 = 104 = 22 Oct 1808 - Josepha C 16 - Francesco Paolo & Cajetana
1795 May 21 - son Giovanni Vito born[95]
    328 = 66 = 22 May 1795 b yest - Joannes Vitus G
    - Francesco Paolo & Cajetana C
1797 Aug 1 - daughter Vita Giovanna born[96] (died 1818)[97]
    358 = 92 = 2 Aug 1797 b yest - Vita Joanna G
       - Francesco Paolo & Cajetana G
    death
    340 = 185 = 15 Oct 1818 - Vita G 23 unm
    d/o Francesco Paolo & Cajetana

---

[91]Maria Santissima delle Grazie, Terrasini, Palermo, Sicily, Italy, Baptismal register, 1789-1801, v. 15, p. 22, Joanna Providentia C baptism, 1791; *Family Search.org*, "Battesimi 1778-1801," image 277 of 437.

[92]Maria Santissima delle Grazie, Terrasini, Palermo, Sicily, Italy, Death Register, v. 78 continued, p. 102, Joanna G, 1791; *Family Search.org*, "Morti 1788-1799," image 23 of 83.

[93]Maria Santissima delle Grazie, Terrasini, Palermo, Sicily, Italy, Baptismal register, 1789-1801, v. 15, p. 38, Josepha Nicolina C baptism, 1792; *Family Search.org*, "Battesimi 1778-1801," image 298 of 437.

[94]Maria Santissima delle Grazie (Chiesa Madre [Mother Church]), Terrasini, Palermo, Sicily, Italy, Death Register, v. 80 (1799-1835) p. 104, Josepha Cusmano, 1808; *Family Search.org*, "Morti 1782-1835," image 258 of 480.

[95]Maria Santissima delle Grazie, Terrasini, Palermo, Sicily, Italy, Baptismal register, 1789-1801, v. 15, p. 66, Joannes Vitus C baptism, 1795; *Family Search.org*, "Battesimi 1778-1801," image 328 of 437.

[96]Maria Santissima delle Grazie, Terrasini, Palermo, Sicily, Italy, Baptismal register, 1789-1801, v. 15, p. 92, Vita Joanna G baptism, 1797; *Family Search.org*, "Battesimi 1778-1801," image 358 of 437.

[97]Maria Santissima delle Grazie (Chiesa Madre [Mother Church]), Terrasini, Palermo, Sicily, Italy, Death Register, v. 80 (1799-1835) p. 185, Vita Gusmano, 1818; *Family Search.org*, "Morti 1782-1835," image 340 of 480.

1800 July 25 - daughter Maria Anna Pietra born[98] (died 1802)[99]
     398 = 128 = 26 July 1800 b yest - Maria Anna Petra G
        - Francesco Paolo G & Gaetana Palazzolo
   death
     182 = 33 = 15 Jan 1802 - Maria Anna G 1y 6m
        - Franciscus & Cajetana
1804 Dec 13 - son Pietro Giuseppe born[100] (died Dec 23)[101]
     100 = 41 = 14 Dec 1804 b yest - Petrus Joseph G
        - Francisco Paolo G & Cajetana Palazzolo
   death
      230 = 78 = 23 Dec 1804 - Petrus G 9d - Francesco Paolo & Cajetana
1806 Dec 16 - wife Gaetana Palazzolo C died[102]
     245/6 = 43 = 16 Dec 1806 - Cajetana G 47
        - wife of Francesco Paolo G
        d/o Petro & Rosa Palazzolo
1821 August - died[103]
     360 = 204 = 3 or 5 Aug 1821 - Francesco Paolo G
        wid late Cajetana Palazzolo
        s/o Mr Joannes & Anna Maria

---

[98]Maria Santissima delle Grazie, Terrasini, Palermo, Sicily, Italy, Baptismal register, 1789-1801, v. 15, p. 128, Maria Anna Petra G baptism, 1800; *Family Search.org*, "Battesimi 1778-1801," image 398 of 437.

[99]Maria Santissima delle Grazie (Chiesa Madre [Mother Church]), Terrasini, Palermo, Sicily, Italy, Death Register, v. 80 (1799-1835) p. 33, Maria Anna Gusmano, 1802; *Family Search.org*, "Morti 1782-1835," image 182 of 480.

[100]Maria Santissima delle Grazie, Terrasini, Palermo, Sicily, Italy, Baptismal register, 1801-1814, v. 16, p. 41, Petrus Joseph C baptism, 1804; *Family Search.org*, "Battesimi 1801-1820," image 100 of 369.

[101]Maria Santissima delle Grazie (Chiesa Madre [Mother Church]), Terrasini, Palermo, Sicily, Italy, Death Register, v. 80 (1799-1835) p. 78, Petrus Gusmano, 1804; *Family Search.org*, "Morti 1782-1835," image 230 of 480.

[102]Maria Santissima delle Grazie (Chiesa Madre [Mother Church]), Terrasini, Palermo, Sicily, Italy, Death Register, v. 80 (1799-1835) p. 43, Cajetana Gusmano, 1806; *Family Search.org*, "Morti 1782-1835," image 245/6 of 480.

[103]Maria Santissima delle Grazie (Chiesa Madre [Mother Church]), Terrasini, Palermo, Sicily, Italy, Death Register, v. 80 (1799-1835) p. 204, Francesco Paolo Gusmano, 1821; *Family Search.org*, "Morti 1782-1835," image 360 of 480.

Children of Francesco Paolo and Gaetana Palazzolo

5. Anna Maria Giuseppa 1781
5. Rosa Francesca 1783-1850 + Matteo Bommarito (1809)
5. **Antonia** Alberta 1785-1801
5. Giovanni Carlo 1787-1788
5. Grazia Giuseppa 1789
5. Giovanna Providenza 1791-1791
5. **Giuseppa** Nicolina 1792-1808
5. **Giovanni** Vito 1795-1871 + Francesca Paola Bommarito
5. **Vita** Giovanna 1797-1818 - unm
5. Maria Pietra 1800-1802
5. Pietro Giuseppe 1804-1804

Our ancestor, Giovanni Vito (known as Giovanni) was the only son who survived to adulthood. An earlier Giovanni (Giovanni Carlo) died as an infant, as did a later son, Pietro Giuseppe (named after maternal grandfather Pietro Palazzolo).

Of the girls, only Rosa made it to married adulthood. One girl, Vita Giovanna, lived to age 21 but never married.

Of the other girls, it is certain (there are records) that one (Giovanna Providenzia) died in infancy and one (Maria Pietra) died at age 1 ½ . It is probable that two others - Anna Maria Giuseppa (1781) and Grazia Giuseppa (1789) - also died young, because there was another girl named Giuseppa - Giuseppa Nicolina - born after them, in 1792. Poor Giuseppa died at 16; her sister Antonia Alberta at 15.

Incidentally, although both Rosa and Giovanni married Bommaritos, the Bommaritos were not also siblings. Matteo's parents were Giovanni & Maria Anna Ventimiglia; Francesca Paola's were Salvatore & Catarina.

Generation 5: Giovanni & Francesca Paola Bommarito

Note: Giovanni is actually generation 7, but I found the earlier people by accident later in my searches, and I didn't want to go back and re-number everything - so I have continued to refer him as being of Generation 5.

Born in 1795, one of the 11 children of Francesco Gusmano & Gaetana Palazzolo, he was the only son to make it to adulthood. His grandfather and some of his uncles were given the Magistro/Maestro honorific, but his father, one of the younger sons, was not - so presumably they were going down in the world, if only a little. He was named after his paternal grandfather.

It is possible that he worked as a baker. Both his son and at least two of his grandsons were bakers, and his son's death certificate claimed his father was one too. So.

He married Francesca Paola Bommarito in 1822 (and there is - or was - a Bommarito bakery in Detroit), and together they had 13 children, two of whom seem to have been named Giovanni! I have no explanation for this, unless one was named Giovanni Vito (say) and the other Giovanni-something-else. The church records are clear - two separate Giovannis, both claiming to be unmarried sons of Giovanni & Francesca Paola, getting married to two different women on two different dates - and both giving their children the family names and having the same collection of people acting as godparents for their children. It is a puzzle. [Oddly enough, the same thing is true of his son Angelo: two sons named Giovanni. One married Anna Serra in 1886 and moved to Detroit, one married Providenzia Aluja in 1893 and stayed in Terrasini, at least until 1907.]

Another reason to think they were not as well-off as they once had been is that their sons start disappearing from the records, so I expect they moved on to greener pastures. It is certain that one of their Giovanni sons (our ancestor) moved to the town of Mazzara (now Mazara del Valle) in the Trapani province. At least 14 of their grandchildren moved to Detroit, with most of *their* children coming along - or making their own separate way(s) there - as well.

He died in 1871. I don't know when Francesca Paola died.

Timeline Giovanni Gusmano & Francesca Paola Bommarito
Giovanni b 1795, died 1871 - Francesca Paola b, d

1795 May 21 - born[104] - son of Francesco Paolo and Gaetana Palazzolo
    baptized 22 May - Maria Santissima delle Grazie, Terrasini
    328 = 66 = 22 May 1795 b yest - Joannes Vitus G
        - Francesco Paolo & Cajetana C
*1820 - revolt against Ferdinand I, King of the two Sicilies - put down by
Austria*
1822 Nov 21 - married Francesca Paola Bommarito
    banns[105]
    358 = 51 = 7 July 1822 - 1ˢᵗ Giovanni C bach Terr
        - Francesco Paolo G & Gaetana Palazzolo
       Francesca Paola Bommarito bach Terr - Salvatore & Caterina B
    marriage[106]
    491 = 116 = 21 Nov 1822 - Joannes G, unm
        - Francesco Paolo G & Cajetana Palazzolo
       Francesca Paola Bommarito - Salvatore & Catharina Bommarito
1823 June 9 - daughter Gaetana Julia (named after paternal grandmother)
born[107] - died 1831, age7
    28 = 97 = 9 June 1823 b today - Cajetana Julia
        - Joanne G & Francesca Paola Bommarito
       (Godmother - Julia Serra)
    death[108] - age 7
    439 = 278 = 30 Aug 1831 - Cajetana G 7
        - Joannes & Francesca Paola Bommarito

---

[104]Maria Santissima delle Grazie (Chiesa Madre [Mother Church]), Terrasini, Palermo, Sicily, Italy, Baptismal register, 1789-1801, v. 15, p. 66, Joannes Vitus Gusmano baptism 1795; *Family Search.org*, "Battesimi 1778-1801," image 328 of 437.

[105]Maria Santissima delle Grazie, Terrasini, Palermo, Sicily, Italy, Liber Denunciandorum, v. 72, 1814-1843, p. 51, Giovanni C banns 1822; *Family Search.org*, "Documenti Matrimoniali 1787-1843," image 358 of 492.

[106]Maria Santissima delle Grazie, Terrasini, Palermo, Sicily, Italy, Marriage register, v. 43, 1807-1835, p.116, Joannes Gusmano marriage 1822; *Family Search.org*, "Matrimoni 1757-1835," image 491 of 580.

[107]Maria Santissima delle Grazie (Chiesa Madre [Mother Church]), Terrasini, Palermo, Sicily, Italy, Baptismal register, 1815-1827, v. 17 [part 2, 1820-1827], p. 97, Cajetana Julia Gusmano baptism 1823; *Family Search.org*, "Battesimi 1820-1827," image 28 of 78.

[108]Maria Santissima delle Grazie (Chiesa Madre [Mother Church]), Terrasini, Palermo, Sicily, Italy, Death Register, v. 80 (1799-1835) p. 278, Cajetana G death 1831; *Family Search.org*, "Morti 1782-1835," image 439 of 480.

1825 June 7 - son Francesco (named after paternal grandfather) born[109]
     55 = 124 = 8 June 1825 b yest - Franciscus
     - Joanne G & Francesca Paola Bommarito
        (Godparents - Franciscus & Joachima Abbate)
     - married Maria Gratia Alfano
     death[110] - age 60
     226 = 159 = 25 Feb 1884 - Francesco Paolo G 60
        - Joannes & Francesca Paola Bommarito
1827 Nov 13 - son Salvatore (named after maternal grandfather) born[111]
     160 = 11 = 14 Nov 1827 b yest - Salvatore G
       - Joanne G & FP Bommarito
       (Godmother - Serafina, wife of Laurentius Lumetta)
     - married Rosalia Randazzo
     death[112] - age 69
     94 = 43 = 2 Nov 1896 - C Salvator 69
       - Joannes & Francesca Paola Bommarito
1830 April 25 - son Vincenzo born[113] - (d 1833)
     196 = 43 = 25 Apr 1830 b today- Vincentia G
       - Joanne G & FP Bommarito
       (Godmother - Josepha Palazzolo w/o Cajetanus)
     death[114] - age 3
     455 = 294 = 22 Sept 1833- Vincentius G 3
       - Joannes & Francesca Paola Bommarito

---

[109]Maria Santissima delle Grazie (Chiesa Madre [Mother Church]), Terrasini, Palermo, Sicily, Italy, Baptismal register, 1815-1827, v. 17 [part 2, 1820-1827], p. 124, Franciscus Gusmano baptism 1825; *Family Search.org*, "Battesimi 1820-1827," image 55 of 78.

[110]Maria Santissima delle Grazie, Terrasini, Palermo, Sicily, Italy, Death register, v. 86, 1871-1887, p. 159, Francesco Paolo G, 1884; *Family Search.org*, "Morti 1871-1892," image 226 of 476.

[111]Maria Santissima delle Grazie (Chiesa Madre [Mother Church]), Terrasini, Palermo, Sicily, Italy, Baptismal register, 1827-1835, v. 19, p. 11 , Salvator Gusmano baptism 1827; *Family Search.org*, " Battesimi 1818-1869," image 160 of 485.

[112]Maria Santissima delle Grazie, Terrasini, Palermo, Sicily, Italy, Death register, v. 88, 1893-1910, p. 43, Salvator C death 1896; *Family Search.org*, "Morti 1893-1910," image 94 of 207.

[113]Maria Santissima delle Grazie (Chiesa Madre [Mother Church]), Terrasini, Palermo, Sicily, Italy, Baptismal register, 1827-1835, v. 19, p. 43, Vincentia Gusmano baptism 1830; digital images, *Family Search.org*, "Battesimi 1818-1869," image 196 of 485.

[114]Maria Santissima delle Grazie (Chiesa Madre [Mother Church]), Terrasini, Palermo, Sicily, Italy, Death Register, v. 80 (1799-1835) p. 294, Vincentius G death 1833; *Family Search.org*, "Morti 1782-1835," image 455 of 480.

1832 June 21 - son Michele Angelo born[115] -
 229 = 71 = 21 June 1832 b today - Michael Angelus G
  - Joanne G & FP Bommarito
  (Godparents Michael Cappuccio? & Carmela ?)
 married Grazia Buffa, children to Detroit
1834 May 18 - daugher Giuseppa Grazia born[116]
 258 = 94 = 18 May 1834 b today - Josepha Gratia G
  - Joanne G & FP Bommarito
  (Godmother - Gratia Ventimiglia w/o Joachim)
 death[117] - age 75
 183 = 131 = 20 Jan 1908 - Josepha C 75
  - Joannes & Francesca Paola Bommarito
18xx - son Giuseppe born (no birth record found) - m Rosaria Buffa, at least
one child to Detroit
 marriage[118]
 200 = 161 = 7 Feb 1858 - Joseph G unm Terr
 - Joannes & Francesca Paola Bommarito
  Rosaria Buffa unm - Joannes & Petra di Maggio
1836 May 3 or 4 - son Giovanni born[119] - m Maria Assunta Giliberti, children
to Detroit
 328 = 3 = 6 May 1836 (3) - Joannes G
  - Joannes G & Francesca Paola Bommarito

---

[115]Maria Santissima delle Grazie (Chiesa Madre [Mother Church]), Terrasini,
Palermo, Sicily, Italy, Baptismal register, 1827-1835, v. 19, p. 71, Michael Angelus
Gusmano baptism 1832; digital images, *Family Search.org*, image 229 of 485.
[116]Maria Santissima delle Grazie (Chiesa Madre [Mother Church]), Terrasini,
Palermo, Sicily, Italy, Baptismal register, 1827-1835, v. 19, p. 94, Josepha Gratia
Gusmano baptism 1830; digital images, *Family Search.org*, "Battesimi 1818-1869,"
image 258 of 485.
[117]Maria Santissima delle Grazie, Terrasini, Palermo, Sicily, Italy, Death register, v.
88, 1893-1910, p. 131, Josepha C death 1908; *Family Search.org*, "Morti 1893-
1910," image 183 of 207.
[118]Maria Santissima delle Grazie, Terrasini, Palermo, Sicily, Italy, Marriage register,
v. ? cont., 1836-1858, p. 161 , Joseph G marriage 1858; *Family Search.org*,
"Documenti Matrimoniali 1836-1858," image 200 of 202.
[119]Maria Santissima delle Grazie (Chiesa Madre [Mother Church]), Terrasini,
Palermo, Sicily, Italy, Baptismal register, 1835-1869, v. 20, p. 3, Joannes Gusmano
baptism 1836; *Family Search.org*, " Battesimi 1818-1869," image 328 of 485.

1838 April 28 - son Filippo born[120] - married Anna Orlando, widow &
children (except for one) to Detroit

    358 = 29 = 28 Apr 1838 b today - Philippus G

     - Joanne G & Francesca Paola Bommarito

    death[121] - age 54

    272 = 200 = 17 June 1886 - Philippus C, 54

        - Joannes & Francesca Paola Ventimiglia

1840 Aug 2 - son Giovanni born[122] - m Ignatia Napolitano, children to
Detroit

    403 = 74 = 2 Aug 1840 b today - Joannes

        - Joanne G & Francesca Paola Bommarito

1842 - son Pietro born (no birth record found)

    death[123] - age 3

    391 = 16 = 28 Aug 1845 - Petrus C 3y - Joannes & FP Bommarito

1844 July 24 - daughter Gaetana born[124]

    49 = 9 = 25 July 1844 b yest - Cajetana C

        - Joanne G & Francesca Paula Bommarito

    (Godmother Gratia Bommarito w/o Cajetano Catalano)

1847 May 14 - daughter Caterina (named after maternal grandmother) born
[125] - died 1897

    98 = 49 = 14 May 1847 b today - Catharina C

        - Joanne G & Francesca Paola Bommarito

---

[120]Maria Santissima delle Grazie (Chiesa Madre [Mother Church]), Terrasini,
Palermo, Sicily, Italy, Baptismal register, 1835-1869, v. 20, p. 29, Philippus
Gusmano baptism 1838; digital images, *Family Search.org*, "Battesimi 1818-1869,"
image 358 of 485.

[121]Maria Santissima delle Grazie, Terrasini, Palermo, Sicily, Italy, Death register, v.
86, 1871-1887, p. 200, Philippus C death 1886; *Family Search.org*, "Morti 1871-
1892," image X of 272.

[122]Maria Santissima delle Grazie (Chiesa Madre [Mother Church]), Terrasini,
Palermo, Sicily, Italy, Baptismal register, v. 20, 1835-1869, p. 74, Joannes Gusmano
baptism 1840; digital images, *FamilySearch.org*, "Battesimi 1818-1869," image 403
of 485.

[123]Maria Santissima delle Grazie, Terrasini, Palermo, Sicily, Italy, Death Register, v.
83, 1843-1859, p. 16, Petrus C death 1845; *FamilySearch.org*, "Morti 1818-1859,"
image 391 of 562.

[124]Maria Santissima delle Grazie (Chiesa Madre [Mother Church]), Terrasini,
Palermo, Sicily, Italy, Baptismal register v 21, 1844-1853, p. 9, Cajetana Cusmano
baptism 1844; *Family Search.org*, " Battesimi 1844-1859," image 49 of 437.

[125]Maria Santissima delle Grazie (Chiesa Madre [Mother Church]), Terrasini,
Palermo, Sicily, Italy, Baptismal register v 21, 1844-1853, p. 49, Catherina
Gusmano baptism 1847; digital images, *Family Search.org*, "Battesimi 1844-1859,"
image 98 of 437.

(Godparents Salvator G & Maria Anna Grillo unm d/o?)
          99 = 47 = 10 May 1897 - Cusumano Catarina 52? -
                    Joannes & Francesca Paola Bommarito
          death[126] - age 52
          99 = 47 = 10 May 1897 - Cusumano Catarina 52
                    - Joannes & Francesca Paola Bommarito
1848 - Palermo commune established - suppressed 1849
1859 Sept 11 - son Giovanni married Maria Assunta Giliberti[127]
          339 = 196 = 11 Sept 1859 - Joannes G - Joanne & FP Bommarito
                    Maria Assunta Giliberti - Gratiano G & Gratia Lucido
1860 April/May - rebellion against the Bourbons - unification of Italy 1861
1867 May 12 - son Giovanni married Ignazia Napolitano[128]
          194 = 57 = 12 May 1867 - Joannes G - Joannes & FP Bommarito
                    Ignatia Napolitano
1871 Nov 14 - died[129]
          66 = 9 = 14 Nov 1871 - Joannes G, 70?
          - Francesco Paolo & Gaetana Palazzolo
1896 Apr 3 - son Angelo died[130]
          89 = 37 = 3 Apr 1896 - C Angelus 63
          - Joannes & Francesca Paola Bommarito
1896 Nov 2 - son Salvatore died[131]
          94 = 43 = 2 Nov 1896 - C Salvator 60 or 69
          - Joannes & Francesca Paola Bommarito

---

[126]Maria Santissima delle Grazie, Terrasini, Palermo, Sicily, Italy, Death register, v. 88, 1893-1910, p. 47, Catherina C death 1897; *Family Search.org*, "Morti 1893-1910," image 90 of 207

[127]Maria Santissima delle Grazie (Chiesa Madre [Mother Church]), Terrasini, Palermo, Sicily, Italy, Marriage register, v. 45, 1862-1878, p. 196, Joannes Gusmano marriage 1859; *Family Search.org*, "Matrimoni 1814-1878," image 339 of 453.

[128]Maria Santissima delle Grazie (Chiesa Madre [Mother Church]), Terrasini, Palermo, Sicily, Italy, Marriage register, v. 45, 1862-1878, p. 57, Joannes Gusmano marriage 1867; digital images, *Family Search.org*, "Matrimoni 1814-1878." image 194 of 453.

[129]Maria Santissima delle Grazie (Chiesa Madre [Mother Church]), Terrasini, Palermo, Sicily, Italy, Death register, v. 86, 1871-1887, p. 9, Joannes Gusmano, 1871; *Family Search.org*, "Morti 1871-1892," image 66 of 476.

[130]Maria Santissima delle Grazie (Chiesa Madre [Mother Church]), Terrasini, Palermo, Sicily, Italy, Death register, v. 88, 1893-1910, p. 37, Angelus Gusmano, 1896; *Family Search.org*, "Morti 1893-1910," image 89 of 207.

[131]Maria Santissima delle Grazie (Chiesa Madre [Mother Church]), Terrasini, Palermo, Sicily, Italy, Death register, v. 88, 1893-1910, p. 43, Salvator Gusmano, 1896; digital images, *Family Search.org*, "Morti 1893-1910," image 94 of 207.

1897 May 10 - daughter Catarina died[132]
	99 = 47 = 10 May 1897 - Cusumano Catarina 52
	- Joannes & Francesca Paola Bommarito
1908 Jan 20 - daughter Giuseppa died[133]
	183 = 131 = 20 Jan 1908 - Josepha C 75
	- Joannes & Francesca Paola Bommarito

---

[132]Maria Santissima delle Grazie (Chiesa Madre [Mother Church]), Terrasini,
Palermo, Sicily, Italy, Death register, v. 88, 1893-1910, p. 47, Catarina Cusumano,
1897; digital images, *Family Search.org*, "Morti 1893-1910," image 99 of 207.
[133]Maria Santissima delle Grazie (Chiesa Madre [Mother Church]), Terrasini,
Palermo, Sicily, Italy, Death register, v. 88, 1893-1910, p. 131, Josepha Cusumano,
1908; digital images, *Family Search.org*, "Morti 1893-1910," image 183 of 207.

Children of Giovanni & Francesca Paola Bommarito

6. Gaetana Julia 1823-1831
6. **Francesco** 1825-1884 + Maria Grazia Alfano (1850)
6. **Salvatore** 1827-1896 + Rosalia Randazzo (1854)
6. Vincenzo 1830-1833
6. Michele **Angelo** 1832-1896 + Grazia Buffa (1853)
6. Giuseppa Grazia 1834-1908
6. Giuseppe 18xx + Rosaria Buffa (1858)
6. **Giovanni** 1836 - 1908 (Mazzara) + Maria Assunta Giliberti (1859)
6. **Filippo** 1838-1886 + Anna Orlando (1867)
6. Giovanni 1840 - + Ignatia Napolitano
6. Pietro 1842-1845
6. Gaetana 1844-
6. Catarina 1847-1897

Three of the children died young: Gaetana Julia at age 7, Vincenzo at age 3, and Pietro at age 3. I don't know what happened to the second Gaetana (born 1844).

Two of the girls lived to a decent old age, but I haven't (yet) found marriage or other records for them. Giuseppina died at age 75, and Catarina at age 52.

Francesco died at about age 60 in Terrasini; he and Maria Grazia Alfano had several children, all baptized in Terrasini, but I haven't found anything but their baptismal and sometimes death records.

Salvatore died in Terrasini at age 69, so he might have been living there all his life, but only one child was baptized there, so it is possible that he lived elsewhere for a while.

Angelo, like his father, named at least two of his sons Giovanni. One of them emigrated to Detroit, as did all his other surviving sons, one remained in Terrasini until at least 1907. I don't know what happened to his daughters.

I don't know what happened to Giuseppe & Rosaria Buffa, but two of their daughters (Rosalia and Grazia) emigrated to Detroit.

Filippo married Anna Orlando; he died in Terrasini in 1886, age 48. After his death, all his children (except the eldest, Francesca Paola, married to Rosolino Giliberti) as well as his widow Anna emigrated - first to Oakfield,

New York, then to Detroit. His son, Francesco Paolo, married brother Giovanni's granddaughter Rosalia.

Then there are the two Giovannis.

--Our great-great grandfather, who was a baker, married Maria Assunta Giliberti. It would appear he moved to Mazzara when his sons did (in about 1886); he died there in 1908. One of his sons, our ancestor Giovanni, moved on to Detroit; son Graziano seems to have stayed in Mazzara.

–The other Giovanni married Ignatia Napolitano and seems to have stayed mostly in Terrasini. I have no information about him except what is in the church records, and I have no idea what he did for a living or when he died. After the birth of daughter Marianna in 1888, he disappears from the records, so possibly he moved to another city, or possibly he emigrated. Three of his children did emigrate, and ended up in Detroit.

For the records I have on the children of Giovanni & Francesca Paola, see Volume 2. There will also be more records for later descendants in The Detroit Cusmanos.

Generation 6: Giovanni & Maria Assunta Giliberti

There are a fair number of records for our Great-great Grandfather Giovanni; unfortunately they are contradictory.

He was born in the mid-1830s, to Giovanni and Francesca Paola Bommarito. His death certificate says he was born 1834 (died 1908, age 74). [It also lists his parents as Giovanni and Francesca Paola Mazzola (I think, it is not very easy to read). Mazzola is the name of this Giovanni's daughter-in-law, so I think there was a simple mistake here.] There is a baptism for a Giovanni born in 1836, and another born 1840. Generally speaking, that occurs when a child dies: the next available baby is given the name. But I haven't been able to find a death record for the first Giovanni.

To add to the confusion, there are two adult Giovannis, sons of Giovanni and Francesco Paola Bommarito, floating around in the records, and it isn't clear if the baptisms refer to either (or both) of them. Our Giovanni got married in 1859 to Maria Assunta Giliberti, and the other Giovanni got married in 1867, to Ignazia (Agnes) Napolitano - at a time when Maria Assunta was still alive. Both of them are listed in the marriage register as unmarried sons of Giovanni and Francesca Paola.

So. Either the priests made a mistake in the marriage (or birth) registers OR there were two Giovannis born to Giovanni and Francesca Paola. If you compare the records available, you will see that (1) our Giovanni seems to have been older than the other Giovanni - so that they could have been two separate people - and also (2) that one man *could* have fathered all those children - our Giovanni's children were, with the exception of the late-born Joseph, all born before the other Giovanni started having children. So it doesn't help much. One odd thing is that they traveled in the same circles - Anna Orlando, wife of brother Philip, was godmother to a child of each of the Giovannis. My personal guess is that they were two separate people - maybe one of them was named, say, Giovanni Baptista? Because I cannot believe that the priests would not notice that one man was marrying two different women. And also - there were banns! Surely someone else, if not the priests, would have noticed.

Another point (yes, sigh) - Giovanni's brother Angelo, who married Grazia Buffa, also had two sons named Giovanni. Same story - one Giovanni -"unmarried son of Angelo & Grazia" - married Anna Serra in 1886 and emigrated to Detroit in about 1901; another Giovanni - "unmarried son of Angelo & Grazia" - married Providenzia Aluja in 1893 and stayed in Terrasini until at least 1907.

To get back to the narrative.

Giovanni was a baker, and, according to his death record, his father was a baker too.

In 1859, September 11, he married Maria Assunta Giliberti, the daughter of Graziano Giliberti and Grazia Lucido. Their first child, a son, named Giovanni after his paternal grandfather, was born in 1860 [this is our great-grandfather Giovanni, the one who emigrated to the US]. In 1864, they had another son, named Graziano after Maria Assunta's father - and then no more children until Joseph born 1871. [His brother and sister-in-law, Philip and Anna Orlando, acted as godparents to Joseph; Giovanni and Maria Assunta had been godparents to Philip and Anna's first daughter, Francesca Paola in 1868.] [Francesca Paola, incidentally, would eventually marry Rosolino Giliberti - although I have not yet figured out just what relation he was to Maria Assunta.] Those are all the children I have found for these two - and I have found no further records for Joseph, not death or marriage or baptism-of-children. This is extremely rare! I suspect there were more children - possibly in the records of a different parish.

I suspect this because Giovanni lived in interesting times. Things started heating up politically in the 1800s. In 1820, there was a revolution; the King (Ferdinand I of the two Sicilies) capitulated, but the "great powers" - especially Austria, which controlled northern Italy - could not let the concessions stand, and the revolt was brutally suppressed. In 1837, in the east, the cities of Catania and Siracusa rose again, again unsuccessfully. In 1848, the "year of revolution" all over Europe, a provisional government was proclaimed in Palermo - but it lasted only 18 months, and was - again - brutally suppressed (which led to a rise in banditry - hmm, could that have anything to do with all those children of unknown parents?). In 1860, in April, a group of insurgents attempted to take Palermo; they were forced to accept a cease-fire (April 17 - on the beach at Favarotta) but their actions may have helped convince Garibaldi that the invasion of Sicily was worth the risk. When he landed on May 11, they immediately took up arms again, and May 15 slaughtered the Bourbon army. "They" were peasants, led by the bandit Giuseppe Badalamenti (the Badalamentis later became famous Mafiosi) of Cinisi. So the whole area was in an uproar - and that was exactly when and where Giovanni and Maria Assunta were beginning their family. (GG Giovanni was born in June 1860.)

Unfortunately things did not get better for the Sicilians after the unification:

That [the idea that the land would be governed by the Sicilians, for their benefit] was the illusion of the men who killed and died for Garibaldi - and the fantasy of Garibaldi himself. It had evaporated within a year of the Bourbon collapse, when Garibaldi's bankrollers from Turin and Milan descended on Sicily with money, lawyers, and

the benign approval of the Italian state. The old aristocratic fiefs were
dismembered and sold to the highest bidders.[134]

    After the unification of Sicily and Italy in 1861, fertile estates
were steadily acquired by men who were seldom interested in the new
methods . . . . Their interests, their profit margins, were served by
keeping Sicily in the darkness, not in forcing it into the light.[135]

This is why I wonder about our ancestors' class and political affiliations.
Were they part of the insurgency? According to Viviano, between seven and
eight thousand Sicilians joined Garibaldi, but maybe as many as twenty
thousand were involved informally, in local squadrons. And "a high
proportion were young men from the Castellamare towns and villages, drawn
to a sixty-mile-long swath of battleground between Marsala and Palermo
with Terrasini at its northern flank."[136]

    So what were our ancestors doing?

    Sometime between 1885 and 1887, Giovanni's sons Giovanni and
Graziano moved to Mazzara (now Mazara del Valle) in the Trapani province,
and I suspect Giovanni and Maria Assunta accompanied them. They all
worked as bakers.

    Son Giovanni emigrated to the US in 1901 [where he worked as a
baker], and eventually all his family joined him there. Graziano apparently
remained in Mazzara, although he visited Giovanni in Detroit on at least 3
occasions.

    This Giovanni died in Mazzara in 1908. I have not found any further
records for Maria Assunta.

---

[134]Frank Viviano, *Blood washes blood : a true story of love, murder, and redemption
under the Sicilian Sun* (New York: Washington Square Press (published by Pocket
Books), 2001), p. 231.

[135]Ibid., p. 127

[136]Ibid., p. 77.

Timeline 6. Giovanni & Maria Assunta Giliberti

Giovanni b 1834 Terrasini -d 1908 Mazzara, Maria Assunta b? d?

1834-1840 - born, Terrasini, Palermo, Sicily
    - son of Giovanni & Francesca Paola Bommarito
    1834 - born (based on death certificate - died 1908, age 74)[137]
    1836 May 6 - baptized Maria Santissima delle Grazie, Terrasini[138]
        328 = 3 = 6 May 1836 (3) - Joannes G
        - Joannes G & Francesca Paola Bommarito
    1840 Aug 2 - baptized Maria Santissima delle Grazie, Terrasini[139]
        403 = 74 = 2 Aug 1840 b today - Joannes
        - Joanne G & Francesca Paola Bommarito
1859 Sept 11 - married Maria Assunta Giliberti
    339 = 196 = 11 Sept 1859 - Joannes G - Joanne & FP Bommarito[140]
        Maria Assunta Giliberti - Gratiano G & Gratia Lucido
1860 June 19 - son Giovanni born
    289 = 128/9 = 19 June 1860 b today - Joannes G
        - Joanne G & Maria Assunta Giliberti[141]
    24 = #81 - 19 June 1860 - Giovanni

---

[137]Mazara del Vallo, Trapani, "Registro degli Atti di Morte [Registry of Acts of Death] 1908" : entry # 336, Giovanni Cusumano; digital images, *Antenati [Ancestors]*, Trapani, Mazara del Vallo, Morti [Deaths] 1908 (http://www.antenati.san.beniculturali.it/v/Archivio+di+Stato+di+Trapani/Stato+civile+italiano/Mazara+del+Vallo/), image #148 (screen 4); Ministerio dei beni e delle attivita culturale e del tourismo [Ministry of health and cultural activity and tourism], Direzione generale per gli archivi [Directorate-General for Archives], Archivio di Stato di Trapani [State archives of Trapani], Stato civile italiano [Italian civil records], Mazara del Vallo.

[138]Maria Santissima delle Grazie (Chiesa Madre [Mother Church]), Terrasini, Palermo, Sicily, Italy, Baptismal register, 1835-1869, v. 20, p. 3, Joannes Gusmano baptism 1836; *Family Search.org*, "Battesimi 1818-1869," image 328 of 485.

[139]Maria Santissima delle Grazie (Chiesa Madre [Mother Church]), Terrasini, Palermo, Sicily, Italy, Baptismal register, v. 20, 1835-1869, p. 74, Joannes Gusmano baptism 1840; *FamilySearch.org*, "Battesimi 1818-1869," image 403 of 485.

[140]Maria Santissima delle Grazie (Chiesa Madre [Mother Church]), Terrasini, Palermo, Sicily, Italy, Marriage register, v. 45, 1862-1878, p. 196, Joannes Gusmano marriage 1859; *Family Search.org*, "Matrimoni 1814-1878," image 339 of 453.

[141]Maria Santissima delle Grazie (Chiesa Madre [Mother Church]), Terrasini, Palermo, Sicily, Italy, Baptismal register, v. 26, 1854-1861, p. 128-9, Joannes Gusmano baptism 1860; *Family Search.org*, "Battesimi 1854-1861," image 289 of 323.

s/o Giovanni & Maria Assunta Giliberti - [142]

(Godparents - Vita Zerilli w/o Nicolo)

1863 - Maria Assunta acted as godmother to the son of Giuseppe Gusmano & Rosaria Buffa

74 = #6 = 19 Jan 1863 - Giovanni G b yest - Giuseppe & Rosaria Buffa[143]

(Maria Assunta Giliberti)

1864 May 25 - son Graziano born[144]

191 = 44-5 = 26 May 1864 b yest - Gratianus G

- Joannes & Maria Assunta Giliberti

1866 - Maria Assunta acted as godmother to the daughter of Angelo Gusmano & Grazia Buffa

232 = p. 84 = 18 May 1866 - Petra Maria - Angelo G & Gratia Buffa[145]

(Maria Assunta G w/o Joannes)

1867 May 12 - the other Giovanni married Ignazia (Agnes) Napolitano[146]

1868 Feb 20 - the other Giovanni's son Giovanni born, named after paternal grandfather[147] - died 1869

1868 - Giovanni and Maria Assunta acted as godparents for his niece, Francesca Paola

---

[142]Maria Santissima delle Grazie (Chiesa Madre [Mother Church]), Terrasini, Palermo, Sicily, Italy, Baptismal register, v. 27, 1859-1863, record #81, Giovanni Gusmano baptism 1860; *Family Search.org*, "Battesimi 1859-1878," image 24 of 481.

[143]Maria Santissima delle Grazie (Chiesa Madre [Mother Church]), Terrasini, Palermo, Sicily, Italy, Baptismal register, v. 27, 1859-1863, p. 6, Giovanni Gusmano baptism 1863; *FamilySearch.org*, "Battesimi 1859-1878," image 74 of 481.

[144]Maria Santissima delle Grazie (Chiesa Madre [Mother Church]), Terrasini, Palermo, Sicily, Italy, Baptismal register, v. 28, 1862-1872, p. 44-5, Gratianus Gusmano baptism 1864; *FamilySearch.org*, "Battesimi 1859-1878," image 191 of 481.

[145]Maria Santissima delle Grazie (Chiesa Madre [Mother Church]), Terrasini, Palermo, Sicily, Italy, Baptismal register, v. 28, 1862-1872, p. 84, Petra Maria Gusmano baptism 1866; *FamilySearch.org*, "Battesimi 1859-1878," image 232 of 481.

[146]Maria Santissima delle Grazie (Chiesa Madre [Mother Church]), Terrasini, Palermo, Sicily, Italy, Marriage register, v. 45, 1862-1878, p. 57, Joannes Gusmano marriage 1867; *Family Search.org*, "Matrimoni 1814-1878," image 194 of 453.

[147]Maria Santissima delle Grazie (Chiesa Madre [Mother Church]), Terrasini, Palermo, Sicily, Italy, Baptismal register, v. 28, 1862-1872, p. 114, Joannes Gusmano baptism 1868; *Family Search.org*, "Battesimi 1859-1878," image 264 of 481.

283 = 133 = 17 Nov 1868 b yest - Francisca Paola - Phillipi G & Anna Orlando[148] (Joannes G & Maria Assunta)

1869 April 29 - the other Giovanni's son Philip born, named after maternal grandfather[149]

1871 Jan 23 - the other Giovanni's daughter Francesca Paola born, named after paternal grandmother[150]

1871 June 1 - son Joseph born

    336 = 182 = 2 June 1871 b yest - Joseph G

        s/o Joanne & Maria Assunta Giliberti[151]

        (Godparents - Phlippus G & Anna Orlando)

1872 Oct - the other Giovanni's daughter Rosaria born, named after maternal grandmother[152] - this may have been Rosario - died before 1878

1874 Nov 11- the other Giovanni's daughter Grazia born[153]

1877 March 8 - the other Giovanni's son Giovanni born[154]

1878 Oct 27 - the other Giovanni's daughter Rosaria born[155]

---

[148]Maria Santissima delle Grazie (Chiesa Madre [Mother Church]), Terrasini, Palermo, Sicily, Italy, Baptismal register, v. 28, 1862-1872, p. 133, Francesca Paola Gusmano baptism 1868; *FamilySearch.org*, "Battesimi 1859-1878," image 283 of 481.

[149]Maria Santissima delle Grazie (Chiesa Madre [Mother Church]), Terrasini, Palermo, Sicily, Italy, Baptismal register, v. 28, 1862-1872, p. 146, Philippus Gusmano baptism 1869; *FamilySearch.org*, "Battesimi 1859-1878," image 298 of 481.

[150]Santa Rosalia Favarotta (daughter church), Terrasini, Palermo, Sicily, Italy, Baptismal register v. 25, 1854-1871, p. 89, Francesca Paola Gusmano baptism 1871; *Family Search.org*, "Battesimi 1854-1861," image 93 of 323.

[151]Maria Santissima delle Grazie (Chiesa Madre [Mother Church]), Terrasini, Palermo, Sicily, Italy, Baptismal register, v. 28, 1862-1872, p. 182, Joseph Gusmano baptism 1871; *FamilySearch.org*, "Battesimi 1859-1878," image 336 of 481.

[152]Maria Santissima delle Grazie (Chiesa Madre [Mother Church]), Terrasini, Palermo, Sicily, Italy, Baptismal register, v. 28, 1862-1872, p. 204, Rosaria Gusmano baptism 1872; *FamilySearch.org*, "Battesimi 1859-1878," image 363 of 481.

[153]Maria Santissima delle Grazie (Chiesa Madre [Mother Church]), Terrasini, Palermo, Sicily, Italy, Baptismal register, v. 30, 1873-1881, p. 39, Gratia Gusmano baptism 1874; *Family Search.org*, "Battesimi 1873-1889," image 102 of 792.

[154]Maria Santissima delle Grazie (Chiesa Madre [Mother Church]), Terrasini, Palermo, Sicily, Italy, Baptismal register, v. 30, 1873-1881, p. 93, Joannes Gusmano baptism 1877; *FamilySearch.org*, "Battesimi 1873-1889," image 155 of 792.

[155]Maria Santissima delle Grazie (Chiesa Madre [Mother Church]), Terrasini, Palermo, Sicily, Italy, Baptismal register, v. 30, 1873-1881, p. 128, Rosaria Gusmano baptism 1878; *FamilySearch.org*, "Battesimi 1873-1889," image 190 of 792.

1880 Dec 11 - alt-Giovanni's son Rosario born[156]
1881? - the other Giovanni's daughter Sarah born????
1882, 1883 - Maria Assunta acted as godmother to her granddaughter Maria Assunta

> 376 = 8 = 22 March 1882 b yest - Maria Assunta
> > d/o Joannes Cusumano & Antonina Mazzola[157]
> > (Godmother - Maria Assunta Giliberti)
> 417 = 43 = 24 March 1883 b yest - Maria Assunta
> > d/o Joannes Gusmano & Antonia Mazzola[158]
> > (Maria Assunta Giliberti)

1883 Feb 6 - alt-Giovanni's twins Maria Anna and Catharina born[159]
1884 Dec 26 - alt-Giovanni's son Giovanni born[160]
1885-1887? - moved to Mazzara, in company with his sons???
1888 Feb 17 - alt-Giovanni's daughter Marianna born[161]

---

[156]Maria Santissima delle Grazie (Chiesa Madre [Mother Church]), Terrasini, Palermo, Sicily, Italy, Baptismal register, v. 30, 1873-1881, p. 188, Rosario Gusmano baptism 1880; *FamilySearch.org*, "Battesimi 1873-1889," image 261 of 792.

[157]Maria Santissima delle Grazie (Chiesa Madre [Mother Church]), Terrasini, Palermo, Sicily, Italy, Baptismal register, v. 31, 1882-1889, p. 8, Maria Assunta Cusumano baptism 1882; *Family Search.org*, "Battesimi 1873-1889," image 376 of 792.

[158]Maria Santissima delle Grazie (Chiesa Madre [Mother Church]), Terrasini, Palermo, Sicily, Italy, Baptismal register, v. 31, 1882-1889, p. 43, Maria Assunta Cusumano baptism 1883; *FamilySearch.org*, "Battesimi 1873-1889," image 417 of 481.

[159]Maria Santissima delle Grazie (Chiesa Madre [Mother Church]), Terrasini, Palermo, Sicily, Italy, Baptismal register, v. 31, 1882-1889, p. 40, Catharina & Maria Anna Gusmano baptism 1883; *Family Search.org*, "Battesimi 1873-1889," image 414 of 792.

[160]Maria Santissima delle Grazie (Chiesa Madre [Mother Church]), Terrasini, Palermo, Sicily, Italy, Baptismal register, v. 31, 1882-1889, p. 120, Joannes Gusmano baptism 1884; *FamilySearch.org*, "Battesimi 1873-1889," image 504 of 792.

[161]Maria Santissima delle Grazie (Chiesa Madre [Mother Church]), Terrasini, Palermo, Sicily, Italy, Baptismal register, v. 31, 1882-1889, p. 248, Marianna Gusmano baptism 1888; *FamilySearch.org*, "Battesimi 1873-1889," image 682 of 792.

1908 Sept 13 - died, Mazara, Trapani, Sicily
        Screen 4 image 148 #327 - 14 Sept 1908 (yest?) - Cusumano Giovanni
- via Garibaldi[162]
        Giovanni 74 years old, baker, res Mazara, b Terrasini
        father Giovanni, mother Francesca Paola M?
         - married to Maria Assunta Giliberti

Children of Giovanni and Maria Assunta Giliberti

7. Giovanni 1860-1943 + Antonina Mazzola (1881) -> **Detroit**
7. Graziano 1864 + Francesca Arena (1890 Mazzara)
7. Giuseppe 1871

    Both Graziano and Giovanni moved to Mazzara in the early 1880s,
where they worked as bakers. Giovanni (our ancestor) and his wife Lena
Mazzola seem to have alternated for a while between Mazzara and Terrasini
(they have children baptized in both places). Graziano apparently stayed in
Mazzara pretty much continually. He married there in 1890.
    Giovanni emigrated to Detroit in 1901 and over the next 10 years his
family joined him there. Graziano was in Detroit on at least four occasions,
but seems to have always returned to Mazzara.
    About Giuseppe, nothing more is known (by me).

---

[162]Mazara del Vallo, Trapani, "Registro degli Atti di Morte [Registry of Acts of
Death] 1908" : entry #327, Giovanni Gusmano [Image 148, screen 4, 1908].

Generation 7: Giovanni & Lena Mazzola
- Terrasini, Sicily - Detroit, Michigan

Great Grandpa Giovanni was born on June 19, 1860 to Giovanni Cusumano and Maria Assunta Giliberti. He was the oldest male child and therefore he was named after his father's father. He was baptized in the big church in the center of Terrasini - Maria Santissima delle Grazie - the same day he was born.

He had at least two brothers, Graziano, named after his mother's father, and Giuseppe. There may have been more, but if so, they weren't born and baptized in Terrasini. His father was a baker, and both he and brother Graziano were bakers - and maybe Giuseppe too, although I haven't been able to trace him.

In 1881 - March 10 - he married Antonina (Lena) Mazzola, and their first child, a daughter named Maria Assunta after his mother, was born a year later. She died when she was only two months old. A year later (1883), another little girl was born, also named Maria Assunta, and she survived. Both girls had their grandmother as godmother.

In 1885, a second little girl was born. She should have been named Lorenza, after her mother's mother, but instead she was named Rosalia, after the patron saint of Palermo. I have wondered if maybe this was the result of a vow.

Shortly after Rosalia was born, the family moved to Mazzara, in the Trapani province. I wonder what the story behind the move was - mostly Sicilians stayed where they were, so this was an uncommon thing. (Although not so much for our ancestors, apparently!)

In Mazzara, Giovanni worked as a baker again - as did his brother Graziano, who had also moved.

In Mazzara, Giovanni and Lena had a son, Giovanni, named after Giovanni's father. He was born in 1887 and died 8 months later in 1888. In 1889, a girl, named Grazia (after Giovanni's grandmother?) was born. In 1891, another Giovanni was born (he died when he was a year old, in 1892). Also in 1891, a few days after Giovanni was born, little Grazia died, 1 year 8 months old.

They seem to have alternated between Mazzara and Terrasini for the next few years: another baby Grazia was baptized in Terrasini in 1892, but died in Mazzara in 1894; our Grandpa Jack (another Giovanni) was born in Terrasini in 1895, and uncle Chris (named after Lena's father)was born in Mazzara in 1899.

How did they bear all that loss?

In 1901, Great Grandpa Giovanni came to America. He said he was going to New York, but must have moved to Detroit fairly soon afterwards, because in 1903, Grandpa Jack, 7 years old, came over with his uncle Graziano - and he said he was going to his father in Detroit.

Incidentally, Graziano did not remain in Detroit, at least not for long. He visited Giovanni in 1909, 1912, and 1914. In 1912, he brought along his son, Giovanni. I don't think cousin Giovanni remained in Detroit either, but I am not sure.

In 1905, both his daughters emigrated, separately. Rosalia had married her cousin (2nd cousin I think) Paul in early 1905, and joined him in Oakfield, New York. Maria Assunta went directly to Detroit, and married Graziano Serra a month or two later. In 1909, Lena and Chris emigrated. Sometime before 1913, Rosalia and her family moved to Detroit, so from then on, the whole family was there.

They all lived in Little Italy, in the parish of Holy Family, which had been set up to be a specifically Italian parish. Great Grandpa lived on Woodbridge, in a three-family house (after Grandpa Jack and Grandma Ruth were married, they lived with them for a while). The Serras lived on Larned Street - Graziano had a grocery store. Paul and Rosalia lived in various places - Riopelle, Lafayette - but from 1935 at least they lived on Chestnut Street. Great Grandpa still worked as a baker, and Lena helped him out in the bakery. [In 1918, his nephew Giuseppe worked as a driver for Cusumano Bakery on Clinton Street.??] Mom remembers them living on Fort Street, in an old Fire Station, but I haven't found any records of them there. (Giovanni disappeared from the city directories and censuses after 1935.)

Lena died in 1937, and Giovanni in 1943. They are both buried in Mt Olivet cemetery, 6-Mile & Dequindre, but only Lena has a stone.

Mom remembered him as a bit of a dandy, and also a womanizer (that has been confirmed by a cousin I met online). She thought he had a crossed eye (like mine) but his arrival document (the ship manifest) says he was actually blind in one eye.

Timeline Giovanni & Lena Mazzola
Giovanni b 1860 Terrasini, d 1943 Detroit; Lena b 1858 Terrasini, d 1937 Detroit

1860 June 19 - born, Terrasini, Palermo, Sicily[163] - son of Giovanni & Maria Assunta Giliberti
> baptized Maria Santissima delle Grazie, Terrasini
> 289 = 128/9 = 19 June 1860 b today - Joannes G
>> - Joanne G & Maria Assunta Giliberti
> 24 = #81 - 19 June 1860 - Giovanni
>> s/o Giovanni & Maria Assunta Giliberti - [164]
> (Vita Zerilli w/o Nicolo)

1881 March 10 - married Lena Mazzola[165]
> Atti di Matrimonio - numero 7 - 1881, 10? March
>> - can't read the hour -
> In front of me - Pietro Palazzolo, something and Official of the Civil State, in my official capacity, appeared before me

> 1. Gusmano Giovanni, 21 years old, single, something (I think panottiere? baker?)
> born in Terrasini, resident of Terrasini, son of Giovanni resident of Terrasini and of Maria Assunta Giliberti? resident of Terrasini;
> 2. Mazzola Antonina, 23 years old, single, villica, born in Terrasini, resident of Terrasini, daughter of Cristoforo resident of Terrasini and of Vitale Lorenza resident of Terrasini

---

[163]Maria Santissima delle Grazie (Chiesa Madre [Mother Church]), Terrasini, Palermo, Sicily, Italy, Baptismal register, v. 26, 1854-1861, p. 128-9, Joannes Gusmano baptism 1860; *Family Search.org*, "Battesimi 1854-1861," image 289 of 323.

[164]Maria Santissima delle Grazie (Chiesa Madre [Mother Church]), Terrasini, Palermo, Sicily, Italy, Baptismal register, v. 27, 1859-1863, record #81, Giovanni Gusmano baptism 1860; *Family Search.org*, "Battesimi 1859-1878," image 24 of 481.

[165]Palermo (Palermo), Ufficio dello stato civile, "Registro degli atti di Matrimonio [Register of Marriages], 1881" : entry #7, Giovanni Gusmano; digital images, *FamilySearch.org*,
"Italia, Palermo, Palermo, Stato Civile (Tribunale), 1866-1910"
(https://familysearch.org/ark:/61903/3:1:3QSQ-G97B-27ZM?cc=2051639&wc=MC TM-1TG%3A351055601%2C353722501%2C353605302 : 22 May 2014), Palermo > Terrasini > image 1991 of 2313; citing Tribunale di Cagliari (Cagliari Court, Cagliari).

who requested me to marry them. To this effect they presented me with documents described below, and upon examination of these there was no [not sure here, but I think there was nothing missing], and I placed them into the volume of annexes to this register, so that nothing precludes the celebration of their marriage, I read to the couple the articles 130, 131, and 132 of the Civil Code, and when I demanded of the man if (who?) he intended to take as his wife he presented Mazzola, Antonina, and to her who? she intended to take as husband she presented Gusmano, Giovanni, and having given me each response affermatively and fully understanding also the witnesses indicated below, I pronounced in the name of the law that they were united in marriage. To this act were present:

Biondo Antonino 22 civile? and

Ottijane? Giuseppe 58? civile?

both resident in this commune. The documents presented

[here is a handwritten list of docs I can't read]

signed by Giovanni, the witnesses, and Pietro Palazzolo (not Antonina)

1882 March 21 - daughter Maria Assunta born[166]
    baptized Maria Santissima delle Grazie, Terrasini
    22 March 1882 b yest - Maria Assunta
    - Joannes Cusumano & Antonina Mazzola
        (Maria Assunta Giliberti)

1882 June 17 - dau Maria Assunta died[167]
    192 = 129 = 17 June 1882 - Maria Assunta, 2 mo,
    d/o Joannes & Antonina Mazzola

1883 March 23 - daughter Mary Assunta born Terrasini[168]
    baptized March 24 Maria Santissima delle Grazie, Terrasini
    417 = 43 = 24 March 1883 b yest - Maria Assunta
        d/o Joannes Gusmano & Antonia Mazzola
        (Maria Assunta Giliberti)

---

[166]Maria Santissima delle Grazie (Chiesa Madre [Mother Church]), Terrasini, Palermo, Sicily, Italy, Baptismal register, v. 31, 1882-1889, p. 8, Maria Assunta Cusumano baptism 18 *Family Search.org*, "Battesimi 1873-1889," image 376 of 792.

[167]Maria Santissima delle Grazie (Chiesa Madre [Mother Church]), Terrasini, Palermo, Sicily, Italy, Death register, v. 86, 1871-1887, p. 192, Maria Assunta Cusumano, 1882; *Family Search.org*, "Morti 1871-1892." image 192 of 476.

[168]Maria Santissima delle Grazie (Chiesa Madre [Mother Church]), Terrasini, Palermo, Sicily, Italy, Baptismal register, v. 31, 1882-1889, p. 43, Maria Assunta Cusumano baptism 1883; *FamilySearch.org*, "Battesimi 1873-1889," image 417 of 792.

1885 Oct 29 - daughter Rose b Terrasini[169]

    baptized Oct 30 Maria Santissima delle Grazie, Terrasini

    #250 = 30 Oct 1885 b yest - Rosalia C

    - Giovanni C & Antonina Mazzola

        (Girolamo Palazzolo s/o Nicolo)

    548 = 152 = 30 Oct 1885 b yesterday

    - Rosalia d/o Joannes C & Antonina Mazzola

        (Hieronymus Palazzolo)

1885-7 - moved to Mazzara (now Mazara del Vallo) in the Trapani province

1887 Dec 22 - son Giovanni b Mazzara[170]

    screen 5 image 219 #651 Giovanni Cusumano 23 Dec (b 22)

        piazza #5 - Antonia Mazzola - Giovanni Cusumano

1888 Aug 17 - son Giovanni died Mazzara (8m)[171]

    Screen 2 image 84 #336 - 27 Aug 1888 - Giovanni Cusmano 8 mos -

        piatta Clinica? - s/o Giovanni baker & Antonia Mazzola

1889 May 26 - daughter Grazia b Mazzara[172]

    screen 3 imge 108 #310 Grazia Cusumano 28 May (b 26)

        - piazza Coliseo? -Antonia Mazzola - Giovanni C

---

[169]Maria Santissima delle Grazie (Chiesa Madre [Mother Church]), Terrasini, Palermo, Sicily, Italy, Baptismal register, v. 32, 1884-1889, record # 250, Rosalia Cusumano baptism 1885; *Family Search.org*, "Battesimi 1884-1887 image 57 of 103. AND Maria Santissima delle Grazie, Terrasini, Palermo, Sicily, Italy, Baptismal register, v. 31, 1882-1889, p. 152, Rosalia C baptism 1885; *Family Search.org*, "Battesimi 1873-1889," image 548 of 792.

[170]Mazara del Vallo, Trapani, "Registro degli Atti di Nascita [Registry of Acts of Birth] 1887" : entry #651, Giovanni Cusumano; digital images, *Antenati [Ancestors]*, Trapani, Mazara del Vallo, Nati [Births] (http://www.antenati.san.beniculturali.it/v/Archivio+di+Stato+di+Trapani/Stato+civil e+italiano/Mazara+del+Vallo/), image # 219 (screen 5); Ministerio dei beni e delle attivita culturale e del turismo [Ministry of health and cultural activity and tourism], Direzione generale per gli archivi [Directorate-General for Archives], Archivio di Stato di Trapani [State archives of Trapani], Stato civile italiano [Italian civil records], Mazara del Vallo.

[171]Mazara del Vallo, Trapani, "Registro degli Atti di Morte [Registry of Acts of Death] 1888" : entry #327, Giovanni Cusmano; digital images, *Antenati [Ancestors]*, Trapani, Mazara del Vallo, Morti [Deaths] 1888 (http://www.antenati.san.beniculturali.it/v/Archivio+di+Stato+di+Trapani/Stato+civil e+italiano/Mazara+del+Vallo/), image # 84 (screen 2); Ministerio dei beni e delle attivita culturale e del turismo [Ministry of health and cultural activity and tourism], Direzione generale per gli archivi [Directorate-General for Archives], Archivio di Stato di Trapani [State archives of Trapani], Stato civile italiano [Italian civil records], Mazara del Vallo.

[172]Mazara del Vallo, Trapani, "Registro degli Atti di Nascita [Registry of Acts of Birth] 1889" : entry #310, Gratia Cusumano [Image 108, screen 3, 1889].

1891 Jan 19 - son Giovanni b Mazzara[173]
     screen 1 image 22 #57 Giovanni Gusmano 22 Jan (b 19th)
        Antonia Mazzola - Giovanni Gusmano 39 panottiere?
1891 Jan 25 - daughter Grazia died Mazzara (1y 8m)[174]
     Screen 1 image 8 #22 - 25 Jan 1891 - Gratia Cusumano, 1 yr 2 mo - via
        Garibaldi -   d/o Giovanni baker & Antonia Mazzola
1892 Feb 27 - son Giovanni died Mazzara (1 y)[175]
     Screen 1 image 13 # 52 - 27 Feb 1892 - Giovanni Gusmano, 1 yr -
        piatta Clinica? - s/o Giovanni baker & Antonia Mazzola
1892-1899 - back and forth between Terrasini and Mazzara
1892 Nov 29 - daughter Grazia b Terrasini[176]
     baptized Nov 30 Maria Santissima delle Grazie, Terrasini
     153 = 106 = 30 Nov 1892 b yest - Gratia C
        - Joanne & Antonina Mazzola
        (Filomena Delia w/o Vito Mazzola) [Lena's sister-in-law]
1894 June 13 - daughter Grazia died Mazzara (1y, 6m - b Terrasini)[177]
     Screen 2 image 56 #207 - 13 June 1894 - Gratia Cusmano 1yr 6mo
     b Terrasini- - via Arustanca? d/o Giovanni baker & Antonina M
1895 Aug - son Giovanni b. Terrasini[178]
     baptized Aug 10 Maria Santissima delle Grazie, Terrasini
     the baptismal info says he was born 3 days - he always said he was
born Aug 9
     250 = #178 = 10 Aug 1895 - Giovanni C
     - Giovanni & Antonia Mazzola (born the other)
        godfather Giovanni C of Salvatore
     429 = 61 = 10 Aug 1895 (3) - Joannes Cusumano

---

[173]Mazara del Vallo, Trapani, "Registro degli Atti di Nascita [Registry of Acts of Birth] 1891" : entry #57, Giovanni Gusmano [Image 22, screen 1, 1891].

[174]Mazara del Vallo, Trapani, "Registro degli Atti di Morte [Registry of Acts of Death] 1891" : entry #22, Gratia Cusumano [Image 8, screen 1, 1891].

[175]Mazara del Vallo, Trapani, "Registro degli Atti di Morte [Registry of Acts of Death] 1892" : entry #52, Giovanni Gusmano [Image 13, screen 1, 1892].

[176]Maria Santissima delle Grazie (Chiesa Madre [Mother Church]), Terrasini, Palermo, Sicily, Italy, Baptismal register, v. 33?, 1889-1893, p.106, Gratia Cusumano baptism 1892; *Family Search.org*, "Battesimi 1889-1903," , image 153 of 621.

[177]Mazara del Vallo, Trapani, "Registro degli Atti di Morte [Registry of Acts of Death] 1894" : entry #207, Gratia Cusmano [Image 56, screen 2, 1894].

[178]Maria Santissima delle Grazie (Chiesa Madre [Mother Church]), Terrasini, Palermo, Sicily, Italy, Baptismal register, v. 34, 1893-1897, record #178, Giovanni Cusumano baptism 1895; *FamilySearch.org*, "Battesimi 1889-1903,"image 250 of 621 AND Baptismal register, v. 35, 1893-1902, p. 61; *FamilySearch.org*, "Battesimi 1889-1903," image 429 of 621.

s/o Joannes & Antonina Mazzola
godfather Joannes C of Salvatore

1899 April 29- son Christopher b. Mazzara[179]

There is no actual record online, but he is in the index. The month & year are from other sources (WWI Draft Registration, for one).[180]

1901 - emigrated to US[181]

Ship Karamania - Naples to New York - arrived 25 Nov 1901
Gusmano, Giovanni - 41 - male - occupation baker - destination New York (cousin S Orlando - 18? Union St)

Name	Gusmano, Giovanni
age	41
sex	male
marital status	married
occupation	baker
read/write?	yes
ethnicity	Italian
last place of res	Terrasini
landing	New York
final destination	New York
ticket to final dest?	No
paid for	by himself
how much money?	$10
in US before?	no
going to someone?	pretty unreadable - maybe cousin S Olando
their address?	Union St
ever in almshouse?	no
polygamist?	no
under contract?	no
health?	good
deformed?	no- blind in one eye (maybe - diffy to read)

---

[179]Mazara del Vallo, Trapani, "Registro degli Atti di Nascita [Registry of Acts of Birth] 1899" : index entry, Cusumano, Cristofaro di Giovanni [Image 113, screen 3, 1899].

[180]"U.S. World War I Draft Registration Cards, 1917-1918," database with images, *Ancestry.com* (http://ancestry.com: accessed 28 August 2016), card for Christopher Cusmano, serial no. 3532 Draft Board 6, Wayne County, Michigan; imaged from Family History Library microfilm.

[181]Manifest, *Karamania*, 25 November 1901, page 205, line 16, Giovanni Gusmano, 41; images, "Passenger Lists, 1820-1957," *Ancestry.com* (http: ancestry.com: accessed 6 September 2016). The page had been taped, and the tape made the image quite difficult to read.

*The fellow next to him on the list was also going to cousin S Orlando, 78
Union St - his name was Sebastian Mercantile, age 26, laborer - but I can't
read what town he was from, whether Terrasini or Mazzara.*
1903 - son Giovanni emigrated, in company with Uncle Graziano Cusmano,
a baker.[182]
First appearance in *Detroit City Directories*
1904 Cusumano, John, baker, h. 262 Woodbridge (Detroit) (Cusimano, with
Fruntiere, Louis)[183]
       Joseph, baker, bds 262 Woodbridge
1905 Cusumano, John, baker, h 262 Woodbridge[184]
1905 March 15 - daughter Rosalia married Francesco Paolo Gusmano in
Terrasini.[185]
1905 April 6 - daughter Maria Assunta emigrated.[186]
1905 June 3 - daughter Maria Assunta married Graziano Serra, Detroit[187]
1905 Sept 2 - daughter Rosalia emigrated (to husband in Oakfield, NY)[188]
1906 Cusumano, John, baker, h. 262 Woodbridge[189]
    Serra Graziano gro 140 Larned e h do (p. 1909)
1907 Cusumano, John baker bds. 260 Woodbridge[190]
1908 ditto h. 262 Woodbridge[191]

---

[182]Manifest, *Nord America*, 7 May 1903, page 33, line 14, Giovanni Gusmano, 7;
images, "Passenger Lists, 1820-1957," *Ancestry.com* (http: ancestry.com : accessed
6 September 2016).

[183]R. L. Polk, compiler, *Detroit City Directory, 1904* (Detroit, MI: R. L. Polk & Co,
1904), p 917; database with images, Ancestry.com (http://www.ancestry.com :
accessed 18 September 2016).

[184]*Detroit City Directory, 1905*, p. 911.

[185]Maria Santissima delle Grazie (Chiesa Madre [Mother Church]), Terrasini,
Palermo, Sicily, Italy, Marriage register, v. X, 1904-1909, p.19, Francesco Paolo
Gusmano marriage 1905; *Family Search.org*, "Matrimoni 1905-1911," image 46 of
264.

[186]*Statue of Liberty - Ellis Island Foundation*, database with images
(http://www.ellisisland.org : accessed 3 September 2016), "Ship Manifest: Manifest
for *Lombardia*," handwritten on form, entry for Maria Cusumano, age 22, arrived 21
April 1905.

[187]"Michigan, Marriage Records, 1867-1953," database with images, Ancestry.com
(http://ancestry.com : accessed 25 Aug 2016), certificate image, Graziano Serra
[indexed Grazino Seno], 2 June 1905, no. 45938; citing Michigan Department of
Community Health, Division for Vital Records and Health Statistics.

[188]Manifest, *Neapolitan Prince*, 2 September 1905, p.51, line 17, Rosalia Cusumano,
age 19; images, "New York Passenger Lists, 1820-1957," *Ancestry.com*
http://ancestry.com : accessed 27 August 2016).

[189]*Detroit City Directory, 1906*, p. 752 and p. 1909.

[190]*Detroit City Directory, 1907*, p. 875.

[191]*Detroit City Directory, 1908*, p. 826.

1908 Sept 14 - father Giovanni died, in Mazzara[192]

      Screen 4 image 148 #327 - 14 Sept 1908 (yest?) - Cusumano Giovanni - via Garibaldi

           Giovanni 74 years old, baker, res Mazara, b Terrasini
           I think it says his parents were Giovanni baker? b in Terrasini and Francesca Paola Mazzola, wife, b in Terrasini and he was married to Maria Assunta Giliberti

1909 - son Chris and wife Antonina Mazzola emigrated[193]

1910 Census - Michigan, Wayne Co, Detroit, ED 64 sheet 11 - taken 17 Apr 1910[194] - 262 Woodbridge -

      Cusmano, John head m w 47 married 28 y, b Italy, mf b Italy, immigrated 1901, speaks Italian, baker, bakery, owns, doesn't read or write, rents home.

      Lolina wife f w 50 married 28 y, 6?overwritten 4 children, 4 still living, b. Italy, parents b. Italy,   immigrated 1909, doesn't read or write.

      John son m w 15 single, b. Italy, immigrated 1902, speaks English, helper in bakery, reads, writes, attended school this year.

      Christopher, son m w 11, single, b. Italy immigrated 1909, speaks English, reads, writes, attended school

1910-1911 - daugher Rosalia & family moved to Detroit.

1911 Cusmano John coremkr bds 262 Woodbridge[195]

1913 Cusman Jno lab h 262 Woodbridge[196]

      Cosemanno Paul lab 170 Riopelle

1915 Cushmano Jno baker h 262 Woodbridge e[197]

      Cushmano Jno jr autowkr b 262 Woodbridge e

Mom said he had a house on Fort Street, but I never found any address except the Woodbridge one - unless this fellow (below) is him? It's especially curious that there is a Joseph with him in 1918, since in his very first appearance in the City Directories in 1904 - at which time he is on Woodbridge, not Fort - there is a Joseph with him, also a baker. I am wondering about the elusive younger brother Joseph b 1871???

---

[192]Mazara del Vallo, Trapani, "Registro degli Atti di Morte [Registry of Acts of Death] 1908" : entry #327, Giovanni Cusumano [Image 148, screen 4, 1908].

[193]Manifest, *Regina d'Italia*, 16 June 1909, page 168, line 9, Cristofaro Cusumano, 9; images, "Passenger Lists, 1820-1957, " *Ancestry.com* (http: ancestry.com : accessed 6 September 2016).

[194]1910 U.S. census, Wayne County, Michigan, population schedule, Detroit ward 5, enumeration district (ED) 64, sheet 11a, dwelling 112 rear, family 173, John Cusmano; image, *Ancestry.com* (http://ancestry.com : accessed 6 September 2016); citing NARA microfilm publication T624, roll 681.

[195]*Detroit City Directory, 1911*, p. 873.

[196]*Detroit City Directory, 1913*, p. 748.

[197]*Detroit City Directory, 1915*, p. 820.

1915 Cusmano Jno lab h 219 Fort e
1916 Cusmano Jno baker h 219 Fort e
1918 Cusumano Jno h219 Fort - with Jos
  Cusumano Jos lab b219 Fort - with Jno
1916 Cushmano John baker h 262 Woodbridge e[198]
1918 - Joseph (s/o cousin Giovanni & Rosa Zerilli)
  = driver for Cusumano Bakery 337 Clinton
  (according to his WWI Draft Registration)
1919 Cusumano John 374 Clinton (p. 2166 - street directory section)
  262 Woodbridge - Laktas Elie / Ahee George baker r (p. 2513)
1920 Federal Census - Michigan, Wayne Co, Detroit. ED 160, p. 2[199]
  262 Woodbridge - 3 families
  Ellis, Anthony (wife Julia) rents
  Mendel, Magel (rents) and Claryzek? Mike (boards)
  Casamano, John - head - owns - mortgaged. male white 60 married.
    immigrated 1901. alien.can read and write. born Italy, native
    tongue Italian. father&mother b. Italy, native tongue Italian.
    can speak English.baker. delicatessen.
   Lena wife f w 60 married immigrated 1901. alien can read write,
    born Italy, parents b. Italy (native tongue Italian) can speak
    English
   John son m w 23 single immigrated 1905 naturalized 1917 can
    read write b. Italy etc. can speak English. machinist-
    machine shop
   Christopher son m w 19 single immigrated 1909 alien can
    read write b. Italy etc. can speak English. helper -
    machine shop
1920/21 p. 1057 (image 571) Coseman Jno baker 978 (262) Woodbridge[200]
  also in Bakers, image 1472 - Coseman Jno 978 (262) Woodbridge
1921 Jan 29 - son John married Ruth Stanton[201]

---

[198]*Detroit City Directory, 1916*, p. 922.
[199]1920 U. S. Federal census, Wayne County, Michigan, population schedule, Detroit, ward 5, enumeration district (ED) 160, sheet 2 b, dwelling 28, family 23, John Casanano; image, *Ancestry.com* (http://ancestry.com: accessed 6 September 2016); citing NARA microfilm publication T625, roll 802.
[200]*Detroit City Directory, 1920/21*, p. 1057.
[201]Wayne County, Michigan, marriage certificate no. 209075 (1921), Cusman-Stanton; photocopy, Cusman family archives; privately held by Lee Bothwell, Alden, MI, 2016.

1921-22 Cusumano, Jno baker h978 Woodbridge[202] (Incidentally, this was
the same house - the street numbering changed.)
        Jno Jr mach ditto
        Chris lab r978 Woodbridge e
1922-23 Cusmano Chris lab r978 Woodbridge[203]
    Cusumano Jno baker h978 Woodbridge
        Jno jr mach h978 Woodbridge
1924/25 Cusimano, John 978 Woodbridge (street index) - he was not in the
name listings[204]
1925/26 Cusimano John h978 Woodbridge[205]
1930 Michigan Federal Census - Wayne County - Detroit [Roll 1035, Bk 2 -
Image 15] SD 21,[206] ED 82-112, Sheet 8a stamp 175, written 3310) - Ward of
city 5, Block #183 - taken 7 Apr 1930 line 37 - 978 Woodbridge - 3 families
    Delia, Gasper mw 53 Italy & wife Marianne 43 Italy
    Bommarito, Joseph 21 Missouri & wife Fannie 18 Missouri
    Cusmano, John head rents $25 mw 70 married at 27, can read & write,
        all Italy, emigrated 1900, not naturalized, speaks English
        Lena wife 70 married at 27 no read & write, all Italy, emigrated
        1910, not naturalized, doesn't speak English
        Christopher son 27 s? 28?, can read & write, all Italy, emigrated
        1910, not naturalized, speaks English, laborer auto factory, not a
        veteran
1930/31 Cusamano John (Lena) lab h 978 Woodbridge[207]
1931-32 Cusman John (Lena) h978 E Woodbridge[208]
1932-33 Cusmano John (Anna) lab h978 E Woodbridge[209]
1934 Cusmano John (Lena) h978 E Woodbridge[210]
    Christopher autowkr r978 E Woodbridge
1935 Cusmano Christopher lab r978 Woodbridge[211]
    John (Lena) lab h978 E Woodbridge

---

[202]*Detroit City Directory, 1921-22*, p. 873.

[203]*Detroit City Directory, 1922-23*, p. 839.

[204]*Detroit City Directory, 1924-25*, (I don't have the page number, sorry)

[205]*Detroit City Directory, 1925-26*, p. 787.

[206]1930 U.S. census, Wayne County, Michigan, population schedule, Detroit ward 5,
enumeration district (ED) 82-112, sheet 8a, dwelling 30, family 87, John Cusmann;
image, *Ancestry.com* (http://ancestry.com : accessed 29 Aug 2016); citing FHL
microfilm: 2340770; NARA microfilm publication T626.

[207]*Detroit City Directory, 1930-31*, p. 617.

[208]*Detroit City Directory, 1931-32*, p. 538.

[209]*Detroit City Directory, 1932-33*, p. 463.

[210]*Detroit City Directory, 1934*, p. 521.

[211]*Detroit City Directory, 1935*, p. 503.

19xx moved to Fort Street (Mom's recollections have him living at Fort Street)

> "Grandpa kept a bakery in his garage at Fort Street. He was separated from Grandma Lena. Grandma Lena and Chris slept in the basement of the house and Grandpa slept over the garage."

1937 June 1 - Lena died,[212] buried Mt Olivet (Section 51, Tier 50, Space 47)[213]

1937 Nov 25 - son Christopher married Rose Evola[214]

1940 census - not found

1943 Feb 25 - died.[215] Buried Mt. Olivet Cemetery, 6-Mile & Dequindre (Section 51, Tier 50, Space 48)[216]

---

[212]"Michigan, Death Records, 1867-1950," database with images, *Ancestry.com* (http://ancestry.com: accessed 7 September 2016), entry for Antonina Cusumano, 1937 (state file no. 226099); Michigan Department of Community Health, Division for Vital Records and Health Statistics, Lansing, Michigan.

[213]Mt. Elliott Cemetery Association, database, (http://www.mtelliott.com/genealogy/ : accessed 31 August 2016), Mt. Olivet Cemetery (Detroit, Wayne, Michigan), entry for Antonina Cusumano (1 June 1937).

[214]"Michigan Marriage Records, 1867-1952," database, *Ancestry.com* (http://ancestry.com: accessed 25 August 2016), entry for Christopher Cusmano, 1937 (state file no.194213); citing Michigan Department of Community Health, Division for Vital Records and Health Statistics, film no. 290 (82 Wayne 194100-197369).

[215]"Michigan Death Records, 1867-1950," database, *Ancestry.com* (http://ancestry.com: accessed 20 Sept 2016), entry for Giovanni Cusumano, 25 Feb 1943, file no. 303791; citing Michigan Department of Community Health, Division for Vital Records and Health Statistics.

[216]*Findagrave.com*, database and images (http://findagrave.com: accessed 25 August 2016), memorial page for Giovanni Cusumano (1860-1943), Find A Grave Memorial no. 144066987, created by "Angie," citing Mt. Olivet Cemetery, Detroit, Wayne, Michigan.

Children of Giovanni and Lena (Antonina) Mazzola

8. Maria Assunta 1882-1882
8. Maria Assunta 1883-1945 + Graziano Serra (1905) -> **Detroit**
8. Rosalia 1885-1965 + Francesco Paolo Gusmano (1905)
>->**New York, Detroit**
8. Giovanni 1887-1888
8. Grazia 1889-1891
8. Giovanni 1891-1892
8. Grazia 1892-1894
8. Giovanni 1895-1949 + Ruth Aletha Stanton (1921) -> **Detroit**
8. Cristofaro 1899-1974 + Rose Evola (1937) -> **Detroit**

Of their 9 children, only 4 survived to adulthood: Maria Assunta (who married Graziano Serra), Rosalia (who married her cousin Paul), our Grandpa Jack, and Uncle Chris (who married Rose Evola). The first three were born in Terrasini; Uncle Chris was born in Mazzara. All of them (and Giovanni and Lena themselves) emigrated to Detroit, but they made separate journeys (except for Chris, who came over with Lena).

For more information about Grandpa Jack's siblings, see below:

Maria Assunta & Graziano Serra	- 89-99
Rosalia & Paul Cusmano	- 100-111
Chris & Rosie	- 112-116

Generation 7 - Graziano & Francesca Arena
Terrasini, Palermo, Sicily - Mazara del Valle, Trapani, Sicily

*In the Terrasini Baptismal records, I found only 3 children for Giovanni &
Maria Assunta: Giovanni, Graziano & Giuseppe.
Giovanni is our Great Grandfather, Graziano is Jack's uncle, who took him
to the US, Giuseppe is . . . well, I found nothing more about him in the
records I looked at. He might be the Joseph who is living with G-Grand
Giovanni in Detroit in 1904, but I'm not sure.*

Great Grandpa's brother Graziano was born 25 May 1864 in Terrasini.
Sometime after 1885, the whole family (I think) moved to Mazzara (now
Mazara del Valle) in the Trapani Province. Graziano was a baker, as were
his father and brother.

In 1890, he married Francesca Arena, and in 1891, their first child, a
son, named Giovanni after his (Graziano's) father, was born. He died in
1892, when he was 8 months old. In 1893, they had a daughter, named Maria
Assunta after his mother; she died when she was 6 months old.

In 1895, they had another Giovanni, and this one survived (he visited
the US with his father in 1912). In 1896, they had another Maria Assunta,
and I think she survived also - I haven't found a death record for her. But in
1900, they had more bad luck - twins Desiderio and Maria were stillborn. I
haven't found any more children for them.

In 1901, Graziano's brother Giovanni emigrated to the US, and in 1903
he took his nephew Giovanni (our Grandpa Jack) to Detroit to be with him.
I'm not sure how long Graziano remained in Detroit, but he did go back to
Sicily. He visited Giovanni in 1909, 1912 (accompanied by his own
Giovanni, now 18 years old) and 1914. It is possible he was a "bird of
passage," a person who worked in the US, but returned regularly to Sicily.

The records available online only go to 1911 or so, so this is all I have
found out about him.

Timeline Graziano 1864-

1864 May 25 - born Terrasini, Palermo, Sicily[217] - son of Giovanni & Maria
Assunta Giliberti - baptized Maria Santissima delle Grazie, Terrasini
191 = 44-5 = 26 May 1864 b yest - Gratianus G
- Joannes & Maria Assunta Giliberti

---

[217]Maria Santissima delle Grazie (Chiesa Madre [Mother Church]), Terrasini,
Palermo, Sicily, Italy, Baptismal register, v. 28, 1862-1872, p. 44-5, Gratianus
Gusmano baptism 1864; *Family Search.org*, "Battesimi 1859-1878," image 191 of
481.

1890 Dec 30 - married Francesca Arena

    image 73 #143 - 30 Dec 1890 - Graziano Gusmano, 26 b Terrasini res Mazara panattiere

    s/o Giovanni & Maria Assunta Giliberti both res Mazara

    Francesca Arena 22 - Francesco & Maria Anna Lucca?

1891 Oct 17 - son Giovanni born[218]

    screen 4 or 5 image 205 #599 Giovanni Gusmano 18 Oct (b 17) via Porta Palermo - Francesca Arena - Graziano G

1892 July 2 - son Giovanni died (8 mo)[219]

    Image 44 #174 - 2 July 1892 - Giovanni Gusmano 8 mos? - via porto Palermo - s/o Gratiano baker & Francesca Arena

1893 March 18 - daughter Maria Assunta born[220]

    screen 2 image 55 #166 Cusumano Maria Assunta 20 March (b 18th) - via Porta Palermo - Francesca Arena - Graziano Cusumano pastaio? 43?

1893 Oct 12 - daughter Maria Assunta died (6 mo)[221]

    Screen 2 image 76 #291 - 12 Oct 1893 - Maria Assunta Cusumano, 2x mo? - via? - d/o Graziano baker & Francesca Arena

---

[218]Mazara del Vallo, Trapani, "Registro degli Atti di Nascita [Registry of Acts of Birth] 1891" : entry #599, Giovanni Cusumano; digital images, *Antenati [Ancestors]*, Trapani, Mazara del Vallo, Nati [Births] (http://www.antenati.san.beniculturali.it/v/Archivio+di+Stato+di+Trapani/Stato+civile+italiano/Mazara+del+Vallo/), image #205 (screen 4 or 5); Ministerio dei beni e delle attivita culturale e del tourismo [Ministry of health and cultural activity and tourism], Direzione generale per gli archivi [Directorate-General for Archives], Archivio di Stato di Trapani [State archives of Trapani], Stato civile italiano [Italian civil records], Mazara del Vallo.

[219]Mazara del Vallo, Trapani, "Registro degli Atti di Morte [Registry of Acts of Death] 1892" : entry #174, Giovanni Cusmano; digital images, *Antenati [Ancestors]*, Trapani, Mazara del Vallo, Morti [Deaths] 1892 (http://www.antenati.san.beniculturali.it/v/Archivio+di+Stato+di+Trapani/Stato+civile+italiano/Mazara+del+Vallo/), image # 44 (screen 1?); Ministerio dei beni e delle attivita culturale e del tourismo [Ministry of health and cultural activity and tourism], Direzione generale per gli archivi [Directorate-General for Archives], Archivio di Stato di Trapani [State archives of Trapani], Stato civile italiano [Italian civil records], Mazara del Vallo.

[220]Mazara del Vallo, Trapani, "Registro degli Atti di Nascita [Registry of Acts of Birth] 1893" : entry #166, Maria Assunta Cusumano [Image 55, screen 2, 1893].

[221]Mazara del Vallo, Trapani, "Registro degli Atti di Morte [Registry of Acts of Death] 1893" : entry #291, Maria Assunta Cusumano [Image 76, screen 2, 1893].

1894 Sept 5 - son Giovanni born[222]

    screen 4 image 150 #412 Giovanni G 7 Sept (b 5th) vico Pieta

        Francesca Arena - Graziono G panattiera

1896 Jan 18 - daughter Maria Assunta born[223]

    screen 1 - image 20 #54 - Cusumano Maria Assunta - 1896 Jan 18

    (b 14th) via Vico Pieta - Francesca Arena w/o Graziano Cusumano

1900 Nov 22 - twins Desiderato and Maria stillborn[224]

    Screen 6 image 246 #682 - Desiderato Cusumano - 22 Nov 1900 - via

    vico Pieta -   Francesca Arena w/o Grazio? C

        #683 - Maria C ditto all (b dead)

1903 - went to the US, in the company of his nephew Giovanni

    1903 May 7 - *Nord America* - Napoli - New York[225]

        Gusmano, Graziano 38 male single baker reads/writes Italy south

last res Mazzara going to Detroit MI no ticket? Money $10 never

before in US - going to brother Giovanni 136 Lain

        Gusmano, Giovanni 7 ms doesn't read/write Italy south going to

Detroit MI - no ticket - money 5 - ditto (going to brother Giovanni)

        In the book, it lists Cusmano, Graziano and Gusmano, Giovanni

1908 Sept 14 - father Giovanni died, in Mazzara[226]

    Screen 4 image 148 #327 - 14 Sept 1908 (yest?) - Cusumano Giovanni

    - via Garibaldi

    Giovanni 74 years old, baker, res Mazara, b Terrasini

his parents Giovanni baker? b in Terrasini and Francesca Paola

Mazzola, wife, b in Terrasini -married to Maria Assunta Giliberti

1909 - to US - but I am having trouble accessing the manifest - it is mis-
linked

    On Ancestry also there is a problem. The index says:

    ship *Calabria* - Palermo to New York - arriving 29 March 1909

    Graziano Cusmano, age 45, Mazara

---

[222]Mazara del Vallo, Trapani, "Registro degli Atti di Nascita [Registry of Acts of Birth] 1894" : entry #412, Giovanni Gusmano [Image 150, screen 4, 1894].

[223]Mazara del Vallo, Trapani, "Registro degli Atti di Nascita [Registry of Acts of Birth] 1896" : entry #54, Maria Assunta Cusumano [Image 20, screen 1, 1896].

[224]Mazara del Vallo, Trapani, "Registro degli Atti di Nascita [Registry of Acts of Birth] 1900" : entry #682 and #683, Desiderato and Maria Cusumano [Image 246, screen 6, 1900.

[225]Manifest, *Nord America*, 7 May 1903, page 33, line 14, Giovanni Gusmano, 7; images, "Passenger Lists, 1820-1957," *Ancestry.com* (http: ancestry.com : accessed 6 September 2016).

[226]Mazara del Vallo, Trapani, "Registro degli Atti di Morte [Registry of Acts of Death] 1908" : entry #327, Giovanni Cusumano [Image 148, screen 4, 1908].

1912 - to US, in the company of his son Giovanni

SS Canada - Palermo (1 May) to New York (13 May) 1912[227]

line 12 - Gusmano Giovanni 18 m s laborer - from Mazara - at home = mother Arena, Francesca - going to Detroit, Mi - to uncle Giovanni - I think the street is 262 Bridgewood [which must be Woodbridge!]

line 13 - Gusmano, Graziano 47 m married laborer from Mazara - at home = wife Arena, Francesca - going to Detroit MI - to brother Giovanni 262 Bridgewood - was in US before 1910, 1903

1914 - to US

SS Canada - Palermo (13 May) to New York (25 May) 1914[228]

line 4 - Gusmano, Graziano, 50 m laborer, at home = wife Arena, Francesca, Mazara - going to Detroit MI - to brother Giovanni 262 Bridgewood - was in US before can't read the years

Timeline Joseph 1871-

1871 June 1 - born Terrasini, Palermo, Sicily[229]

Baptized 2 June, Maria Santissima delle Grazie, Terrasini

336 = 182 = 2 June 1871 b yest - Joseph G

s/o Joanne & Maria Assunta Giliberti

(Phlippus G & Anna Orlando) [Giovanni's brother & wife]

???1904 Cusumano, John, baker, h. 262 Woodbridge (Detroit) (Cusimano, with Fruntiere, Louis)[230]

Joseph, baker, bds 262 Woodbridge

Mom said Great Grandpa had a house on Fort Street, but I never found any address except the Woodbridge one - unless this fellow is him? It's especially curious that there is a Joseph with him in 1918, since in his very first appearance in the City Directories in 1904 - at which time he is on

---

[227]*Statue of Liberty-Ellis Island Foundation*, database with images (http://www.ellisisland.org : accessed 19 March 2017), "Ship Manifest: Manifest for *Canada*," handwritten form, list 86, page 178, line 13 entry for Graziano Gusmano, age 47, arrived 13 May 1912.

[228]*Statue of Liberty-Ellis Island Foundation*, database with images (http://www.ellisisland.org : accessed 19 March 2017), "Ship Manifest: Manifest for *Canada*," handwritten form, list 65, page 90, line 4 entry for Graziano Gusmano, age 50, arrived 25 May 1914.

[229]Maria Santissima delle Grazie (Chiesa Madre [Mother Church]), Terrasini, Palermo, Sicily, Italy, Baptismal register, v. 28, 1862-1872, p. 182, Joseph Gusmano baptism 1871; *Family Search.org*, "Battesimi 1859-1878," image 336 of 481.

[230]R. L. Polk, compiler, *Detroit City Directory, 1904* (Detroit, MI: R. L. Polk & Co, 1904), p 917; database with images, Ancestry.com (http://www.ancestry.com : accessed 18 September 2016).

*Woodbridge, not Fort - there is a Joseph with him, also a baker. I am
wondering about the elusive younger brother Joseph b 1871???*
1915 Cusmano Jno lab h 219 Fort e
1916 Cusmano Jno baker h 219 Fort e
1918 Cusumano Jno h219 Fort - with Jos
Cusumano Jos lab b219 Fort - with Jno

Generation 8: Giovanni (Jack) & Ruth Stanton
Terrasini, Palermo, Sicily - Detroit, Wayne, Michigan

Grandpa Jack was born August 9, 1895 to Giovanni Cusmano and Antonina (Lena) Mazzola. He was baptized in the church of Maria Sanctissima delle Grazie a few days later. [He was baptized on August 10, and that record says he was born 3 days earlier, but he always gave his birthdate as August 9.] His godfather was another Giovanni, "of Salvatore," and there are many people that could be, but the closest would be his father's cousin.

His father was a baker, as was his grandfather and (probably) great-grandfather. At the time he was born his parents had two living children, his sisters Maria Assunta and Rosalia, but there had been several other babies born who lived only a few years, including two previous Giovannis.

Jack and his sisters were born in Terrasini, but his brother Chris was born in Mazzara (now Mazara del Valle) as were several of the babies who didn't make it. It seems as though his parents (and his uncle Graziano and possibly his grandparents as well) moved to Mazzara sometime after Rosalia was born in 1885, but after 1892 there was a bit of going back and forth - baby Grazia was baptized in Terrasini in 1892, but died in Mazzara in 1894; Grandpa Jack was born in Terrasini in 1895, and uncle Chris was born in Mazzara in 1899.

In 1901, Great-Grandpa Giovanni emigrated to the US. He told the immigration authorities that he was going to his cousin, Salvatore Orlando, who lived on Union Street in New York (I haven't figured out just exactly who this is. His uncle Filippo was married to Anna Orlando.) GGrandma and the children were left behind, apparently in Mazzara; the girls were in their teens (Maria 18, Rosalia 16), but Grandpa Jack was only 5, and Chris was a baby of 2.

In 1903, when he was 7 years old, Grandpa Jack emigrated. His uncle Graziano came along with him (but he didn't stay; he had a family of his own in Mazzara). By this time G-Grandpa Giovanni was in Detroit, working as a baker, and already living on Woodbridge. He (Grandpa Jack) probably had to help G-Grandpa in the bakery: he was listed as a helper in the bakery in the 1910 census, when he was 15.

His sister Rosalia - age 20 - got married to her father's cousin Paul (Francesco Paolo, son of Filippo and Anna Orlando) in March 1905 in Terrasini and joined him in Oakfield, NY in September of that year. Sister Maria Assunta (age 22) left for the US in April 1905, and married Graziano Serra in Detroit in June. (I wonder if either - or both - of the marriages was arranged by the parents.) So Lena was left in Mazzara with Chris (age 6). They came over when Chris was 9 or 10, in 1909.

Grandpa Jack was without his mother for 7 years, between the ages of 7 and 14.

He didn't work in the bakery after 1910 - maybe because Chris and Lena were now available as helpers. (But he loved bakeries and found them irresistible - as did his daughter Betty, who could not drive past a bakery to save her life.) In 1911 (age 16), he was listed in the City Directory as a "coremaker" (I'm not sure exactly what that is!) and then as a laborer, auto-worker, machinist.

In 1917 and 1918, all males born between 1873 and 1900 (ages 18-45) - had to register for the draft. Grandpa Jack, age 21, did so on June 5. He claimed his parents as dependents, and said his occupation was a tinner (I think) at the Dominion Stamping Plant in Wakeville, Ontario.

He enlisted - or was drafted - on May 28, 1918, and on August 9 of that year was granted US citizenship. He was at that time at Camp Wheeler in Georgia. Citizenship was not automatically granted to aliens who served in the US military, but it was expedited: you no longer had to file a declaration of intention, and the residency requirements were reduced or waived. (The residency requirements possibly wouldn't have mattered to Grandpa Jack.) For many years, Grandpa Jack was the only member of his family to be a citizen; I don't know if G-Grandpa ever became a citizen; Chris was naturalized sometime between 1930 and 1940.

At Camp Wheeler, he was described as: age 23 years, height 5 feet 8 inches, color white, complexion fair, color of eyes blue, color of hair brown, visible distinguishing marks none. His discharge a year later said: "When enlisted he was 22 years of age and by occupation a ???tuner. [I think tinner?] He had brown eyes, brown hair, dark complexion, and was 5 feet, 5 inches in height." So in a year, his eyes turned from blue to brown, his complexion from fair to dark, and he lost 3" and 1 year! I think he must have had hazel eyes - and as for his age, August 9 was his birthday, so you could call him either 22 or 23 in 1918.

Grandpa served in France and Germany. He left the US in September, 1918. While in Germany, he took a 4-week course in auto-repairing (he got a grade of 72). He didn't have any horrible war stories to tell: (items in quotations are from my Mom, Betty) "Dad used to tell us stories of when he was in the Army. Trading provisions with German guards on the other side of a bridge - catsup for potatoes etc. About monkey dropping coconuts on German soldiers etc. etc." He was discharged from the army - rank, corporal - on August 23, 1919 at Camp Sherman, Ohio. He got a travel allowance to get back to Detroit and a $60 bonus, and in 1920 he was living at home with his parents and brother, and working as a machinist in a machine shop.

Meanwhile in 1920, a young girl from southern Indiana moved to Detroit. Grandma Ruth's Aunt Mildred (who was only 10 years older than

she was) was married and living on 14th Street near Grand Boulevard; she
convinced her mother (Grandma Becky) and Ruth to come live with her.
Grandma worked as a cigar roller for a while (she had done that back in
Indiana too) and at some time she got a job at a dimestore on Woodward.
Later on, Mildred & Jack divorced and Mildred and Ruth lived on Pallister
(also near Grand Boulevard). Both places are fairly far from the Italian
neighborhoods, so I am not sure how Grandma and Grandpa met. Maybe at a
ballroom: she (and Mildred) loved going dancing, and there were plenty of
places to do so: the Pier Ballroom on Belle Isle, the Polonaise Ballroom at
the Amusement Park, the Majestic Ballroom and the Arcadia.

She was crazy about him (and vice versa)."Grandma Becky would read
the coffee grounds for Mom and tell her fortune. 'She was going to make up
with Jack [so apparently they had fights!]---He loved her---She was going to
meet him at the ballroom.' all the things she knew Mom wanted to hear."
They did silly things together: "when they were dating he used to come over
to their (Ruth & Mildred's) apartment. They'd turn the lights out for a while
- then on quickly - then spend a while stomping the cockroaches." She
dressed up in his army uniform and posed for a picture. Later on, when they
were married, she would play practical jokes on him: fill his wine bottle with
vinegar, put an onion instead of an apple in his lunchbox, make a sandwich
with fake bologna. Sicilians are not jolly people, and Grandma Ruth was
funny and cheerful and lively: she must have been quite a revelation to him.

They got married by a Justice of the Peace on January 29, 1921. This
was a HUGE break with tradition. Sicilians believe in like-with-like:
merchant with merchant, peasant with peasant, fisherman with fisherman.
They also are fond of cross-cousin marriages, where a child will marry the
child of his/her mother's brother (I'm not sure why this is called cross-cousin
marriage - it seems like a regular cousin marriage to me). At the very least,
they prefer marriages between people from the same town, who speak the
same dialect. And Grandma Ruth was not only not Sicilian, she was not
Catholic. I wonder how his parents took it.

As far as her parents go, when she told Grandma Bess the man she had
married was Italian (I was told Ruth herself didn't know he was Italian until
they signed the marriage register; that he had told her his name was John
Christiansen), she was worried about the monkey that would (undoubtedly)
be living with them. [Because all Italians were organ-grinders.]

So.

After the wedding the bridal party (and I don't know who was in it
besides her Aunt Mildred; the other witness was just a fellow who worked in
the office) went to the Liberty Theater and saw "Hearts of the World."
Grandpa loved movies, especially Abbott and Costello, and he would take
whole walnuts and crack them, and whole grapefruits and peel them, when he

went. (John Franklin said they always knew he was in the audience by the smell of grapefruit - and then they would have to be careful to sneak out before him.)

At first they lived in a one-room apartment, but soon they moved in with his parents in the house on Woodbridge. (Unless the one-room apartment was the one with his parents!) I remember Grandma saying that they used to buy one book a week, and read it out loud, to help Grandpa Jack with his English. (I have some of those books, an odd collection: *Tess of the Storm Country* as well as *The Clansman*, among others.) He worked as a machinist, at the Hudson Motor Car Co[231] (Connor Plant), and not long after they were married, he got a job for his father-in-law, Grandpa Rufus, there. Later on, he got a job for his nephew there too. So it must have been a fairly decent place to work - although he did go out on strike once - and got frostbitten ears and toes while on the picket line.

Aunt Delores was born 2 November 1922, while they were living with his parents. Her middle name was Lena, after Grandpa Jack's mother, according to Sicilian tradition. By 1924 they had their own house, on Woodlawn, and the rest of the children, except Shirley, were born there: Bessie Jean - named after Ruth's mother, Grandma Bess - born 28 April 1924; John Dale born 12 February 1926, named after Jack's father; Mary Virginia, born 7 March 1928, was given the name because they were afraid she would die (she had the umbilical cord wrapped around her neck) - and I believe she was the only child that *was* baptized; Gerald Rufus born 11

---

[231]This was a pretty interesting company. It was intended to produce affordable cars, but it was also innovative:

The company had a number of firsts for the auto industry; these included dual brakes, the use of dashboard oil-pressure and generator warning lights, and the first balanced crankshaft, which allowed the Hudson straight-six engine, dubbed the "Super Six" (1916), to work at a higher rotational speed while remaining smooth, developing more power for its size than lower-speed engines. The Super Six was the first engine built by Hudson, previously Hudson had developed engine designs and then had them manufactured by Continental Motors Company. Most Hudsons until 1957 had straight-6 engines. The dual brake system used a secondary mechanical emergency brake system, which activated the rear brakes when the pedal traveled beyond the normal reach of the primary system; a mechanical parking brake was also used. Hudson transmissions also used an oil bath and cork clutch mechanism that proved to be as durable as it was smooth.

The company merged with Nash in 1954 and became American Motors (alas?). The last Hudson was made in 1957. (And, by the way, it was named after J.L. Hudson - the department store guy - who provided the start up capital.)

Info from: Wikipedia contributors, *Wikipedia, The Free Encyclopedia* (https://en.wikipedia.org/w/index.php?title=Hudson_Motor_Car_Company&oldid=7 83246130 : accessed July 1, 2017), "Hudson Motor Car Company."

September 1932. Shirley - Dorothy Shirley, the Dorothy after Grandma's sister - was born 28 August 1935, after they had moved to Stephens in East Detroit.

The house on Woodlawn had a Michigan basement, which Ruth had enlarged to full size, and fixed up as a play place for the kids; they also would sleep there when the weather got hot - until Grandma started worrying about spiders and carried then all back up to the porch. Later on, she ran a Blind Pig in that basement.

There was an old man living across the street, and Ruth used to complain about the time Jack spent playing checkers with him. Jack said, "he is my godfather, I have to show him respect." [I haven't been able to figure out who this fellow was!] They did their shopping on Saturdays, and always brought the kids a special treat afterwards. They went on a lot of picnics, to Chandler Park, and Belle Isle. They had a player piano, and the three oldest kids got music lessons: Aunt Delores piano, Betty violin, Johnny clarinet. I think Aunt Mary took singing lessons for a while.

Sometime after they moved to East Detroit, they got a store on Gratiot, candy and groceries at first, and then later they got a license to sell beer and wine. Grandpa would work at Hudson's all day, and then work at the store when he got home. (This was where she switched his wine with vinegar: he used to run to the back room in between customers to take a swig.) Eventually they built a supermarket next door: Jack's Super Market. In the 1942 City Directory, their address was 21851 Gratiot but in 1946 it was the Stephens address again, so I wonder if the Gratiot address was the address of their store.

From Mom (Betty): "During this time I remember Mom & Dad playing Bingo at Eastwood Park, going to Toledo to gamble, and shooting craps after hours in Merollis Car garage in the back." [I remember the huge Merollis Chevrolet lot on Gratiot - I wonder if that was the same one?]

Eventually - I think maybe around 1946/7, they bought the Limberlost Hotel in Houghton Lake. It was a 9-room hotel, with 4 cottages attached, and there was dancing and dining and of course a bar. [One of the cooks at the Limberlost taught Mom how to make excellent french fries: the secret is to soak them in ice water first, and to cook them twice.] Mom and Del had married by this time, and Mary was living at the Priscilla Inn (a residence hotel for young working women in Detroit), so only John, Jerry and Shirley were with them.

He died on June 18, 1949. He had a heart attack, and everyone thought he was recovering nicely, and then a blood clot got loose and killed him.

The Detroit News - Monday, June 20, 1949 - p. 31 col 8 - Death Notices

(microfilm photocopy)

Cusman - John (Jack) of Houghton Lake, Mich., beloved husband of Ruth; dear father of Mrs. Delores Herpel, Mrs. Betty Bothwell, John, Jr., Mary, Gerald and Shirley; brother of Mrs. Rose Cusmano and Christopher Cusmano; grandfather of two grandchildren. Service from Wm. D. Clyne Funeral Home, 22322 Gratiot ave., East Detroit, Wednesday, 8:30; St. Veronica Church, 9 a.m.

[I don't think he was a member of St. Veronica's, but it was located on Gratiot, near their old stomping grounds.]

He was buried in Mt. Olivet Cemetery, 6-mile & Dequindre - section 17, lot 895, space 1. Many of his Sicilian relatives are buried there also - his parents, his sisters, many of his cousins.

Timeline Jack & Ruth Stanton

Jack b 1895 Terrasini, d 1949 Detroit; Ruth b 1903 Indiana, d 1988

1895 Aug 9 - born Terrasini[232]

    baptized Aug 10 Maria Santissima delle Grazie, Terrasini

the baptismal info says he was born 3 days - he always said he was born Aug 9

    250 = #178 = 10 Aug 1895 - Giovanni C

        - Giovanni & Antonia Mazzola (born the other)

        godfather Giovanni C of Salvatore

    429 = 61 = 10 Aug 1895 (3) - Joannes Cusumano

        s/o Joannes & Antonina Mazzola

        Joannes C of Salvatore

1901 - father emigrated to US

1903 - emigrated to the US[233] (uncle Graziano took him over)

    1903 May 7 - ***Nord America*** - Napoli - New York

        Gusman, Graziano 38 male single baker reads/writes Italy south last res Mazzara going to Detroit MI no ticket? Money 10 never before in US - going to brother Giovanni 136 Lain

        Gusman, Giovanni 7 male single doesn't read/write Italy south going to Detroit MI - no ticket - money 5 - ditto (going to brother Giovanni)

---

[232]Maria Santissima delle Grazie (Chiesa Madre [Mother Church]), Terrasini, Palermo, Sicily, Italy, Baptismal register, v. 34, 1893-1897, record #178, Giovanni Cusumano baptism 1895; *FamilySearch.org*, "Battesimi 1889-1903," image 250 of 621 AND Baptismal register, v. 35, 1893-1902, p. 61; *FamilySearch.org*, "Battesimi 1889-1903," image 429 of 621.

[233]Manifest, *Nord America*, 7 May 1903, page 33, line 14, Giovanni Gusmano, 7; images, "Passenger Lists, 1820-1957," *Ancestry.com* (http: ancestry.com: accessed 6 September 2016).

Detroit City Directories[234]

1904 Cusumano, John, baker, h. 262 Woodbridge (Cusimano, with
      Fruntiere, Louis)
            Joseph, baker, bds 262 Woodbridge
1905 Cusumano, John, baker, h 362 Woodbridge
1906 Cusumano, John, baker, h. 262 Woodbridge
1907 ditto   bds. 260 Woodbridge
1908 ditto   h.   362 Woodbridge

1910 Census[235]

MI, Wayne, Detroit, ED 64 sheet 11 - taken 17 Apr 1910 - 262 Woodbridge -
      Cusmano, John head m w 47 married 28 y, b Italy, mf b Italy,
            immigrated 1901, speaks Italian, baker, bakery, owns, doesn't
            read or write, rents home.
      Lolina wife f w 50 married 28 y, 6?overwritten 4 children, 4 still
            living, b. Italy, parents b. Italy, immigrated 1909, doesn't read or
            write.
      John son m w 15 single, b. Italy, immigrated 1902, speaks English,
            helper in bakery, reads, writes, attended school this year.
      Christopher, son m w 11, single, b. Italy immigrated 1909, speaks
            English, reads, writes, attended school

Detroit City Directories[236]

?1911 Cusmano John coremkr bds 262 Woodbridge
1913 Cusman Jno lab h 262 Woodbridge
1915 Cushmano Jno baker h 262 Woodbridge e
       Cushmano Jno jr autowkr b 262 Woodbridge e
1916 Cushmano John baker h 262 Woodbridge e[237]

---

[234]R. L. Polk, compiler, *Detroit City Directory, 1904* (Detroit, MI: R. L. Polk & Co,
1904), p 917; database with images, Ancestry.com (http://www.ancestry.com:
accessed 18 September 2016). And subsequent directories, for 1905, 1906, 1907,
1908.
[235]1910 U.S. census, Wayne County, Michigan, population schedule, Detroit ward 5,
enumeration district (ED) 64, sheet 11a, dwelling 112 rear, family 173, John
Cusmano; image, *Ancestry.com* (http://ancestry.com: accessed 6 September 2016);
citing NARA microfilm publication T624, roll 681.
[236]R. L. Polk, compiler, *Detroit City Directory for the year commencing August 15th,
1911* (Detroit, MI: R. L. Polk & Co, 1911) p nos; database with images,
Ancestry.com, "U.S. City Directories, 1822-1995" (http://www.ancestry.com:
accessed 24 September 2016). And subsequent directories for 1913, 1915.
[237]*Detroit City Directory, 1916*, p. 922.

1917 June 5 - WWI Draft Registration[238] (stamped 209. written 5986 - registration card written 19481 no. 335)

>   John Cusmano, age 21
>   262 E Woodbridge, Detroit
>   b Aug 9, 1895 - alien - b Terrasini, Palermo, Italy
>   occupation: tinner? turner? Dom. Stamping Plant, Wakevill, Ont
>   dependents - father & mother
>   single, caucasian, med height, med build, brown eyes, brown hair

1918 May 29 - enlisted (or inducted?) in US Army

1918 Aug 9 - certificate of naturalization - no 1085536[239]

>   Petition, Volume M-6, Number 1358 m
>   Description of holder Age 23 years; height 5 feet 8 inches; color white; complexion fair; color of eyes blue; color of hair brown; visible distinguishing marks none
>   name, age and place of residence of wife none
>   names ages and places of residence of minor children none
>   stamp: US District Court   SS John Cusmans
>   Western Division, So. Dist of GA
>   Be it remembered that John Cusmans then residing at number Co D 121st Infantry, Camp Wheeler, Georgia [crossed out blanks for city and street etc) who previous to his naturalization was a citizen/subject of Italy, having applied to be admitted a citizen of the United States of America pursuant to law, and at a special term of the US District Court of So. Dist of Georgia held at Macon GA on the ninth day of August in the year of our Lord nineteen hundred and eighteen, the court having found that the petitioner [had resided continuously within the United States for at least five years and in this state/territory/district for at least one year immediately preceding the date of the filing of his petition and that said petitioner][crossed out] intends to reside permanently in the United States, had in all respects complied with the law in relation thereto, and that he was entitled to be so admitted, it was thereupon ordered by the said court that he be admitted as a citizen of the United States of America.

---

[238]"U.S. World War I Draft Registration Cards, 1917-1918," database with images, *Ancestry.com* (http://ancestry.com: accessed 28 August 2016), card for John Cusmano, serial no. 335?, Draft Board 6, Wayne County, Michigan; imaged from Family History Library microfilm.

[239]U.S. District Court, to John Cusmans, certificate of naturalization, 9 August 1918; photocopy, Cusman family archives; privately held by Lee Bothwell, Alden, MI, 2016.

1919 Aug 29 - honorable discharge from the army[240]

   To All whom it may Concern:

This is to certify, that John Cusmano, 1346360, corporal, Co "B:, 4th Inf, 3rd Div

The United States Army, as a Testimonial of Honest and Faithful Service is hereby honorably discharged from the military service of the United States by reason of E.T.S. per par. 16 w.d. cu. 252-1919 Said John Cusmano was born in Terrissini Palermo in the State of Italy. When enlisted he wa 22 years of age and by occupation a Tinner. He had Brown eyes, Brown hair, Dark complexion, and was 5 feet 5 inches in height.

   Given under my hand at Camp Sherman, O. This 29 day of Aug., one thousand nine hundred and nineteen

   signed (unreadable) [Fred D Zinz, major infantry U.S.A commanding

handwritten note: certified for Michigan bonus by J. S. Barton (?)

- This was on the back of the discharge:

Enlistment Record

name: John Cusmano grade: cpl

enlisted or inducted: May 29, 1918 at Detroit, Mich

serving in first enlistment period at date of discharge.

prior service: none

non-commissioned officer: apptd cpl 8/21/19

marksmanship, gunner qualification or rating: none

horsemanship: not mounted

battles, engagements, skirmishes, expeditions: none

decorations, medals, badges, citations: none

knowledge of any vocation: [blank]

wounds received in service: none

physical condition when discharged: good

typhoid prophylaxis completed: 6/14/18

paratyphoid prophylaxis completed: 6/14/18

married or single: single

character: excellent

remarks: no awol. No absence under G.O. 45 1914

Entitled to travel pay to Detroit, Mich and $60 bonus

Served in France and Germany. Left US

Sept 30, 1918. Arrived in US

signature of soldier: John Cusmano

---

[240]Fred D. Zinz, major infantry, USA, to John Cusmano, honorable discharge from the U.S. Army, 29 August 1919; photocopy, Cusman family archives; privately held by Lee Bothwell, Alden, MI, 2016.

signature something
commanding 1469
stamped: Camp Sherman, Ohio - Aug 29, 1919 - Paid in full including
bonus $109.72
William J Thompson, captain Q.M.O
Aug 23, 1919
1920 Federal Census - Michigan, Wayne Co, Detroit. ED 160, p. 2[241]
262 Woodbridge - 3 families
-Ellis, Anthony (wife Julia) rents
-Mendel, Magel (rents) and Claryzek? Mike (boards)
Casamano, John - head - owns - mortgaged. male white 60
married.immigrated 1901. alien. can read and write. born Italy,
native tongue Italian. father&mother b. Italy, native tongue
Italian. can speak English.baker. delicatessen.
Lena wife f w 60 married immigrated 1901. alien can read write,
born Italy, parents b. Italy (native tongue Italian) can speak
English
John son m w 23 single immigrated 1905 naturalized 1917 can read
write b. Italy etc. can speak English. machinist- machine shop
Christopher son m w 19 single immigrated 1909 alien can read write
b. Italy etc. can speak English. helper - machine shop
1921 Jan 29 - married Ruth Aletha Stanton[242]
No. 209075 (stamped) Marriage License - Wayne County, Michigan.
To any person legally authorized to solemnize marriage, Greeting:
Mr. John Cusman and M Ruth Stanton affidavit having been filed in
this office, as provided by Public Act No 128, Laws of 1887, as
amended, by which it appears that said
John Cusman is 24 years of age, color is white, residence is Detroit,
and birthplace was Mich., occupation metal worker, father's name
John, and mother's maiden name was Lena Mazzola, had been
previously married NO time; and that said Ruth Stanton is 18 years of
age, color is white, residence is Detroit and birthplace was Mich.,
occupation is –, father's name Rufus, and mother's maiden name
Bessie Dorr, and who has been previously married NO time . . . 29?
Jan 1921

---

[241] 1920 U. S. Federal census, Wayne County, Michigan, population schedule,
Detroit, ward 5, enumeration district (ED) 160, sheet 2 b, dwelling 28, family 23,
John Casanano; image, *Ancestry.com* (http://ancestry.com: accessed 6 September
2016); citing NARA microfilm publication T625, roll 802.
[242] Wayne County, Michigan, marriage certificate no. 209075 (1921), Cusman-
Stanton; photocopy, Cusman family archives; privately held by Lee Bothwell, Alden,
MI, 2016.

Certificate of Marriage

between Mr. John Cusman and M Ruth Staton

I hereby certify that, in accordance with the above license, the persons herein mentioned were joined in marriage by me at Detroit, County of Wayne, Michigan, on the 29th day of January, A.D. 1921 in the presence of Raymond J. Milrow, of Detroit Michigan and Miss Mildred Stevens of Detroit Michigan

John F McKinlay, Justice of the Peace

1921-22 Detroit City Directory - Cusumano, Jno baker h978 Woodbridge[243]

Jno Jr mach ditto

Chris lab r978 Woodbridge e

1922 Nov 2 - daughter Delores Lena born

1922-23 Detroit City Directory - Cusmano Chris lab r978 Woodbridge

Cusumano Jno baker h978 Woodbridge

Jno jr mach h978 Woodbridge

1923-24 - moved to Woodlawn

1924 April 28 - daughter Bessie Jean (Betty) born

1924/25 Detroit City Directory

- Cusman, John metalworker h 9138 Woodlawn Av

1925/26 Detroit City Directory

- Cusman John metalwrkr h9138 Woodlawn

1926 Feb 12 - son John Dale born

1928/29 Detroit City Directory

- Cusman John (Ruth) foremn h 9338 Woodlawn

1928 March 7 - daughter Mary Virginia born

1930 census - Michigan - Wayne Co - Detroit - Pct 17 - SD22, ED82-693, Sheet 19a - Apr 10[244] -   9338 Woodlawn

Cusman, John head 600r no mw34 m25 no Mi It It foreman autofactory WW

Ruth wife fw26 m17 no Ind Ind Ind

Delores dau fw7s no Mich Mich Ind

Betty daughter fw5s yes ditto

John son mw4s no ditto

---

[243]R. L. Polk, compiler, *Detroit City Directory, 1921-22* (Detroit, MI: R. L. Polk & Co, 1921); also subsequent years by the same title: (1921-22), 1922-23), (1931-32), (1932-33), (1934), (1935). I accessed all these city directories at the Wisconsin State Historical Society Library (Madison, WI); most of them were on microfilm, and at the time, I did not get the exact bibliographic information for them. Some of them are now available at Ancestry.com, but not all, so I apologize for not having all the bib info.

[244]1930 U.S. census, Wayne County, Michigan, population schedule, Detroit precinct 17, enumeration district (ED)82- 693, sheet 19a, dwelling 382, family 7, John Cusman [indexed Casnav!]; image, *Ancestry.com* (http://ancestry.com : accessed 29 Aug 2016); citing FHL microfilm: 2340794; NARA microfilm publication T626.

Mary daughter fw2s no ditto

1930/31 Detroit City Directory

   - Cusman John J (Ruth) frmn h9338 Woodlawn

1931-32 Detroit City Directory

   - Cusman John T (Ruth) fender h9338 Woodlawn

     John (Lena) h978 E Woodbridge

1932 Sept 11 - son Gerald Rufus (Jerry) born

1932-33 Detroit City Directory

   -Cusman John J (Ruth) fcty wkr h9338 Woodlawn

     John (Anna) lab h978 E Woodbridge

1934 Detroit City Directory

   - Cusman John J (Ruth) sheet metal worker h9338 Woodlawn

  Cusmano John (Lena) h978 E Woodbridge

     Christopher autowkr r978 E Woodbridge

1935 Detroit City Directory

   -Cusman John (Ruth) sheet metal worker h 9338 Woodlawn av

  Cusmano Christopher lab r978 Woodbridge

     John (Lena) lab h978 E Woodbridge

1935 Aug 28 - daughter Dorothy Shirley born

1940 census - Michigan Macomb East Detroit, wd 1 SD7 Ed50-13 Sheet 19a
- April 22, 1940 - line 14[245]

    16131 Stephens - owns house, 4700 - Cusman, John head m w 45
married - 8th grade
born Michigan (hah) 1935 lived Detroit, Wayne, Mi - sheet metal
worker, auto co

      Ruth A fw 36 m 7th b Indiana clerk retail groc store

      Delores dau 17 / Bessie J 15 / John D 13 / Mary V 11 /

      Gerald R 7 / Dorothy S 4

extra questions: father & mother born Italy, early language Italian, yes
a veteran, served in war, yes ss#, yes old age pension deductions.

1941 - WWII Draft Registration - U1210[246]

    John Cusmano

---

[245] 1940 U. S. Census, Macomb County, Michigan, population schedule, East Detroit, ward 1, enumeration district (ED) 50-13, sheet 19a, household 380, John Cusman [indexed Corman!]; image, *Ancestry.com* (http://ancestry.com: accessed 9 September 2016); citing NARA microfilm publication T627, roll 1782.

[246] "U.S. World War II Draft Registration Cards, 1942," database with images, *Ancestry.com* (http://ancestry.com: accessed 27 August 2016), card for John Cusmano, serial no. 1212; citing The National Archives at St. Louis, Draft Registration Cards for Fourth Registration for Michigan, 04/27/1942 - 04/27/1942; NAI Number: 623283; Records of the Selective Service System; Record Group Number: 147.

21851 Gratiot, E Detroit, Macomb

tel Roseville 9017

age 46 - b 8-9-95 - Terrasini, Palermo, Italy

contact person: Ruth Cusmano - same address

employer: Hudson Motor Car Co

   Connors Plant, Detroit, Wayne, MI

1942 - Polk's East Detroit, Roseville, Fraser and Vicinity (Macomb County, Michigan) City Directory 1942[247]

Cusman, Delores L clk Fan Tan Mkt (Center Line) r 21851 Gratiot av (ED)

  John (Ruth) asst frmn Hudson MCCo (Detroit)

    h 21851 Gratiot av (ED)

  Ruth (Mrs) gro & beer 21851 Gratiot av r do

1946 - Polk's East Detroit etc. City Directory 1946[248]

Cusman, Betty J civil serv r16131 Stephens dr (ED)

  Delores L r16131 Stephens dr

  John (Ruth A) fcty wkr Hudson's MCCo (Det) h 16131 Stephens dr

  John D jr USA r16131 Stephens dr

  Mary V student r16131 Stephens dr

  Ruth A Mrs beer dir 21845 Gratiot av (ED) r16131 Stephens dr

1946 May 25 - daughter Betty married Scott Bothwell

1946 June 8 - daughter Delores married Harold Herpel

194x - bought Limberlost Hotel - Houghton Lake, MI

1949 June 18 - died[249] - buried Mt Olivet (Section 17, Lot 895, Space 1)

  John Cusman - m w m - b 9 Aug 1895 Italy - d 18 June 1949 Detroit - age 53

  f John Cusman - m Lena [index says Leana][250]

---

[247]*Polk's East Detroit. Roseville, Fraser and vicinity (Macomb County) City Directory, 1942* (Detroit, MI: R. L. Polk & Co, 1942), 84; database with images, Ancestry.com (http://www.ancestry.com: accessed 9 September 2016).

[248]*Polk's East Detroit. Roseville, Fraser and vicinity (Macomb County) City Directory, 1946* (Detroit, MI: R. L. Polk & Co, 1946), 80; database with images, Ancestry.com (http://www.ancestry.com: accessed 9 September 2.016).

[249]Social Security Administration, "United States Social Security Death Index," database, Ancestry.com (http://ancestry.com: accessed 25 August 2016), entry for John Cusman, 1949, SS no. 381-01-5855.

[250]"Michigan, Death Records, 1867-1950," database, *Ancestry.com* (http://ancestry.com: accessed 21 September 2016), entry for John Cusman, 18 June 1949 (file no. 396640); Michigan Department of Community Health, Division for Vital Records and Health Statistics, Lansing, Michigan.

Children of Jack (Giovanni) and Ruth Aletha Stanton

9. Delores Lena 1922 - 2002 - m Harold Herpel - 3 children
9. Bessie Jean 1924 - 2013 m Kearney Scott Bothwell - 3 ch ildren
9. John Dale   1926 - 1971 - + Maxine Reese - 1 child, + Barbara
9. Mary Virginia 1928 - 2012 - m Luther Cornett - 2 children
9. Gerald Rufus 1932 - 1983 - m. Virginia Forten - 2children + stepdaughter
9. Dorothy Shirley 1935 - m John Franklin - 3 children

Maria Assunta 1883 - 1945
new information from Kathleen Stork, wife of David, grandson of Maria

Assunta means taken, and the name Maria Assunta commemorates the Assumption into heaven of the Virgin Mary. There was also a Saint Maria Assunta - but she was only born in 1878, so I don't think our Maria was named after her. It is more likely she was named after her grandmother, Maria Assunta Giliberti. [Jan 2018 - the church in Carini, where our ancestors lived in the 1500s, was Maria SS Assunta.]

1883 March 23 - born Sicily
1905 Apr 21 - arrived in US aboard the *Lombardia*[251]
    Palermo (6 April 1905) to Detroit (21 April 1905) stamped 106
        line 20 Cusumano, Maria 22 f s from Mazzara -
        To father Cusmano Giovanni 130 Lain St Detroit
[For some reason, all our people claim they are heading for 130 or 140 Lain St in Detroit. There *is* no Lain Street in Detroit - I checked the street directory section in the Detroit City Directories - so I don't know what was going on. The Serras had a grocery store at 140 LARNED Street. Giovanni himself lived on Woodbridge.]
1905 June 3 - married Graziano Serra, Detroit, MI[252]
    record #45938 - Graziano Serra, 36, res Detroit, b Italy, laborer,
        father Salvatore, mother Antonia Finazzi
      - Maria A Cusumano, 22, res Detroit, b Italy, housewife,
          father John, mother Antoina Mazzol
      official - Francis Beccherini, rector
      witnesses - Salvatore Zerillo, Detroit - Rosa Salomeano, Det
1906 Detroit City Directory[253]
   Serra Graziano gro 140 Larned e h do
     Salvatore gro 135 Larned
     Saml macaroni 180 Brush hw se 137 Larned e

---

[251]*Statue of Liberty - Ellis Island Foundation*, database with images (http://www.ellisisland.org : accessed 3 September 2016), "Ship Manifest: Manifest for *Lombardia*," handwritten on form, entry for Maria Cusumano, age 22, arrived 21 April 1905.
[252]"Michigan, Marriage Records, 1867-1953," database with images, Ancestry.com (http://ancestry.com : accessed 25 Aug 2016), certificate image, Graziano Serra [indexed Grazino Seno], 2 June 1905, no. 45938; citing Michigan Department of Community Health, Division for Vital Records and Health Statistics.
[253]*Detroit City Directory for the year commencing August 1st., 1906* (Detroit, MI: R.L. Polk & Co, 1906), 1909; database with images, "U.S. City Directories 1822-1995," *Ancestry.com* (http://ancestry.com: accessed 25 Aug 2016).

1907 Detroit City Directory[254]
Serra Graziano gro 140 Larned e h do
        Salvatore gro 140 Larned e
        Saml 197 Larned e
1907 - son Sam born
1908 - son John born
1909 Detroit City Directory[255]
        Serra Graziano gro 140 Larned
        Serra S & Bro (Samuel& NS) macaroni mnfrs 127 Fort e
1910 - dau Lena born
1910 Michigan Wayne Detroit wd 3 - SD1, ED35, Sheet 8b - 22 Apr - 140
Larned[256]
        Sarra, Graciano mw 30 - married 1x - 5yrs - It -> em 1901 alien -
            storekeeper grocery store
            Mary 25 It -> em 1901 alien
            Sam 3 MI / John 2 MI / Lena 0?/12 MI
        one side - next to Nicolas Sarra 45 / Josie 45/ Sam 19
            / Lena 16 / Joe 10 / Mary 1 1/12
            Nicholas = manufacturer macaroni - Sam = baker bakery
        other side next to Toko, Joe 45 m1 18y 1902 peddler
            Grace wife 35 m 1 18 y 4ch/4 liv 1902 /
            Noa 18 m1 (line connecting her to Philip Cusman) 1902
            Joe 14 / Sam 11 / Joseph 5
            Cusman, Philip son-in-law 26 1901 peddler fruit
        then Toko, Sam - with lodger Alfonso Cusman 50 m1 27 1902
            lab fish store
        then Mazzolo, Mike 32 - and family
            Mazzolo, Sam 38 - and family
        then Froudaro, Frank 50 +

---

[254]R. L. Polk, compiler, *Detroit City Directory, 1907* (Detroit, MI: R. L. Polk & Co),
1907; also subsequent years by the same title: (1910), (1935). I accessed all these city
directories at the Wisconsin State Historical Society Library (Madison, WI); most of
them were on microfilm, and at the time, I did not get the exact bibliographic
information for them. Some of them are now available at Ancestry.com, but not all,
so I apologize for not having all the bib info.
[255]*Detroit City Directory for the year commencing August 1st., 1909* (Detroit, MI:
R.L. Polk & Co, 1909), 726; database with images, "U.S. City Directories 1822-
1995," *Ancestry.com* (http://ancestry.com: accessed 25 Aug 2016). Another entry -
retail grocers, p. 2959.
[256]1910 U.S. census, Wayne County, Michigan, population schedule, Detroit ward 3,
enumeration district (ED) 35, sheet 8b, dwelling 116, family 141, Graziano Serra
[indexed Sraciano Sarra]; image, *Ancestry.com* (http://ancestry.com: accessed 25
Aug 2016); citing NARA microfilm publication T624, roll 681.

son in law Christ Cusemano 30 m1 3y 1901 peddler fruit
wife Liza 20 m1 3y 2/0
further down - Mazzolo, Joe 58 m1 34 / Loria 59 7/7 /
Felipa 22 m1 6y 3/3
/ Rose 19 m1 3y 1/1 / Sam 17 / Robert 14
sons in law Amato, Thom 25 m1 6y- Sam 5, Joe 4, Toni 7/12
and Batalamenti, Toni 27 m1 8y - Bertha 2

1910 *Detroit City Directory*

Serra, Anthony mold h 172 Champlain
Graziano gro 140 Larned e h do
Nicholas h 136 Larned e
Rosato saloon 568 Rivera bus do
Saml baker bd 136 Larned
Saml macaroni mft r 1274 e h 197 Larned e

1912 - son Nick born

1914 - son Giuseppe born (d 1916)

1917 - dau Rose born

1920 Mi Wayne Detroit wd 5 SD145 ED160 sheet 13b[257]

210 E. Forth St - Serra, Christiano [indexed Christina Sarras] 50, em 1899 alien, It It It, store keeper, groceries

Mary wife 35 em 1903 alien, It It It
Samuel son 15 MI It It / John son 14 MI It It
Lena dau 10 MI It It
Nick son 8 MI It It / Rose dau 2 4/12 MI It It

1920 Detroit City Directory[258] - lots of Serras

Serra, Graziano h 1002 (210) Fort e
Jos body mkr h 25662 (126) Hendricks
Nicholas b 1472 (379) Congress e

1921 - dau Sarah born

1930 Sept 14 - husband Graziano died[259]

---

[257] 1920 U. S. Federal census, Wayne County, Michigan, population schedule, Detroit, ward 5, enumeration district (ED) 160, sheet 13b, dwelling 135, family 235, Christiano Serra [indexed Christina Sarras]; image, *Ancestry.com* (http://ancestry.com: accessed 26 Aug 2016); citing NARA microfilm publication T625, roll 802.

[258] *R. L. Polk & sons 1920-21 Detroit City Directory, v. LVIII*, Detroit, MI: R.L. Polk & Co, 1920), 2049; database with images, "U.S. City Directories 1822-1995," *Ancestry.com* (http://ancestry.com: accessed 25 Aug 2016).

[259] *Findagrave.com*, database and images (http://findagrave.com: accessed 25 August 2016), memorial page for Graziano Serra (1877-1930), Find A Grave Memorial no. 43582507, created by "Angie," citing Mt. Olivet Cemetery, Detroit, Wayne, Michigan.

1930 MI Wayne Detroit wd 5 SD21 ED82-113 sheet 17b[260]
1002 Fort - Serra, John head 22 Mi It It prop grocery store
        Nick brother 19 Mi It It clerk grocery story
    Serra, Maria mother 45 wd It It It
        Mary sister 21 Mi It It
1935 Detroit City Directory
lots of Serras
    Mary (wid Graziano S) 1002 E Fort   Saml (Mary) 1006 E Fort
    Saml J (Rose) 750 Lakepoint
Fort - between Hastings and Rivard
      964 Mazzola Saml
      1002 Serra Mary Mrs gro (wid Graziano)
      1006 Serra Saml (Mary)
1940 Mi Wayne Detroit wd 5 SD1 ED84-187 sheet 8b April 10[261]
1002 E Fort st upstairs - Serra, Maria 55 wd b Italy alien same house 1935
      (Next page)   Lena 28 MI
          Nick 26
          Rose 20 bookkeeper wholesale produce
          Sarah 17
1006 E Fort down - Serra, Sam 33 Mi - truck driver wholesale produce
          Mary 31
          Harry 11
          Mary 8
1945 August 23 - died, buried Mt Olivet[262]
    Maria Assunta Serra [transcribed Lena] - f w wid - b 1883 Italy - d 20 Aug 1945 Detroit
    f Giovanni Cusmano [transcribed Gronanni] - m Lena Mazzola [transcribed Marcola]
    Mt Olivet.

---

[260] 1930 U.S. census, Wayne County, Michigan, population schedule, Detroit ward 5, enumeration district (ED) 82-113, sheet 17b, dwelling 142, family 22, John Serra; image, *Ancestry.com* (http://ancestry.com : accessed 25 Aug 2016); citing FHL microfilm: 2340770; NARA microfilm publication T626.

[261] 1940 U. S. Census, Wayne County, Michigan, population schedule, Detroit, ward 5, enumeration district (ED) 84-187, sheet 8b, household 161, Maria Serra; image, *Ancestry.com* (http://ancestry.com : accessed 25 Aug 2016); citing NARA microfilm publication T627, roll 1846.

[262] "Michigan Death Records, 1867-1950," database, *Ancestry.com* (http://ancestry.com : accessed 21 Sept 2016), entry for Maria Assunta Serra [indexed Lena], 20 Aug 1945, no. 340575; citing Michigan Department of Community Health, Division for Vital Records and Health Statistics.

(Mt. Olivet Cemetery {This might be them, but the death date for Graziano is not good[263] -)

> Graziano Serra - Location: Section 21, Lot 1061, Space 1 - date of interment: 10/31/1945 (There was another Graziano Serra, whose date of interment was 07/20/1909)
> Maria Serra - Location: Section 21, Lot 1061, Space 2 - date of interment: 08/23/1945

However, the Find-a-Grave entry for Graziano (cited above) sounds more reasonable:

> Graziano Serra born Nov. 5, 1877, Terrasini Favarotta, Città Metropolitana di Palermo,Sicilia, Italy - died Sep. 14, 1930, Detroit, Wayne County, Michigan, USA of Broncho Pneumonia, Pulmonary Congestion
> A note says he was the son of Son of Salvatore Serra and Antonina Finazzo, husband of Maria Assunta Cusumano, brother of Blasio Serra, Giuseppe Serra

Children of Maria Assunta and Graziano Serra

Sam 1906-1988

1906 July 29 - born[264]
1910 Michigan Wayne Detroit wd 3 - SD1, ED35, Sheet 8b - 22 Apr - 140 Larned[265]

> Sarra, Graciano mw 30 m1 - 5yrs - It -> em 1901 alien
> > - storekeeper grocery store
> > Mary 25 It -> em 1901 alien
> > Sam 3 MI / John 2 MI / Lena 0?/12 MI

---

[263]Mt. Elliott Cemetery Association, database, (http://www.mtelliott.com/genealogy/ : accessed 25 August 2016), Mt. Olivet Cemetery (Detroit, Wayne, Michigan), entry for Maria Serra (23 August 1945).

[264]Michigan Department of Vital and Health Records, "Michigan, Death Index, 1971-1996," database, *Ancestry.com* (http://ancestry.com : accessed 26 August 2016), entry for Sam Serra.

[265]1910 U.S. census, Wayne County, Michigan, population schedule, Detroit ward 3, enumeration district (ED) 35, sheet 8b, dwelling 116, family 141, Graziano Serra [indexed Sraciano Sarra]; image, *Ancestry.com* (http://ancestry.com : accessed 25 Aug 2016); citing NARA microfilm publication T624, roll 681.

1920 Mi Wayne Detroit wd 5 SD145 ED160 sheet 13b[266]
210 E. Forth St - Serra, Christiano [indexed Christina Sarras] 50, em 1899
alien, It It It, store keeper, groceries
        Mary wife 35 em 1903 alien, It It It
        Samuel son 15 MI It It / John son 14 MI It It
        Lena dau 10 MI It It
          Nick son 8 MI It It / Rose dau 2 4/12 MI It It
1927 April 23 - married Maria Anna Serra in Windsor[267]
        [There were different boxes to be filled out, which is why some
        things are repeated]
        Salvatore Serra - Maria Anna Serra
        wit Philip Zerilla - 3068 Hardy St, Detroit MI
            - Ninfa Umetta - Box 5362 RFD#2, Warren MI
        city of Windsor, county of Essex, Ontario
        23rd day of April 1927
        parents - Graziano Serra b Italy - Maria Assunta Cusumano
            Nicholas Serra b Italy - Josephine Ventimiglia
        reg# 4652
        J E Pas . . . n - 15 Clarkson E Windsor, Ontario - Catholic
        I think it says notice was given in La Voce Popula - newspaper
        published in Detroit - on Feb 18 & 25, 1927
        Salvatore Serrra - Maria Anna Serra
        garage worker
        21 in July next - 18 on March 3, 27
        signed Sam Serra
1930
1940 Mi Wayne Detroit wd 5 SD1 ED84-187 sheet 8b April 10[268]
1002 E Fort st upstairs - Serra, Maria 55 wd b Italy alien same house 1935
        (Next page) Lena 28 MI / Nick 26
           Rose 20 bookkeeper wholesale produce

---

[266] 1920 U. S. Federal census, Wayne County, Michigan, population schedule, Detroit, ward 5, enumeration district (ED) 160, sheet 13b, dwelling 135, family 235, Christiano Serra [indexed Christina Sarras]; image, *Ancestry.com* (http://ancestry.com: accessed 26 Aug 2016); citing NARA microfilm publication T625, roll 802.

[267] Ancestry.com and Genealogical Research Library (Brampton, Ontario, Canada), "Ontario, Canada, Marriages, 1801-1928, 1933-1934," database, *Ancestry.com* (http://ancestry.com: accessed 25 August 2016), entry for Salvatore Serra, 1927; citing Archives of Ontario, MS932, reel 808.

[268] 1940 U. S. Census, Wayne County, Michigan, population schedule, Detroit, ward 5, enumeration district (ED) 84-187, sheet 8b, household 161, Maria Serra; image, *Ancestry.com* (http://ancestry.com: accessed 25 Aug 2016); citing NARA microfilm publication T627, roll 1846.

Sarah 17

1006 E Fort down - Serra, Sam 33 Mi - truck driver wholesale produce
Mary 31 / Harry 11 /   Mary 8

1988 Jan 24 - died - Warren, Macomb, Michigan[269]

John ~1908 - 1952

~1908 - born (Michigan Death Index says 1903)
1910 Michigan Wayne Detroit wd 3 - SD1, ED35, Sheet 8b - 22 Apr - 140
Larned[270]

> Sarra, Graciano mw 30 m1 - 5yrs - It -> em 1901 alien
> - storekeeper grocery store
>> Mary 25 It -> em 1901 alien
>> Sam 3 MI / John 2 MI / Lena 0?/12 MI

1920 Mi Wayne Detroit wd 5 SD145 ED160 sheet 13b[271]

210 E. Forth St - Serra, Christiano [indexed Christina Sarras] 50, em 1899
alien, It It It, store keeper, groceries
> Mary wife 35 em 1903 alien, It It It
> Samuel son 15 MI It It / John son 14 MI It It
> Lena dau 10 MI It It
> Nick son 8 MI It It / Rose dau 2 4/12 MI It It

1930 MI Wayne Detroit wd 5 SD21 ED82-113 sheet 17b[272]

1002 Fort - Serra, John head 22 Mi It It prop grocery store
> Nick brother 19 Mi It It clerk grocery story

Serra, Maria mother 45 wd It It It
> Mary sister 21 Mi It It

---

[269]Michigan Department of Vital and Health Records, "Michigan, Death Index, 1971-1996," database, *Ancestry.com* (http://ancestry.com: accessed 26 August 2016), entry for Sam Serra. Also Social Security Administration, "United States Social Security Death Index," database, Ancestry.com (http://ancestry.com: accessed 25 August 2016), entry for Sam Serra, 1988, SS no. 364-03-8876.

[270]1910 U.S. census, Wayne Co., MI, pop. sched., Detroit ward 3, enumeration district (ED) 35, sheet 8b, dwel. 116, fam. 141, Graziano Serra [indexed Sraciano Sarra].

[271]1920 U. S. Federal census, Wayne Co., MI, pop. sched., Detroit, wd 5, ED 160, sheet 13b, dwelling 135, family 235, Christiano Serra [indexed Christina Sarras].

[272]1930 U.S. census, Wayne County, Michigan, population schedule, Detroit ward 5, enumeration district (ED) 82-113, sheet 17b, dwelling 142, family 22, John Serra; image, *Ancestry.com* (http://ancestry.com: accessed 25 Aug 2016); citing FHL microfilm: 2340770; NARA microfilm publication T626.

1935 Sept 21 - married Lucille Gates, Detroit, Wayne, MI[273]
    Wayne County, Michigan #464426
    John Serra 27 res Detroit, father Gratiano, mother Maria Cusmano
    Lucille Gates 27 res Detroit, father Edward, mother Nellie Adams
    lic 16 Sept 1935 - married 21 Sep 1935 - Francis Beccherini, rector
    wit Salvatore Serra, Florence Rich
1940 -
1952 Oct 16 - died - Detroit, Wayne, Michigan[274]
    John Serra - m w m - b 1903 Detroit - d 16 Oct 1952 Detroit - age 44
    f Graziano Serra - m Maria Cusumano

Lena 1909-1990

1909 Dec 22 - born Michigan[275] - or 26 Dec 1909[276]
1910 Michigan Wayne Detroit wd 3 - SD1, ED35, Sheet 8b - 22 Apr - 140
Larned[277]
    Sarra, Graciano mw 30 m1 - 5yrs - It -> em 1901 alien
      - storekeeper grocery store
      Mary 25 It -> em 1901 alien
      Sam 3 MI / John 2 MI / Lena 0?/12 MI
1920 Mi Wayne Detroit wd 5 SD145 ED160 sheet 13b[278]
210 E. Forth St - Serra, Christiano [indexed Christina Sarras] 50, em 1899
alien, It It It, store keeper, groceries
      Mary wife 35 em 1903 alien, It It It
      Samuel son 15 MI It It / John son 14 MI It It

---

[273]"Michigan Marriage Records, 1867-1952," database, *Ancestry.com*
(http://ancestry.com: accessed 25 August 2016), entry for John Serra, 1935 (state file
no.148969); citing Michigan Department of Community Health, Division for Vital
Records and Health Statistics, film no. 276 (82 Wayne 148100-151359).
[274]"Michigan Death Records, 1867-1950," database, *Ancestry.com*
(http://ancestry.com : accessed 21 Sept 2016), entry for John Serra, 16 Oct
1952, no. 448269; citing Michigan Department of Community Health,
Division for Vital Records and Health Statistics.
[275]Social Security Administration, "U.S., Social Security Applications and Claims
Index, 1936-2007," database, *Ancestry.com* (http://ancestry.com: accessed 25
August 2016), entry for Antonina Serra Crimaudo, 1990, SS no. 382-52-1881.
[276]Michigan Department of Vital and Health Records, "Michigan, Death Index,
1971-1996," database, *Ancestry.com* (http://ancestry.com: accessed 25 August
2016), entry for Antonina Crimaudo.
[277]1910 U.S. census, Wayne Co., MI, pop. sched., Detroit ward 3, enumeration
district (ED) 35, sheet 8b, dwel. 116, fam. 141, Graziano Serra [indexed Sraciano
Sarra].
[278]1920 U. S. Federal census, Wayne Co., MI, pop. sched., Detroit, wd 5, ED 160,
sheet 13b, dwelling 135, family 235, Christiano Serra [indexed Christina Sarras].

Lena dau 10 MI It It

Nick son 8 MI It It / Rose dau 2 4/12 MI It It

1930 MI Wayne Detroit wd 5 SD21 ED82-113 sheet 17b[279]

1002 Fort - Serra, John head 22 Mi It It prop grocery store

Nick brother 19 Mi It It clerk grocery story

Serra, Maria mother 45 wd It It It

Mary sister 21 Mi It It

1940 Mi Wayne Detroit wd 5 SD1 ED84-187 sheet 8b April 10[280]

1002 E Fort st upstairs - Serra, Maria 55 wd b Italy alien same house 1935

(Next page) Lena 28 MI / Nick 26

Rose 20 bookkeeper wholesale produce

Sarah 17

1006 E Fort down - Serra, Sam 33 Mi - truck driver wholesale produce

Mary 31 / Harry 11 /   Mary 8

1940 June 29 - married Francesco Crimaudo - Detroit, Wayne, MI[281]

1990 Sept 18 - died[282]

Nick 1911/ 1914

1920 Mi Wayne Detroit wd 5 SD145 ED160 sheet 13b[283]

210 E. Forth St - Serra, Christiano [indexed Christina Sarras] 50, em 1899 alien, It It It, store keeper, groceries

Mary wife 35 em 1903 alien, It It It

Samuel son 15 MI It It / John son 14 MI It It

Lena dau 10 MI It It

Nick son 8 MI It It / Rose dau 2 4/12 MI It It

---

[279] 1930 U.S. census, Wayne Co., MI, pop. sched., Detroit wd 5, ED 82-113, sheet 17b, dwel. 142, fam. 22, John Serra.

[280] 1940 U. S. Census, Wayne Co., MI, pop. sched., Detroit, wd 5, ED 84-187, sheet 8b, household 161, Maria Serra.

[281] "Michigan Marriage Records, 1867-1952," database, *Ancestry.com* (http://ancestry.com : accessed 26 August 2016), entry for Lena Serra, 1940 (state file no. 229036); citing Michigan Department of Community Health, Division for Vital Records and Health Statistics, film no. 300 (82 Wayne 227000-230249).

[282] Social Security Administration, "United States Social Security Death Index," database, Ancestry.com (http://ancestry.com : accessed 25 August 2016), entry for Antonina Serra Crimaudo, 1990, SS no. 382-52-1881.

[283] 1920 U. S. Federal census, Wayne Co., MI, pop. sched., Detroit, wd 5, ED 160, sheet 13b, dwelling 135, family 235, Christiano Serra [indexed Christina Sarras].

1930 MI Wayne Detroit wd 5 SD21 ED82-113 sheet 17b[284]
1002 Fort - Serra, John head 22 Mi It It prop grocery store
        Nick brother 19 Mi It It clerk grocery story
    Serra, Maria mother 45 wd It It It
        Mary sister 21 Mi It It
1940 Mi Wayne Detroit wd 5 SD1 ED84-187 sheet 8b April 10[285]
1002 E Fort st upstairs - Serra, Maria 55 wd b Italy alien same house 1935
       (Next page) Lena 28 MI / Nick 26
           Rose 20 bookkeeper wholesale produce
           Sarah 17
1006 E Fort down - Serra, Sam 33 Mi - truck driver wholesale produce
          Mary 31/ Harry 11 /Mary 8
1942 May 16 - married Virginia Fredianelli, Detroit, Wayne, MI[286]

Giuseppe 1914 - 1916

Zinseppe Serra - 210 Fort wd7 - b 18 May 1914 - d 30 Sep 1916 - 2-4-10
    f Zraziane Serra b It - m Maria Cusumano b It
    in Zraziane - Mt Olivet
    "Michigan Death Records, 1867-1950," database with images,
    Ancestry.com (http://ancestry.com : accessed 7 Oct 2016), entry for
    Zinseppe Serra, 30 Sep 1916, state file no. 9235, reg no. 9239; citing
    Michigan Department of Community Health, Division for Vital
    Records and Health Statistics.

Rose 1920

1920 Mi Wayne Detroit wd 5 SD145 ED160 sheet 13b[287]
210 E. Forth St - Serra, Christiano [indexed Christina Sarras] 50, em 1899
alien, It It It, store keeper, groceries
       Mary wife 35 em 1903 alien, It It It
       Samuel son 15 MI It It / John son 14 MI It It
       Lena dau 10 MI It It
       Nick son 8 MI It It / Rose dau 2 4/12 MI It It

---

[284] 1930 U.S. census, Wayne Co., MI, pop. sched., Detroit wd 5, ED 82-113, sheet 17b, dwel. 142, fam. 22, John Serra.

[285] 1940 U. S. Census, Wayne Co., MI, pop. sched., Detroit, wd 5, ED 84-187, sheet 8b, household 161, Maria Serra.

[286] "Michigan Marriage Records, 1867-1952," database, *Ancestry.com* (http://ancestry.com : accessed 26 August 2016), entry for Nick Serra, 1942 (state file no. 268955); citing Michigan Department of Community Health, Division for Vital Records and Health Statistics, film no. 312 (82 Wayne 266300-269589).

[287] 1920 U. S. Federal census, Wayne Co., MI, pop. sched., Detroit, wd 5, ED 160, sheet 13b, dwelling 135, family 235, Christiano Serra [indexed Christina Sarras].

1930
1940 Mi Wayne Detroit wd 5 SD1 ED84-187 sheet 8b April 10[288]
1002 E Fort st upstairs - Serra, Maria 55 wd b Italy alien same house 1935
        (Next page) Lena 28 MI / Nick 26
                Rose 20 bookkeeper wholesale produce
                Sarah 17
1006 E Fort down - Serra, Sam 33 Mi - truck driver wholesale produce
                Mary 31 / Harry 11 / Mary 8
1949 Nov 13 - married Vito Lo Duca - Detroit, Wayne, MI (Holy Family)[289]

Sarah 1921-2008

1921 Nov 13 - born (according to Find-a-Grave)
1930
1940 Mi Wayne Detroit wd 5 SD1 ED84-187 sheet 8b April 10[290]
1002 E Fort st upstairs - Serra, Maria 55 wd b Italy alien same house 1935
        (Next page) Lena 28 MI / Nick 26
                Rose 20 bookkeeper wholesale produce
                Sarah 17
1006 E Fort down - Serra, Sam 33 Mi - truck driver wholesale produce
                Mary 31 / Harry 11 / Mary 8
1949 May 22 - married James David Stork[291] - Detroit, Wayne, MI
2008 Nov 26 - died, buried Mt Olivet[292]

---

[288] 1940 U. S. Census, Wayne Co., MI, pop. sched., Detroit, wd 5, ED 84-187, sheet 8b, household 161, Maria Serra.

[289] "Michigan Marriage Records, 1867-1952," database, *Ancestry.com* (http://ancestry.com: accessed 25 August 2016), entry for Rose Serra, 1949 (state file no. 448388); citing Michigan Department of Community Health, Division for Vital Records and Health Statistics, film no. 367 (82 Wayne 446740-450049).

[290] 1940 U. S. Census, Wayne Co., MI, pop. sched., Detroit, wd 5, ED 84-187, sheet 8b, household 161, Maria Serra.

[291] "Michigan Marriage Records, 1867-1952," database, *Ancestry.com* (http://ancestry.com: accessed 25 August 2016), entry for Sarah Serra, 1949 (state file no. 435887); citing Michigan Department of Community Health, Division for Vital Records and Health Statistics, film no. 363 (82 Wayne 433400-436729).

[292] *Findagrave.com*, database and images (http://findagrave.com: accessed 26 August 2016), memorial page for Sarah M Stork (1921- 2008), Find A Grave Memorial no. 31936404, created by Kathleen Fleury Bilbrey, citing Mt. Olivet Cemetery, Detroit, Wayne, Michigan.

Rosalia, 1885 - 1965
new information from descendant Daniel Mallory
And some from descendant Gianni Cortese

She married a cousin - Paulo Cusmano - and had eight children (our family
memories said she had one daughter, but now I think maybe what was meant
was that she had *a* daughter named Lena.) According to Daniel, 6 survived:
Ann, Lena, Philip, John, Frances, Mary. The 1920 census shows another,
Joseph, born ~1919. Daniel says the other child who died young was a
daughter, Loretta.

1885 Oct 29 - born Terrasini[293]
    baptized Oct 30 Maria Santissima delle Grazie, Terrasini
    #250 = 30 Oct 1885 b yest - Rosalia C
        - Giovanni C & Antonina Mazzola
        (Godfather - Girolamo Palazzolo s/o Nicolo)
    548 = 152 = 30 Oct 1885 b yesterday - Rosalia
        d/o Joannes C & Antonina Mazzola
        (Godfather - Hieronymus Palazzolo)
1905 March 15 - married her father's cousin Francesco Paolo, known as
Paolo (Paul)[294]
    46 = 19 = 15 March 1905 - Francesco Paolo G
      - Filippo & Anna Orlando
    Rosalia G - Joannes & Antonina M
1905 Sept 2 - emigrated - *Neapolitan Prince* (Palermo to NY)[295]
    Cusumano, Rosalia 19 f married - from Terrasini - going to my
    husband Cusumano, Paolo, Box 342 Oakfield, NY
1907 Jan 20 - dau Anna born NY
1908 - son Philip born, died childbirth

---

[293]Maria Santissima delle Grazie (Chiesa Madre [Mother Church]), Terrasini,
Palermo, Sicily, Italy, Baptismal register, v. 32, 1884-1889, record # 250, Rosalia
Cusumano baptism 1885; *Family Search.org*, "Battesimi 1884-1887," image 57 of
103. AND Maria Santissima delle Grazie, Terrasini, Palermo, Sicily, Italy, Baptismal
register, v. 31, 1882-1889, p. 152, Rosalia C baptism 1885; *Family Search.org*,
"Battesimi 1873-1889," image 548 of 792.
[294]Maria Santissima delle Grazie (Chiesa Madre [Mother Church]), Terrasini,
Palermo, Sicily, Italy, Marriage register, v. X, 1904-1909, p.19, Francesco Paolo
Gusmano marriage 1905; *Family Search.org*, "Matrimoni 1905-1911," image 46 of
264.
[295]Manifest, *Neapolitan Prince*, 2 September 1905, p.51, line 17, Rosalia Cusumano,
age 19; images, "New York Passenger Lists, 1820-1957," *Ancestry.com*
(http://ancestry.com: accessed 27 August 2016).

1910 Apr 11 - dau Lena born NY

1910 census[296] - New York, Genessee, Oakfield Twp, SD18 ED29, Sheet 10 a (106/2308) - 29 Apr - Garibaldi Street - line 48 (198-227)

Cusmano, Paul head mw 30 m4 - em 1905 - Italy - laborer gypsum mill

        Rosa wife 26 m4 - em 1906 - Italy -

        Anna 3 - b NY

        Lena 1/12 - b NY

They moved to Michigan sometime before 1913.

Paul's first job was with a cement company at Jefferson and Atwater.[297]

1912-1915 - lived 1470 Orleans[298]

1913 Apr 11 (sic) - son Philip born MI

1913 Detroit City Directory - Cosemanno Paul lab 170 Riopelle

1914 Gusmano Paul lab bds 176 Rivard - with Jno, Jos, Saml

1914- aft 1942 - lived 2671 Chestnut [299] - actually, according to other documents, they lived at 557 Lafayette from 1918-1920 at least, and according to Dan's own report, son John was born at 1470 Orleans in 1915.

1915 March 24 - son John born

1916 May 24 - dau Frances born (died September)[300]

Frances Cusmano - 162 Rivard - b 24 May 1916 - d 7 Sep 1916 - age 3m 17d

    f Paul b It, m Rosie Cusmano b It

    inf Paul - Mt Olivet

1917 July 9 - son Joe born (d 1918)[301]

Joe Cusumano - 162 Rivard - b 8 July 1917 Det - d 30 Mar 1918 - age 8m 22d - fall from high chair

    f Paolo Cusumano b It - m Rosalia Cusumano, b It

    inf Paolo - Mt Olivet

---

[296]U. S. Federal Census, Genessee County, New York, population schedule, Oakfield Township, enumeration district (ED) 29, sheet 10a, dwelling 198, family 227, Paul Cusmano; image, *Ancestry.com* (http://ancestry.com : accessed 27 Aug 2016); citing NARA microfilm publication T624, roll 951.

[297]Mallory, "John Joseph Cusmano."

[298]Mallory, "John Joseph Cusmano."

[299]Mallory, "John Joseph Cusmano."

[300]"Michigan, Death Records, 1867-1950," database with images, *Ancestry.com* (http://ancestry.com : accessed 5 Oct 2016), entry for Frances Cusmano, 7 Sep 1916 (file no. 8638); Michigan Department of Community Health, Division for Vital Records and Health Statistics, Lansing, Michigan.

[301]"Michigan, Death Records, 1867-1950," database with images, *Ancestry.com* (http://ancestry.com : accessed 6 Oct 2016), entry for Joe Cusumano, 30 Mar 1918 (file no. 3260); Michigan Department of Community Health, Division for Vital Records and Health Statistics, Lansing, Michigan.

1918 Sept 12 - WWI Draft Registration for Paul[302]
        serial #4958, order #4223
        Paul Cusumano - 557 Lafayette, Detroit - age 39, born 29 Nov 1879 -
alien, non-declarant
        plaster worker, Union Plaster Co - E Jefferson
        Rose Cusumano, wife, 557 Lafayette
        med height, med build, brown hair & eyes
1919/20 Cusman, Paul - lab. b. 557 Lafayette
1919 - son Joseph b Detroit (d1920)[303]
1920 census[304] - Michigan, Detroit, Wayne - Roll 115 ED 327 sheet 5 line 23
- 557 E Lafayette
56-81 Cusmano Paul 40 1907 (that's the year of emigration - may be 1902)
            Rosa 35 1905
            Anna 13, Gina (I think Lena) 9 b. NY
            Philip 6, John 5, Joseph 1 b. Mich
1920 - dau Frances born
1921 - dau Anna m Vincenzo Bommarito[305]
        219651 - Vincenzo Bommarito 24 res Detroit, b Italy, peddler, father
        Pietro, mother Margaret Giordano [?], not married before
        Anna Cusmano 16 res Detroit, b NY
                father Paul, mother Rose Cusmano
        Official L Eugene Sharp, Justice -
        wit Antonio Cusmano, Antonio Lentini
1921/22 Cusmano Paul lab h2671 Chestnut
1922 - dau Mary born
1922/23 Cusmano Paolo lab h2641 Chestnut

---

[302]"U.S. World War I Draft Registration Cards, 1917-1918," database with images,
Ancestry.com (http://ancestry.com: accessed 27 August 2016), card for Paul
Cusumano, serial no. 4958, Draft Board 13, Wayne County, Michigan; imaged from
Family History Library microfilm.
[303]"Michigan, Death Records, 1867-1950," database with images, *Ancestry.com*
(http://ancestry.com: accessed 6 Oct 2016), entry for Giuseppe Cusumano, 20 Jan
1920 (file no. 711, stamp 672); Michigan Department of Community Health,
Division for Vital Records and Health Statistics, Lansing, Michigan.
[304]1920 U. S. Federal census, Wayne County, Michigan, population schedule,
Detroit, ward 11, enumeration district (ED) 327, sheet 5a, dwelling 56, family 81,
Paul Cusmano; image, *Ancestry.com* (http://ancestry.com: accessed 27 Aug 2016);
citing NARA microfilm publication T625, roll 810.
[305]"Michigan Marriage Records, 1867-1952," database, *Ancestry.com*
(http://ancestry.com: accessed 27 August 2016), entry for Anna Cusmano, 1921 (file
no. 219651); citing Michigan Department of Community Health, Division for Vital
Records and Health Statistics, film no. 160 (1921 Wayne).

1925 - dau Lorenza born (d 1926)[306]

Lorenza Cusumano - 2671 Chestnut - b 8 Aug 1925 Det - d 8 Apr 1926 - 8 mo

     f Paolo Cusumano b Terrasini - m Rosolia Cusumano b Terasini

     inf Paolo - Mt Olivet

1927/28 Cusmano Paul (Rose) lab h2671 Chestnut

1928/29 Cusmano Paul (Rose) h2671 Chestnut

1928-29 - Paul worked for Cusenza, making alcohol[307]

1930 - not found

1930-1960 - Paul worked at Fort and 12th unloading produce from the train for Galardi.[308]

1930/31 Cusmano Paul (Rose) lab h 2671 Chestnut

1931/32 Cusmano Paul (Rose) lab h2671 Chestnut - with Philip

1932/33 Cusmano Paul (Rose) emp Detroit Union Produce Terminal Co h2671 Chestnut

1934 Cusmano Paul (Rose) lab h2671 Chestnut - with Philip, John

1935 Detroit City Directory - Cusmano, Paul (Rose) lab h2671 Chestnut -

     Philip fctywkr r2671 Chestnut

     John fctywkr r2671 Chestnut

1939 Detroit City Directory - Cusmano, Paul (Rose) lab h2671 Chestnut -

     Philip asmblr r2671 Chestnut

     John r2671 Chestnut

1940 census[309] - MI Wayne Detroit wd 11 - SD1st Ed 84-572 sh 6a - April 5 - 2671 Chestnut Ave

Cusumano, Paul 60 alien b Italy - 1935 lived same house - Sicilian - car loader, auto factory

     Rosalia 55 alien b Italy - same house - Sicilian

     Philip 26 b MI assembly auto factory

     John 25 b MI assembly auto factory

     Frances 20 dau / Mary 18

    Cusenza, Leona 12 g-dau - same house

     Leonard 11 g-son

---

[306]"Michigan, Death Records, 1867-1950," database with images, *Ancestry.com* (http://ancestry.com: accessed 6 Oct 2016), entry for Lorenza Cusumano, 8 Apr 1926 (state file no. 582 66362, reg no. 5689); Michigan Department of Community Health, Division for Vital Records and Health Statistics, Lansing, Michigan.

[307]Mallory, "John Joseph Cusmano."

[308]Mallory, "John Joseph Cusmano."

[309]1940 U. S. Census, Wayne County, Michigan, population schedule, Detroit, ward 11, enumeration district (ED) 84-572, sheet 6a, household 105, Paul Cusumano; image, *Ancestry.com* (http://ancestry.com: accessed 27 Aug 2016); citing NARA microfilm publication T627, roll 1858.

194x - WWII Draft Registration for Paul[310]
serial #1704 - Paul (no middle name) Cusmano - 2671 Chestnut, Detroit
        age 63 - b 29 Nov 1880 Italy
        contact - Philip Cusmano, 2671 Chestnut, Detroit
        employer - Terminal, Fort & Crane, Detroit
1960-65 -Paul worked at Beautifeit and Gratiot cleaning beer barrels until
1965.[311]
1965 Jan 31 - Rosalia died[312].
1977 Oct 1 - Paul died[313]
        born 29 Oct 1880[314]; his last residence was St. Clair Shores, Macomb Co.
        They are buried in Mt Olivet.[315]
        Paul Cusmano - Location: Section A - GOTR, Tier 8, Space 175
        Rosalia Cusmano - Location: Section A - GOTR, Tier 8, Space 176

---

[310]"U.S. World War II Draft Registration Cards, 1942," database with images, *Ancestry.com* (http://ancestry.com: accessed 27 August 2016), card for Paul Cusmano, serial no. 1704; citing The National Archives at St. Louis, Draft Registration Cards for Fourth Registration for Michigan, 04/27/1942 - 04/27/1942; NAI Number: 623283; Records of the Selective Service System; Record Group Number: 147

[311]Mallory, "John Joseph Cusmano."

[312]Funeral card for Rosalia Cusmano, Mallory Family Collection, privately owned by Daniel Mallory, email private; scanned image sent to Lee Bothwell, 6 Aug 2006.

[313]"Michigan Death Index, 1971-1996," database, *Ancestry.com* (http://ancestry.com: accessed 27 Aug 2016), entry for Paul Cusmano; citing Michigan Department of Community Health, Division for Vital Records and Health Statistics. Also Michigan Department of Public Health, death certificate (local file) no. 70 (1977), Paul Cusmano; Mallory Family Collection, privately owned by Daniel Mallory, email private; scanned image sent to Lee Bothwell, 29 Aug 2016.

[314] The SS Death Index says he was born 30 Oct 1880; his last residence was Detroit, last benefit Eastpointe. Social Security Administration, "United States Social Security Death Index," database, Ancestry.com (http://ancestry.com: accessed 27 August 2016), entry for Paul Cusmano, 1977, SS no. 363-09-7269.

[315]Mt. Elliott Cemetery Association, database, (http://www.mtelliott.com/genealogy/: accessed 31 August 2016), Mt. Olivet Cemetery (Detroit, Wayne, Michigan), entries for PauL (4 October 1977) and Rosalia (5 February 1965) Cusmano.

Children of Rosalia and Paolo Cusumano

Anna - 1907 - 1982

1907 Jan 20 - born, New York
1910 census - with parents in New York
1920 census - with parents in Detroit
1921 Sept 29 - married Vincenzo Bommarito - Detroit, MI[316]
219651 - Vincenzo Bommarito 24 res Detroit, b Italy, peddler,
       father Pietro, mother Margaret Giordano [?], not married before
  Anna Cusmano 16 res Detroit, b NY, father Paul, mother Rose Cusmano
      Official L Eugene Sharp, Justice -
       wit Antonio Cusmano, Antonio Lentini
  -> 3 children: Margaret, Paul, Pete[317]
1930 MI Wayne Detroit SD 22 ED82-673 sheet 11a - 3889 Holcomb Ave[318]
    Bommarito, Jim 33 m 24 It It It clerk, grocery
      Anna 27 m 17 Mi It It
      Peter 7 MI
1940 MI Wayne Detroit SD 14 ED 84-1229 sheet 1a - 3889 Holcomb[319]
    Bommarito, James 43 store clerk, grocery - same house 1935
      Anna 33 / Peter 17 / Margaret 9

---

[316]"Michigan Marriage Records, 1867-1952," database, *Ancestry.com* (http://ancestry.com: accessed 27 August 2016), entry for Anna Cusmano, 1921 (file no. 219651); citing Michigan Department of Community Health, Division for Vital Records and Health Statistics, film no. 160 (1921 Wayne).

[317]Daniel Mallory, "John Joseph Cusmano,"Mallory Family Collection, privately owned by Daniel Mallory, email private; scanned image sent to Lee Bothwell, 29 Aug 2016.

[318]1930 U.S. census, Wayne County, Michigan, population schedule, Detroit ward 19, enumeration district (ED) 673, sheet 11a, dwelling 174, family 3, Jim Bommarito; image, *Ancestry.com* (http://ancestry.com: accessed 29 Aug 2016); citing FHL microfilm: 2340794; NARA microfilm publication T626.

[319]1940 U. S. Census, Wayne County, Michigan, population schedule, Detroit, ward 19, enumeration district (ED) 84-1229, sheet 1a, household 5, James Bommarito; image, *Ancestry.com* (http://ancestry.com: accessed 29 Aug 2016); citing NARA microfilm publication T627, roll1876.

1942 - WWII Draft Registration for Vincenzo[320]
      serial #2760 - Vincenzo Bommarito - 3889 Holcomb Ave, Detroit
      age 45, born Teruzini, 8 Nov 1896, Italy
      contact - son Peter Bommarito, 3889 Holcomb
      employer - self - grocer 3891 Holcomb
1980 Nov 14 - husband Vincenzo died[321]
1982 Sept 8 - died[322] [SS# 379-70-8871]

Philip - 1908 - died childbirth

Lena - 1910 - 1992 (grandmother of Gianni Cortese)
1910 April 11 - born, NY
1910 census - with parents in New York
1920 census - with parents in Detroit
1926 Oct 23 - married Anthony Cusenza[323]
      Wayne Co no 318748
      Antonino Cusenza 28 res Detroit, b Italy, occ business,
          father Leo, m Leona Bonfilio
      Antonina Cusimano 16 res Detroit, b NY, occ none
          father Paul, mother Rosie Cusimano - mother's consent
      lic 13 Sep 1926 - marriage 23 Oct 1926
          witness - Antonino Ruggiello, Josephine Poma (?)
          Rev John B Marinara, pastor Holy Family
      -> 2 children, Leona & Leonard[324]

---

[320]U.S. World War II Draft Registration Cards, 1942," database with images, *Ancestry.com* (http://ancestry.com: accessed 27 August 2016), card for Vincenzo Bommarito, serial no. 2760; citing The National Archives at St. Louis, Draft Registration Cards for Fourth Registration for Michigan, 04/27/1942 - 04/27/1942; NAI Number: 623283; Records of the Selective Service System; Record Group Number: 147

[321]Social Security Administration, "United States Social Security Death Index," database, Ancestry.com (http://ancestry.com: accessed 27 August 2016), entry for Vincenzo Bommarito, 1980, SS no. 375-34-2650.

[322]Funeral card for Anna Bommarito, Mallory Family Collection, privately owned by Daniel Mallory, email private; scanned image sent to Lee Bothwell, 6 Aug 2006.

[323]"Michigan Marriage Records, 1867-1952," database, *Ancestry.com* (http://ancestry.com: accessed 28 August 2016), entry for Antonina Cusimano, 1926 (state file no.82 14921); citing Michigan Department of Community Health, Division for Vital Records and Health Statistics, film no. 235 (82 Wayne 14050-17299).

[324]Mallory, "John Joseph Cusmano."

192x - daughter Leona born (married Sambone)
1929 Apr 11 - son Leonard (Tony) born [d 26 Aug 1998][325]
    SSDI says 13 March 1929, SS Application file says 12 March 1929
1929 - husband Anthony Cusenza killed[326]
    Cusenza Funeral - Thurs., May 16, 1929 - *Detroit Evening Times*:
    Picture - Plane drops flowers - as thousands mourn.

> Pallbearers carrying the casket bearing Anthony Cusenza, victim
> of an assassin's bullet, from his home, 3492 Algonquin Ave,
> today, for burial in Mt. Olivet Cemetery.
>   Picture - 300 autos and $10,000 in flowers
> An airplane zooming overhead dropped a half ton of rose petals
> on the procession as it moved toward the cemetery. More than
> 300 autos carrying 3,000 mourners formed the cortege. Flowers
> estimated to cost more than $10,000 filled 5 autos to overflowing
> while a blanket of roses was draped over Cusenza's casket.

1930
1937 Sept 25 - married Joseph C. Cortese - Detroit, Wayne, MI[327]
    Joseph age 29 res Detroit b MI - clerk - father Nick, mother Maryn
Grammatico - married once
    Lena age 27 b NY housewife father Paul m Rose Cusmano - married
once -
license 28 July 1937 - m 25 Sept 1937 - Benedict Ferretti priest
        witnesses Frank Cortese, Frances Cusmano
    [According to Jean Williams (Find-a-Grave), *his* first wife was
Antonina "Lena" Poma 1912-1936, with whom he had a son, Nick.[328]]
    -> 2 children - William & Mary[329]

---

[325]Social Security Administration, "U.S., Social Security Applications and Claims Index, 1936-2007," database, Ancestry.com (http://ancestry.com : accessed 29 August 2016), entry for Leonard A. Cusenza, 2007, SS no. 377-20-7238.

[326]"Plane Drops Flowers as Thousands Mourn at Cusenza Funeral," 16 May 1929, Detroit Evening Times; Cusman Family Papers, privately held by Julie Martel [address private]; scanned image sent to Lee Bothwell, ca. 2010. Inherited in [unknown date] by Julie from her grandmother Delores (Cusman) Herpel.

[327]"Michigan Marriage Records, 1867-1952," image, *Ancestry.com* (http://ancestry.com : accessed 27 August 2016), entry for Lena [indexed Lona] Cusenza, 1937 (state file no. 192773); citing Michigan Department of Community Health, Division for Vital Records and Health Statistics, film no. 289 (82 Wayne 190800-194099).

[328]*Findagrave.com*, database and images (http://findagrave.com : accessed 25 August 2016), memorial page for Joseph Cortese (~1908-1967), Find A Grave Memorial no. 14123103, created by Jean Williams, citing Mt Olivet Cemetery, Detroit, Wayne, Michigan.

[329]Mallory, "John Joseph Cusmano."

1940
1967 - husband Joseph Cortese died
1992 April 9 - died[330]
> She is buried in Mt Olivet, as are her two husbands.
> Mt. Olivet Cemetery[331] [Dates here are dates of interment.]
> Joseph Cortese - 09/05/1967 - Section A - GOTR, Tier 5, Space 173
> Lena Cortese - 04/13/1992- Section A - GOTR, Tier 5, Space 174
> Anthony Cusenza - 05/16/1929 - Section 15, Lot 1515, Space 1

Phillip - 1913 MI - 1989

1913 April 11 - born
1920 census - with parents in Detroit
1930 -
Detroit City Directories-
1931/32 Cusmano Philip lab r2671 Chestnut - with Paul
1934 Cusmano Philip lab r2671 Chestnut - with Paul, John
1935 Cusmano Philip fctywkr r2671 Chestnut - with Paul, John
1939 Cusmano, Philip asmblr r2671 Chestnut - with Paul, John
1940 census - with parents in Detroit
1940 Sept 7 - married Frances Manzo - Holy Family - Detroit,Wayne, MI[332]
> -> 1 child Paul
1989 July 19 - Phillip died
2003 April 8 - wife Frances died
> Resurrection Cemetery[333] [the dates here are dates of interment]
> Phillip Cusmano - 07/22/1989 - Section 16, Lot 1169, Space 2
> Frances Cusmano - 04/12/2003 - Section 16, Lot 1169, Space 3

---

[330]Funeral card for Lena Cortese, Mallory Family Collection, privately owned by Daniel Mallory, email private; scanned image sent to Lee Bothwell, 6 Aug 2006.

[331] Mt. Elliott Cemetery Association, database (http://www.mtelliott.com/genealogy/ : accessed 29 August 2016), Mt. Olivet Cemetery (Detroit, Wayne, Michigan), entries for Joseph (5 September 1967) and Lena (13 April 1992) Cortese and Anthony Cusenza (16 May 1929).

[332]"Michigan Marriage Records, 1867-1952," database, *Ancestry.com* (http://ancestry.com : accessed 27 August 2016), entry for Phillip Cusmano, 1940 (state file no. 233332); citing Michigan Department of Community Health, Division for Vital Records and Health Statistics, film no. 301 (82 Wayne 230250-233529).

[333]Mt. Elliott Cemetery Association, database (http://www.mtelliott.com/genealogy/ : accessed 29 August 2016), Resurrection Cemetery (Clinton Township, Macomb, Michigan), entries for Phillip (22 July 1989) and Frances Cusmano (12 April 2003).

John - ~1915 - 2007 (grandfather of Daniel Mallory)

1915 March 24 -born (in Detroit at 1470 Orleans near St. Auburn)

1920 census - with parents in Detroit

1930 -

1934 - worked at Hudson's

Detroit City Directories

1934 Cusmano John r2671 Chestnut - with Paul, Philip

1935 Cusmano John fctywkr r2671 Chestnut - with Paul, Philip

1939 Cusmano, John r2671 Chestnut - with Paul, Philip

1940 census - with parents in Detroit

1940 June 15 - married Ruth Koelsch - Holy Family - Wayne, MI[334]
    -> 2 children: Paul, Rosalia[335]

1940-1943 - lived 3053 Garland, Detroit

1943 Jan - army

1946 April - discharged from army

1946-1955 - worked for Hudson's (Hudson's got bought out in 1955)

1955 - 1957 worked at GM, Ford, car wash at Harper and Connors. 1957 -
1978 worked at Vernors Ginger Ale Distribution Center at Woodward and
Canfield.

1945-1967 - lived 12546 Wade, Detroit

1967- 1977 - lived 16907 Cullingham, Detroit

1977 - lived 16344 Greenland, Macomb[336]

2007 May 30 - died[337] - last residence Bloomfield Hills
    his social security number is not listed, either in the SSDI or the SS
    Applications and Claims index. The latter has the following note: Nov
    1936: Name listed as JOHN CUSMANO; Jan 1945: Name listed as
    JOHN JOSEPH CUSMANO; 09 Jun 2007: Name listed as JOHN J
    CUSMANO

---

[334]"Michigan Marriage Records, 1867-1952," database, *Ancestry.com*
(http://ancestry.com: accessed 27 August 2016), entry for John Cusmano, 1940
(state file no. 227565); citing Michigan Department of Community Health, Division
for Vital Records and Health Statistics, film no. 300 (82 Wayne 227000-230249).

[335]Mallory, "John Joseph Cusmano."

[336]Residences and job information from Mallory, "John Joseph Cusmano."

[337]Social Security Administration, "U.S., Social Security Applications and Claims
Index, 1936-2007," database, Ancestry.com (http://ancestry.com: accessed 27
August 2016), entry for Frances Cusmano Zbercot, 2002, SS no. 383-52-7129.

Frances - May 1916 - d 11 Sept 1916.[338]

Joe born 1917 - d 1918[339]
>   bp 2Sept1917 (b 8July1917)-sponsors Graziano & Giustiana - Holy
>   Family[340]

Joseph 1919 - d 1920[341]
1920 census - with parents in Detroit

Frances - 1920 - 2002
1920 March 21 - born (according to Funeral Card)[342]
1920 May 28 - born (date according to SS Applications & Claims Index)[343]
1930
1940 census - with parents in Detroit
1940 October 5 - married Peter Zbercot - Detroit, Wayne, MI[344]
>   -> 2 children: Veronica, John[345]
1990 May 6 - husband Peter died.

---

[338]"Michigan Death Records, 1867-1950," database with images, *Ancestry.com* (http://ancestry.com: accessed 27 Aug 2016), entry for Francis Cusmano; citing Michigan Department of Community Health, Division for Vital Records and Health Statistics.

[339]"Michigan, Death Records, 1867-1950," database with images, *Ancestry.com* (http://ancestry.com: accessed 6 Oct 2016), entry for Joe Cusumano, 30 Mar 1918 (file no. 3260); Michigan Department of Community Health, Division for Vital Records and Health Statistics, Lansing, Michigan.

[340]Holy Family Catholic Church (Detroit, Michigan), Certificate of Baptism (privately held by Daniel Mallory), Giuseppe Cusumano baptismal certificate (1917), issued 1980; scanned image sent to Lee Bothwell, 29 Aug 2016.

[341]"Michigan, Death Records, 1867-1950," database with images, *Ancestry.com* (http://ancestry.com: accessed 6 Oct 2016), entry for Giuseppe Cusumano, 20 Jan 1920 (file no. 711, stamp 672); Michigan Department of Community Health, Division for Vital Records and Health Statistics, Lansing, Michigan.

[342]Funeral card for Frances Zbercot, Mallory Family Collection, privately owned by Daniel Mallory, email private; scanned image sent to Lee Bothwell, 6 Aug 2006.

[343]Social Security Administration, "U.S., Social Security Applications and Claims Index, 1936-2007," database, Ancestry.com (http://ancestry.com: accessed 27 August 2016), entry for John Cusmano, 2007, SS no. not given.

[344]"Michigan Marriage Records, 1867-1952," database, *Ancestry.com* (http://ancestry.com: accessed 27 August 2016), entry for Frances Cusmano, 1940 (state file no. 234673); citing Michigan Department of Community Health, Division for Vital Records and Health Statistics, film no. 302 (82 Wayne 233530-236769).

[345]Mallory, "John Joseph Cusmano."

2002 May 1 - died[346] - both Frances and Peter J are buried in Resurrection Cemetery[347] (Clinton Twp)   [The dates here are dates of interment.]
Frances P. Zbercot - 05/06/2002 - Section 3, Lot 352, Space 2
Peter J. Zbercot - 05/10/1990- Section 3, Lot 352, Space 1

Mary - 1922 -1999

1922 Feb 2 - born[348]

1930

1940 census - with parents in Detroit

19xx - married James Wayne

-> 1 child, Anthony[349]

19xx - married FNU Drew

1999 May 30 - died[350]

> The SS Applications & Claims Index says she died 24 October 1999, and has the following note: Oct 1941: Name listed as MARY ROSE CUSMANO; Apr 1970: Name listed as MARY ROSE DREW; 05 Nov 1999: Name listed as MARY R DREW.[351]
> buried Oakland Hills Memorial Gardens Cem., Novi, Oakland, MI[352]
> Last residence Plymoth, Wayne, MI

Loretta b 1926

> died at 6 months of pneumonia[353]

---

[346]Funeral card for Frances Zbercot.

[347]Mt. Elliott Cemetery Association, database, (http://www.mtelliott.com/genealogy/ : accessed 29 August 2016), Resurrection Cemetery (Clinton Township, Macomb, Michigan), entries for Peter J. (05/10/1990) and Frances P. (05/06/2002) Zbercot.

[348]Social Security Administration, "U.S., Social Security Applications and Claims Index, 1936-2007," database, Ancestry.com (http://ancestry.com: accessed 29 August 2016), entry for Mary Rose Cusmano, 1999, SS no. 386-16-8170.

[349]Mallory, "John Joseph Cusmano."

[350]Social Security Administration, "United States Social Security Death Index," database, Ancestry.com (http://ancestry.com: accessed 27 August 2016), entry for Mary R Drew, 1999, SS no. 386-16-8170.

[351]Social Security Administration, "U.S., Social Security Applications and Claims Index, 1936-2007," database, Ancestry.com (http://ancestry.com: accessed 29 August 2016), entry for Mary Rose Cusmano, 1999, SS no. 386-16-8170.

[352]*Findagrave.com,* database and images (http://findagrave.com: accessed 25 August 2016), memorial page for Mary R. Drew (1922-1999), Find A Grave Memorial no. 11338426, created by "Laura," citing Oakland Hills Memorial Gardens Cemetery, Novi, Oakland, Michigan.

[353]Mallory, "John Joseph Cusmano."

Christopher
1899 - 1974
Mazzara - Detroit

Chris was born on 29 April 1899, in Mazzara, in the Trapani province (the next one west of Palermo). [I found him in an index[354] for births for the year 1899 - Cusumano, Cristofaro d'Giovanni - 301 - but unfortunately, the record #301 was not online.]

He came to the US in 1909 with his mother Antonina (Lena).[355]
Ship Regina d'Italia from Palermo - arr 16 June 1909

Name	Mazzola, Antonina	Cusimano Cristoforo
Age	52	9
Sex	female	male
Occupation	domestic	child
read/write	yes/yes	yes/yes
nationality	Italy	Italy
last permanent residence	Trapani, Mazzera	Trapani, Mazzera
nearest relative/friend in country from whence immigrant came		
	mother Vitale, Lorencia Mazzara	grandmother as above
final destination	Mich - Detroit	Mich - Detroit
ticket to final dest?	yes	yes
paid for by?	self	self
going to relative/friend?	brother-in-law Cusumano, as above 140 Lain str Detroit	Graciano father
ever in prison? / anarchist / polygamist	no	no
health?	good	good
deformed?	no	no
height	4'11"	
complexion	rosy	
hair	gray	
eyes	chestnut	
identifying marks	-	
place of birth	Trapani, Mazzara	Trapani, Mazzara

---

[354]http://www.antenati.san.beniculturali.it/v/Archivio+di+Stato+di+Trapani/Stato+civ ile+italiano/Mazara+del+Vallo/Nati/1899/suppl+2/007853500_00117.jpg.html

[355]Manifest, *Regina d'Italia*, 16 June 1909, page 168, line 9, Cristofaro Cusumano, 9; images, "Passenger Lists, 1820-1957," *Ancestry.com* (http: ancestry.com: accessed 6 September 2016).

It seems a little odd that Lena says she was going to her brother-in-law Graziano, instead of her husband. It also is a continuing oddity that all our people claim to be going to 140 or 136 or something Lain Street, because I am pretty sure there is no Lain Street in Detroit. I looked at the street listings in the city directories, and there never is a Lain street. However, Graziano Serra, the husband of Giovanni and Lena's daughter Maria Assunta, lived/had a grocery store at 140 **Larned**. Another little genealogical mystery.

He is on the 1910, 1920, 1930 censuses with Giovanni. He registered for the draft in 1918, but apparently was never called up:

1910 Census[356] - Michigan, Wayne Co, Detroit, ED 64 sheet 11 - taken 17 Apr 1910 - 262 Woodbridge -
    Cusmano, John head m w 47 married 28 y, b Italy, mf b Italy, immigrated 1901, speaks Italian, baker, bakery, owns, doesn't read or write, rents home.
    --Lolina wife f w 50 married 28 y, 6?overwritten 4 children, 4 still living, b. Italy, parents b. Italy, immigrated 1909, doesn't read or write.
    -- John son m w 15 single, b. Italy, immigrated 1902, speaks English, helper in bakery, reads, writes, attended school this year.
    -- Christopher, son m w 11, single, b. Italy immigrated 1909, speaks English, reads, writes, attended school
1918 Sept 12 - WWI Draft Registration [357]
    serial #3532, order #A3849
    Christopher Cusmano - 262 E Woodbridge, Detroit, Wayne, MI
    age 18 - b 29 April 1900 - alien non-declarant - Italy
    painter - Com. . . Hastings & Fort, Detroit
    contact Lena Mazzola Cusmano, mother - 262 E Woodbridge
        5'2" 132# lt brown eyes, black hair

---

[356] 1910 U.S. census, Wayne County, Michigan, population schedule, Detroit ward 5, enumeration district (ED) 64, sheet 11a, dwelling 112 rear, family 173, John Cusmano; image, *Ancestry.com* (http://ancestry.com : accessed 6 September 2016); citing NARA microfilm publication T624, roll 681.
[357] "U.S. World War I Draft Registration Cards, 1917-1918," database with images, *Ancestry.com* (http://ancestry.com : accessed 28 August 2016), card for Christopher Cusmano, serial no. 3532 Draft Board 6, Wayne County, Michigan; imaged from Family History Library microfilm.

1920 Federal Census[358] - Michigan, Wayne Co, Detroit. ED 160, p. 2

> 262 Woodbridge - 3 families
>> Ellis, Anthony (wife Julia) rents
>>
>> Mendel, Magel (rents) and Claryzek? Mike (boards)
>
> Casamano, John - head - owns - mortgaged. male white 60 married. emigrated 1901. alien. can read and write. born Italy, native tongue Italian. father&mother b. Italy, native tongue Italian. can speak English.baker. delicatessen.
>> Lena wife f w 60 married emigrated 1901. alien can read write, born Italy, parents b. Italy (native tongue Italian) can speak English
>>
>> John son m w 23 single emigrated 1905 naturalized 1917 can read write b. Italy etc. can speak English. machinist- machine shop
>>
>> Christopher son m w 19 single emigrated 1909 alien can read write b. Italy etc. can speak English. helper - machine shop

Detroit City Directories[359]

1921-22 Cusumano, Jno baker h978 Woodbridge
> Jno Jr mach ditto
>
> Chris lab r978 Woodbridge e

1922-23 Cusmano Chris lab r978 Woodbridge
> Cusumano Jno baker h978 Woodbridge
>
> Jno jr mach h978 Woodbridge

1930 census[360] - Mi, Wayne Detroit SD 21, ED 82-112, Sheet 8a (stamp 175, written 3310) - Ward of city 5, Block #183 - taken 7 Apr 1930 line 37 - 978 Woodbridge - 3 families

> Delia, Gasper mw 53 Italy & wife Marianne 43 Italy
>
> Bommarito, Joseph 21 Missouri & wife Fannie 18 Missouri

Cusmano, John head rents $25 mw 70 married at 27, can read & write, all Italy, emigrated 1900, not naturalized, speaks English
> --Lena wife 70 married at 27 no read & write, all Italy, emigrated 1910, not naturalized, doesn't speak English

---

[358] 1920 U. S. Federal census, Wayne County, Michigan, population schedule, Detroit, ward 5, enumeration district (ED) 160, sheet 2 b, dwelling 28, family 23, John Casanano; image, *Ancestry.com* (http://ancestry.com : accessed 6 September 2016); citing NARA microfilm publication T625, roll 802.

[359] R. L. Polk, compiler, *Detroit City Directory, 1921-22* (Detroit, MI: R. L. Polk & Co, 1921); also subsequent years 1921/22 - 1939.

[360] 1930 U.S. census, Wayne County, Michigan, population schedule, Detroit ward 5, enumeration district (ED) 82-112, sheet 8a, dwelling 30, family 87, John Cusmann; image, *Ancestry.com* (http://ancestry.com : accessed 29 Aug 2016); citing FHL microfilm: 2340770; NARA microfilm publication T626.

--Christopher son 27 s? 28?, can read & write, all Italy, emigrated 1910, not naturalized, speaks English, laborer auto factory, not a veteran

He was still living at home until at least 1935.

Detroit City Directories

1934 Cusmano John (Lena) h978 E Woodbridge
    Christopher autowkr r978 E Woodbridge
1935 Cusmano Christopher lab r978 Woodbridge
    John (Lena) lab h978 E Woodbridge

In 1937, he married Rose Evola. The family story is that it was an arranged marriage, because both the Cusmanos and the Evolas were worried that the children would otherwise never get married. He was a little old (36) but she was only 24. Mom said that Rosie was tall and thin (and I got the idea "elegant") while Chris was a short stocky guy.

1937 Nov 25 - Christopher Cusmano - Rose Evola[361]
    #511069 Wayne County, Michigan 194213
Christopher Cusmano - 36 - res Detroit, b Italy, occ inspector,
    father Giovanni, m Lena Mazzola
Rose Evola - 24- res Detroit, b Detroit, occ none,
    father Joseph, m Fara Lupo
    lic 22 Oct 1937 - m 25 Nov 1937
    - wit F Cusumano?, F Serra - Detroit
    Fr Benedict Ferretti - RC priest

In 1938, their son John Christopher was born. He became a priest. Also in 1938, Chris and Rosie had their own home, on Pennsylvania Ave.

1938 Sept 6 - son John C born

Detroit City Directories:

1938 - Cusmano, Christopher (Rose) autowkr h 5573 Penna av
1939 - Cusmano, Christopher (Rosie) inspr h 5573 Penna av

---

[361]Michigan Marriage Records, 1867-1952," database, *Ancestry.com* (http://ancestry.com: accessed 25 August 2016), entry for Christopher Cusmano, 1937 (state file no.194213); citing Michigan Department of Community Health, Division for Vital Records and Health Statistics, film no. 290 (82 Wayne 194100-197369).

1940 census[362] - MI Wayne Detroit ward 19 - SD 14?Ed 84-1242 sheet 10a -
Apr 10 - 5573 Pennsylvania Ave
     Cusmano, Christopher 39 naturalized b Italy -
         lived same place 1935 - inspector auto fac
       Rose 28 b MI
       John C 1 MI

Sometime after 1940, their daughter Nina was born. I haven't been able to find much out about her, although the obit for her brother John says he was survived by a sister Nina (Mrs. Joseph) Majetic and nieces Christina and Nina and nephew Joey.[363]

Chris died in August, 1974; Rosie in 1989. They were both buried in Resurrection Cemetery (Clinton Township), as was their son John:[364]

Christopher Cusmano - August 19, 1974 - Section 21, Lot 1666, Space 3
Rose Cusmano - March 16, 1989 - Section 21, Lot 1666, Space 4
John C. Cusmano - October 29, 2011 - Section 21, Lot 1927, Space 6

[362] 1940 U. S. Census, Wayne County, Michigan, population schedule, Detroit, ward 5, enumeration district (ED) 84-1242, sheet 10a, household 218, Christopher Cusmano; image, *Ancestry.com* (http://ancestry.com : accessed 25 Aug 2016); citing NARA microfilm publication T627, roll 1877.

[363] *Findagrave.com*, database and images (http://findagrave.com : accessed 25 August 2016), memorial page for Rev Fr John Cusmano (1938-2011), Resurrection Cemetery, Clinton Township, Macomb, Michigan, Find A Grave Memorial no. 79690841, created by "Elizabeth and Ron."

[364] Mt. Elliott Cemetery Association, database, (http://www.mtelliott.com/genealogy/ : accessed 29 August 2016), Resurrection Cemetery (Clinton Township, Macomb, Michigan), entries for Christopher (19 August 1974), Rose (16 March 1989) and John C. Cusmano (29 October 2011).

III. Detroit Cusmanos

Detroit Cusmanos

It wasn't until after the unification of Italy (1861) that Italians had the right to move about freely. I'm not sure what sort of restrictions there were, but before then Italians - Sicilians - mostly stayed put. (Although I have to say, our ancestors seemed to have moved around pretty freely.)

After unification, things were supposed to get better, but they did not. Sicilians were still ruled by foreigners (this time northern Italians) who could understand neither their language nor their unique local problems. What unification brought them was higher taxes, compulsory military service, and the Mafia. Add to this a series of agricultural, environmental, and economic disasters - and the brutal suppression of a popular cooperative movement (think unions) - and suddenly the idea of moving became more attractive.

> "[T]he Sicilians were among the last of the southern Italians to migrate to America in large numbers. However, once they began leaving, their numbers swelled until they constituted more than one quarter of all the Italian American immigrants. . . . Ultimately it would drive more than 1.5 million Sicilians - 40 percent of the island's population - to foreign lands."[365]

The journey over wasn't as bad as it was for the Irish - at least it took less time! (steamships instead of sail) - but it can't have been pleasant, and when they entered the US, they had to undergo a medical inspection - if they failed, they were sent back. There were also a series of questions. (They had filled out a form before they left, and they had to give the same answers when they arrived - or they could be sent back). The questions varied over the years (and the images of the ship manifests online do not contain all the questions and answers), but usually the immigrants were asked: age, occupation, place of birth, last residence, closest relative at home, final destination, if they had a ticket to the final destination (and who paid for it), if they were going to a particular person (who, what address), how much money they had. (It was good to have a ticket to the final destination, bad if someone else paid for it.)

In the beginning most of them were young men (our great-grandfather, age 41, was one of the older ones). Later on they would send for their sons and

---

[365] Jerre Mangione and Ben Morreale, *La Storia: five centuries of the Italian American experience* (New York: Harper Perennial, 1993), 78-9. [Frank Viviano, in *Blood Washes Blood : a true story of love, murder, and redemption under the Sicilian Sun* (New York: Washington Square Press (published by Pocket Books), 2001). 46, gives the number at 2 million, but who's counting?]

wives and other children - or else go back for them. A number of them made several trips back and forth. Some of them did it every year - they were called "birds of passage" - they'd work all summer and go back to Sicily in the winter. Some of *them* were bad guys, and if they hadn't saved enough money for the return trip, they would extort it from their better-off compatriots. Aunt Mary remembers a story about a couple of men demanding Great-Grandpa mortgage the bakery and give them the money; when I heard it, I thought it was the Mafia, but now I'm thinking it might have been this more informal group of extortionists known as the Black Hand. (One Cusmano was blown up by a Black Hand bomb.)

As for occupation, most of them - the southern Italians anyway - were laborers, or "countrymen" (which I think means agricultural laborers), or fishermen, so there weren't a lot of jobs for them. (Our great-grandfather was lucky to be a baker; he always managed to work.)
Many of them were met at the docks and hauled out into the boonies by labor contractors who had them working at back-breaking, dangerous jobs for pennies. (Some of the labor contractors had recruited them back in Sicily, which was why it wasn't good if someone else had paid for your ticket onward - the US authorities disapproved of them.) Others stayed in the port cities, in crowded dilapidated tenements, doing whatever jobs were available, and if there were no jobs, acting as "hucksters:" selling fruits and veg - or fish - from street carts.

In the beginning, they mostly answered that their final destination was New York, or maybe St Louis. It wasn't until after 1900 that a few of them - and then more and more - gave Detroit as their final destination. When our great-grandfather arrived in 1901, he said he was going to a cousin in New York, but by 1903, he was living - and working as a baker - in Detroit. And the word got back to Terrasini. In 1907 there were 3000 Sicilians - mostly from Terrasini or Cinisi - living in Detroit's Little Italy; ten years later there were about 15,000.

When I started looking at the Detroit records, I was appalled at the number of infant deaths there were, but after going through the Sicilian records, I have to say that things were no worse in Detroit, and maybe a little better. There were a lot of deaths from tuberculosis, possibly a result of poor conditions and over-crowding. One poor family had one child who died of malnutrition, another from over-feeding. One died from a fall from a high-chair.

As time went by, the birth rate declined. The second generation still had large families, but it was 6 children instead of 15 - and by the third generation they were having only 3 or 4 children.

They settled in the area around the Church of Saints Peter and Paul (629 E Jefferson) - Jefferson Avenue, Larned, Fort, Hastings, Congress - and they did the same sorts of things they had done in New York and St Louis: day labor, huckstering. Things gradually got easier: the street carts became small store-fronts, or stalls in the Eastern Market, the day-labor turned into steady jobs. And they were lucky: the automobile arrived. Ford started the Detroit Automobile Co in 1899 and by 1908 there were 253 car makers in Detroit. (For a really interesting timeline of the auto industry, see: http://www.scaruffi.com/politics/cars.html.)

When they first arrived, they attended mass at the Church of Sts Peter and Paul, but there were problems. The American Catholic hierarchy was largely Irish, their church had been outlawed for centuries, and they had survived by keeping a low profile; the Italian Catholic church was state supported, politically active (to say the least!), and public. The local Detroit priests were not comfortable with the parades and festivals natural to their Sicilian parishioners - and they didn't speak the language. A plea was sent to the pope, Pius X: "Of the 17 priests at the Jesuit church and college [Sts Peter & Paul had been turned over to the Jesuits in 1877, to form the nucleus of a proposed Catholic college - which eventually became U-Detroit/Mercy], not one could speak Italian. If they had a priest who spoke the language of these newcomers and understood their cultural needs, a church could be built for them. Alternatively, Bishop Foley would have to consider dividing the parish."[366] This was in 1905, and it was decided that a church should be built, but until then, a small chapel was set aside for the Sicilians. (It could have been worse: in one church in New York, the Sicilians were confined to the basement.)

Things hung fire until Father Giovanni Boschi arrived in 1907. He went door-to-door, making friends and gaining trust, and in December a committee was formed to raise money for the new church. (There were no Cusmanos on the committee, but Joseph Mazzola who was married to a Rose Cusmano - and I'm not sure how he was related - was the treasurer.) "The average wage at the time was 11¢ an hour, and their average monthly collection was just under $370."[367] The parish of Holy Family was officially established in 1908

---

[366]Bonnie Leone, *Detroit's Holy Family Church: 100 years of Sicilian tradition* (Charleson, S.C.: Arcadia Publishing, 2008), 7.
[367]Leone, *Holy Family*, 8.

and designated as a Sicilian Church, with Father Boschi as administrator &
priest. The building was finally completed November 1910. (Our great
grandmother walked to this church every day with her collie dog.) And even
after a lot of Sicilians started moving out to the suburbs, they returned to
Holy Family for important events, like marriages and baptisms. And they
fought like hell (successfully) to keep it from being destroyed when the
Chrysler Freeway (I-75) was built (1963 and following).

But all was not rosy. In the early days "Bishop Foley denied burial to a man
because he did not attend church regularly; he would not allow parishioners
to use the Italian flag in the church; and he did not want parishioners to
participate in processions carrying statues, a tradition dear to the hears of
immigrants . . . ."[368] At one point the people kept an uncongenial priest from
entering the church, and demanded the return of his predecessor (Father
Zagni); Father Zagni was recalled, but he - and his successor - snuck out one
night a few months later, locking the church behind them. The church
remained locked for two weeks, and, because the Sicilians still refused to
give up their traditions, they were assigned temporary priests for a year.
Eventually things settled down, although Holy Family remained a thorn in
the side of the archdiocese, which finally asked the Benedictines to take it
over (this was in 1929). The Benedictines continued for 76 years, but "Today
parishioners may feel that history repeats itself. The Benedictines no longer
service Holy Family, and the parish was left without a priest. The diocese, in
administration of the parish again after an interim of many decades, still
wants the parishioners to adapt their culture and traditions to the American
norm. Society leaders have asked for a priest to serve Holy Family, and their
requests have been rejected."[369]

Festa degli schletti

This was one of the street parties so beloved by the Sicilians, and so despised
by the church authorities. The festival of the bachelors was held ONLY in
Terrasini and Detroit - (and now only in Terrasini - Bonnie Leone, in her
book about the parish of Holy Family, published in 2008, says it continued
"until recently.") This is held during Easter week - maybe on Easter Sunday.
Small orange trees are cut and decorated, and the local bachelors take turns
trying to carry one - on the palm of the hand - to place at the door of their
sweetheart. (Bonnie describes it slightly differently: she says the trees are put
by the sweeties' doors in the morning, and then in the afternoon there is a

---

[368]Leone, *Holy Family*, 9.
[369]Leone, *Holy Family*, 10.

contest to see which bachelor can hold the tree - on the palm of the hand -
upright longest.)

~~~~~

Our great-grandfather was one of the first Cusmanos to settle in Detroit.
There was a Calotta Cosimo in the 1900 City Directory, and a Nicholas
Gusmana in 1903 - they were the only earlier ones I could find, although
some of the Mazzola family had arrived as early as 1895. Great Grandpa first
appeared in the City Directory in 1904, with a Joseph Cusmano - his
brother??? - at the same address. He was already living on Woodbridge and
working as a baker (as was Joseph). In 1905, Joseph was gone, but Angelo -
great-grandpa's cousin - had arrived, and in 1906 there were 6 others. This is
not a totally accurate accounting: not everybody was listed in the City
Directory, and our people were disguised under different - and often very
creative - spellings. It was never a very common name, but by 1939 (which is
the last City Directory available online at ancestry), there were 75 in the city
- and this was after some of them had started moving to the suburbs.

And most of them were originally from Terrainsi (or Cinisi) and a majority
of them were related to us. A lot of them were cousins of Great Grandpa
Giovanni: the children of (his uncle) Angelo & Grazia Buffa, the children of
(his uncle) Filippo & Anna Orlando - one of these was his son-in-law as well
- , and the children of (his uncle) the other Giovanni.

And now for the elephant in the room: our connection to the Mafia.

There is that story about the shake-down, and there is the story about the old
man across the street who was Grandpa Jack's godfather. And we did have a
cousin who was married to a mafioso - he was gunned down in his own
home, and he had a HUGE funeral, with airplanes dropping flowers and so
on. Some of the cousins worked for or with him. Other than that, I don't
know. There is also the story that Grandma Ruth wanted to be known as
Cusman instead of Cusmano so as not to be confused with the criminal
elements. I think it was something that was difficult to avoid, but I think our
people mostly tried NOT to be involved.

One time, when they owned the liquor store, Grandma Ruth complained to
Jack that they were being cheated: the delivery guys were claiming they took
away more empties than had been delivered (when full). Grandpa Jack told
her he'd rather trust people and be cheated than cause a fuss. Mom always
took that as an illustration of Jack's beautiful character; I - who do not have
a beautiful character - wonder if he simply knew who he was dealing with.
~~~~~

First Cousins
(of Great-Grandpa Giovanni)
Grandchildren of Giovanni & Francesca Paola Bommarito

Giovanni and Francesca Paola had 13 children, 10 of whom made it to adulthood. Of those, 7 died in Terrasini. Our own ancestor Giovanni died in Mazzara, in the Trapani province, and I don't know when or where the other two died (the death records available online for Terrasini end in 1910). Five of their children had children who emigrated to Detroit. (For the children of other five I could find no further records, so they still might have emigrated, maybe to another city in the US or maybe another one in Sicily.) So. At least 16 of their grandchildren emigrated, possibly more (it was easier to track the sons than the daughters) - and they all but one ended up in Detroit, at least for a while.

Detroit Cusmanos - 1st Cousins of Great Grandpa Giovanni
= Grandchildren of Giovanni & Francesca Paola Bommarito

Descendants of 6. Angelo 1832-1896 + Grazia Buffa (1853)

7. Giovanni 1854

7. Giovanni 1855

7. Salvatore 1858-1866

7. Angelo 1862-1862

7. Giovanni 1862 (sic)-1929 + Anna Serra (1886) -> Detroit

     8. Angelo 1887 -> **Detroit** + Maria Barone (1908 Det)

7. Giovanni ? + Providenza Aluja (1893) *I haven't found records for him in the US*

     8. Angelo 1894-1894

     8. Angelo 1895-1897

     8. Grazia 1897

     8. Angelo 1900

     8. Rosa 1904-1905

     8. Rosa 1906-1907

7. Francesca Paola 1863

7. Pietra Maria 1866

7. Salvatore 1869-1950 + Anna Saputo (1897) -> **Detroit**

     8. Angelo 1899 -1913 Detroit

     8. Michael 1906 (maybe Michael is Nick)

     8. Nick 1910

7. Maria Grazia 1873

7. Angelo 1876-1952 + Rosa Giordano (1908 Det) -> **Detroit**

     8. Grace 1902 + John Lochiechio (1920)

     8. Maria 1904

     8. Pauline 1906 MI

     8. Josephine 1910

7. Giovanni 1

Michigan Death Records make him the son of Angelo & Grazia Buffa and give him a birth date of 15 March 1862, but that is physically impossible: his brother Angelo was born in February 1862, and his sister Francesca Paola in April 1863. Angelo & Grazia had at least two babies they named Giovanni, one baptized 1854, one 1855 - and/or at least two Giovannis who lived to adulthood. One married Anna Serra and moved to Detroit in about 1901, one married Prudenzia Aluja and stayed in Terrasini at least until 1907.
[1862 March 15 - born]

1886 Feb 28 - married Anna Serra[370]

    145 = 111 = 28 Feb 1886 - Joannes C unm - Angelo & Gratia Buffa

          Anna Serra unm - Stephano & Rosaria Bommarito

1887 Dec 24 - son Angelo born[371]

      670 = 240 = 25 Dec 1887 - Angelus (b yest)

          - Joannes C & Anna Serra

      37 = 114 = #325 = 25 Dec 1887 - Angelo C

          - Giovanni C & Anna Serra

1901 emigrated

1902 - wife Anna Serra and son Angelo to US[372]

      Tartar Prince - Palermo - NY arr 5 May 1902

      line 27 Serra Anna 42 fm housewife Terrasini to Detroit -

          to husband Giovanni Cusumano Larned St 203

      line 28 Cusumano Angelo 15 m s workman Terrasini to Detroit - to

          father

1913 - son Angelo m Maria Barone

1920 census[373]

????1920 SD 145 ED 275 sheet 10 - 242 Sherman - Wd 9

      161-209 Cusumano Joe 65 em 1901 It It It - prop grocery store

          Anna 54 em 1902 / Angelo 33 s son em 1902 - machine shop,

          auto factory / Mary 24 s dau em 1902

---

[370]Maria Santissima delle Grazie, Terrasini, Palermo, Sicily, Italy, Marriage register, v. ?, 1878-1891, p. 111, Joannes C marriage 1886; *Family Search.org*, "Matrimoni 1878-1891," image 145 of 238.

[371]Maria Santissima delle Grazie, Terrasini, Palermo, Sicily, Italy, Baptismal register, v. 31, 1882-1889, p. 240, Angelus C baptism 1887; *Family Search.org*, "Battesimi 1873-1889," image 670 of 792. AND Maria Santissima delle Grazie, Terrasini, Palermo, Sicily, Italy, Baptismal register, v. 32 continued?, 1887-1889, p. 114, record no. 325, Angelo C baptism 1887; *Family Search.org*, "Battesimi 1887-1889," image 37 of 90.

[372]Manifest, *Tartar Prince*, 5 May 1902, page 73, line 27, Anna Serra, 42, and line 28, Angelo Cusumano , 15; images, "Passenger Lists, 1820-1957," *Ancestry.com* (http: ancestry.com : accessed 9 Nov 2016).

[373]1920 U. S. Federal census, Wayne County, Michigan, population schedule, Detroit, ward 9, enumeration district (ED) 275, sheet 10, dwelling 161, family 209, Joe Cusumano; image, *Ancestry.com* (http://ancestry.com : accessed 6 September 2016); citing NARA microfilm publication T625, roll 807.

1929 Apr 4 - died[374]
>Giovanni Cusumano - m w m - wife Anna Serra
>b 15 Mar 1862 Terrasini - age 67-23 - d 7 April 1929 Detroit - in US
>>28y
>f Angelo b Terrasini - m Grazia Buffa b Terrasini
>inf Angelo Cusumano 5329 Rohns Av
>Mt Olivet 9 Apr 1929

buried Mt Olivet[375]
>- Giovanni Cusumano - Mar. 15, 1862 Terrasini Favarotta
>>- Apr. 4, 1929 Detroit
>s/o Angelo Cusumano & Grazia Buffa - m Anna Serra
>(d/o Stefano Serra and Maria Rosa Bommarito) February 28, 1886 in
>>Terrasini
>Cerebral Hemorrhage, Apoplexy - Mount Olivet Cemetery -
>- John Cusmano
>Date of Death: APRIL 7, 1929 Date of Interment: 04/09/1929
>Mt. Olivet Cemetery - Section 51, Tier 14, Space 341 (Mt Elliott
>Cemetery Assn)

1930 census[376] - wife and son
1930 Mi Wayne Det pct 19 SD22 ED 82-681 sheet 6a - 5329 Rohns
>84-29 Cusamano, Angelo 42 m 26 It 190? Na machinist auto factory
>>Mary 37 m 21 It 1913
>>Anna mother 75 wd m 46 It 1903 al

---

[374]"Michigan Death Records, 1867-1950," database with images, *Ancestry.com* (http://ancestry.com : accessed 20 Sept 2016), entry for Giovanni Cusumano, 7 April 1929, state file no. 113070, reg no. 5548; citing Michigan Department of Community Health, Division for Vital Records and Health Statistics.

[375]*Findagrave.com*, database and images (http://findagrave.com : accessed 26 August 2016), memorial page for Giovanni Cusumano (1862-1929), Find A Grave Memorial no. 146842888, created by Angie, citing Mt. Olivet Cemetery, Detroit, Wayne, Michigan. AND Mt. Elliott Cemetery Association, database (http://www.mtelliott.com/genealogy/ : accessed 29 August 2016), Mt. Olivet Cemetery (Detroit, Wayne, Michigan), entry for John Cusmano (7 April 1929).

[376]1930 U.S. census, Wayne County, Michigan, population schedule, Detroit precinct 19, enumeration district (ED)82-681, sheet 6a, dwelling 84, family 29, Angelo Cusamano; image, *Ancestry.com* (http://ancestry.com : accessed 28 Sept 2016); citing FHL microfilm 2340794; NARA microfilm T626 roll 1059.

1931 - wife Anna died[377]

   Anna Cusumano 5329 Rohns - husband Giovanni Cusumano
   f w wid - b 10 Feb 1872 Terrasini - 59-3 - d 10 May 1931 Detroit
     f Stefano Serra b Terrasini - m Rosaria Bommarito b Terrasini
     inf Angelo Cusumano 5329 Rohns -   Mt Olivet
– buried Mt Olivet[378]
     - Anna Serra Cusumano - Feb. 10, 1862 Terrasini Favarotta - May 10,
1931 Detroit
     d/o Stefano Serra & Rosaria Bommarito - m Giovanni Cusumano
     (s/o Angelo Cusumano & Grazia Buffa)
       on February 28, 1886 in Terrasini.
     Broncho Pneumonia, Acute Endocarditis - Mount Olivet Cemetery
     Plot: Section 51, Tier 28, Space 682
     - Anna Cusumano
     Date of Death: MAY 10, 1931 Date of Interment: 05/13/1931
     Mt. Olivet Cemetery - Section 51, Tier 28, Space 682

8. Angelo s/o Giovanni & Anna Serra gs/o Angelo & Grazia Buffa
1887 Dec 24 - born[379]
     670 = 240 = 25 Dec 1887 - Angelus (b ieri)
       s/o Joannes Cusumano & Anna Serra
     37 = 114 = #325 = 25 Dec 1887 - Angelo C
       - Giovanni C & Anna Serra?

---

[377]"Michigan Death Records, 1867-1950," database with images, *Ancestry.com* (http://ancestry.com: accessed 20 Sept 2016), entry for Anna Cusumano, 10 May 1931, state file no.144741, reg no. 5917; citing Michigan Department of Community Health,

[378]*Findagrave.com*, database and images (http://findagrave.com: accessed 26 August 2016), memorial page for Anna Serra Cusumano (1862-1931), Find A Grave Memorial no. 143582507, created by Angie, citing Mt. Olivet Cemetery, Detroit, Wayne, Michigan. AND Mt. Elliott Cemetery Association, database (http://www.mtelliott.com/genealogy/ : accessed 29 August 2016), Mt. Olivet Cemetery (Detroit, Wayne, Michigan), entry for Anna Cusumano (10 May 1931).

[379]Maria Santissima delle Grazie, Terrasini, Palermo, Sicily, Italy, Baptismal register, v. 31, 1882-1889, p. 240, Angelus C baptism 1887; *Family Search.org*, "Battesimi 1873-1889," image 670 of 792. AND Maria Santissima delle Grazie, Terrasini, Palermo, Sicily, Italy, Baptismal register, v. 32 continued?, 1887-1889, p. 114, record no. 325, Angelo C baptism 1887; *Family Search.org*, "Battesimi 1887-1889," image 37 of 90.

1902 - to US[380]
>Tartar Prince - Palermo - NY arr 5 May 1902
>line 27 Serra Anna 42 fm housewife Terrasini to Detroit -
> to husband Givanni Cusumano Larned St 203
>line 28 Cusumano Angelo 15 m s workman Terrasini to Detroit - to
>father

Detroit City Directories[381]
?1912 Cusamano Angelo lab h 174 Sherman (Detroit City Directories)
1913 Nov 17 - married Maria Barone[382]
>lic 10 Oct 1913 - Angelo Cusumano 25 res Det b It lab
>>f Giovanni m Anna Serra
>Maria Barone 21 res Det b It domestic
>>f Giuseppe, m Catarina Leto
>marriage 27 Nov 1913 - Josh Boschi pastor
>wit B Salvatore, K Mastranga
 1917 June 2 - WWI Draft Registration[383] - no 203-2 - stamp 1315
>Angelo Cusumano - 142 Sherman - age 29
>b 25 Dec 1887 Palermo declared alien
>automobile machinist Ford
>dep - wife
>short, stout dark hair & eyes - partly bald
1920 census[384] - with parents and wife

---

[380]Manifest, *Tartar Prince*, 5 May 1902, page 73, line 27, Anna Serra, 42, and line 28, Angelo Cusumano , 15; images, "Passenger Lists, 1820-1957, " *Ancestry.com* (http: ancestry.com: accessed 9 Nov 2016).

[381]R. L. Polk & Co's *Detroit City Directory for the year commencing Sept 1, 1912* (Detroit, MI: R. L. Polk & Co, 1912) p. 901; database with images, *Ancestry.com,* "U.S. City Directories, 1822-1995" (http://www.ancestry.com: accessed 24 September 2016). And various subsequent directories.

[382]"Michigan Marriage Records, 1867-1952," database, *Ancestry.com* (http://ancestry.com: accessed 19 Sept 2016), entry for Angelo Cusmano, 1913 (no. 99556); citing Michigan Department of Community Health, Division for Vital Records and Health Statistics, film no. 117 (1913 Wayne - 1914 Branch).

[383]"U.S. World War I Draft Registration Cards, 1917-1918," database with images, *Ancestry.com* (http://ancestry.com: accessed 15 Oct 2016), card for Angelo Cusumano, serial no. 203-2, Draft Board 10, Wayne County, Michigan; imaged from Family History Library microfilm.

[384]1920 U. S. Federal census, Wayne County, Michigan, population schedule, Detroit, ward 9, enumeration district (ED) 275, sheet 10, dwelling 161, family 209, Joe Cusumano; image, *Ancestry.com* (http://ancestry.com: accessed 6 September 2016); citing NARA microfilm publication T625, roll 807.

1920 Michigan Wayne Detroit wd 7 SD 145 ED 275 sheet 10 - 242 Sherman
    161-209   Cusumano Joe 65 em 1901 It It It - prop grocery store
        Anna 54 em 1902
          Angelo 33 s son em 1902 - machine shop, auto factory
          Mary 24 s dau em 1902
?1922/23 Cusumano Angelo autowkr r1934 Sherman (Jos at 1931)
1925/26 Cusumano Angelo clk h5329 Rohns
1927/28 Cusumano Angelo lab DSR r5329 Rohns - with Jos
    Cusumano Jos (Anna) lab h5329 Rohns - with Angelo
1928/29 Cusumano, Angelo (Mary) h5329 Rohns
    Cusumano Jos r 5329 Rohns - with Angelo
1929 - father Giovanni died
    - informant = Angelo Cusumano 5329 Rohns
1930 census[385] - mother living with Angelo & wife
 1930 Mi Wayne Det pct 19 SD22 ED 82-681 sheet 6a - 5329 Rohns
   84-29 Cusamano, Angelo 42 m 26 It 190? Na machinist auto factory
        Mary 37 m 21 It 1913
        Anna mother 75 wd m 46 It 1903 al
1930/31 Cusmano Angelo (Mary) lab 5329 Rohns av
        Jos r 5329 Rohns
1931 - mother Anna Serra Cusumano died
    - informant = Angelo Cusumano 5329 Rohns
1931/32 Cusmano Angelo (Mary) autowkr h5329 Rohns
1932/33 Cusumano Angelo (Mary) h1934 Sherman
1939 Cusumano Angelo (Maria) lab 1934 Sherman
1940 census[386]
  1940 Mi Wayne Detroit wd 9 SD1 ED84-407 sh 1b - 1934 Sherman
  8 Cusumano Angelo 51 It na same house street sweeper wpa for city
       Mary 47 It na

[385] 1930 U.S. census, Wayne County, Michigan, population schedule, Detroit precinct 19, enumeration district (ED)82-681, sheet 6a, dwelling 84, family 29, Angelo Cusamano; image, *Ancestry.com* (http://ancestry.com: accessed 28 Sept 2016); citing FHL microfilm: 2340794; NARA microfilm T626 roll 1059.

[386] 1940 U. S. Census, Wayne County, Michigan, population schedule, Detroit, ward 9, enumeration district (ED) 84-407, sheet 1b, household 8, Angelo Cusumano; image, *Ancestry.com* (http://ancestry.com: accessed 10 Oct 2016); citing NARA microfilm publication T627, roll 1853.

1942 Apr 27 - WWII Draft Registration[387] - ser 802
   - Angelo Cusumano - 1934 Sherman - age 54 b 25 Dec 1887 It
      contact J Lafata 2930 Fort
      emp Ford Rouge Dearborn
      5'3" 175# brown eyes gray hair light complex
1953 - SS Life Claim (made for retirement or disability)
      Angelo Cusumano - 25 Dec 1887, Italy
      Claim Date: 7 Jan 1953   Type of Claim: Life Claim
      Notes: 06 Jan 1953: Name listed as ANGELO CUSUMANO

7. Giovanni 2

Angelo & Grazia had two babies they named Giovanni, one baptized 1854, one 1855 - and/or at least two Giovannis who lived to adulthood. One married Anna Serra and moved to Detroit in about 1901, one married Prudenzia Aluja and stayed in Terrasini at least until 1907.

18xx born
1893 July 2 - married Providenzia Aluja[388]
    38 = 34 = 2 July 1893 - Joannes C unm - Angelo & Gratia Buffa
            Providentia Aluja - Andreas & Rosa Zerilli
1894 April 17 - son Angelo born[389] - died 1894?[390]
    191 = #70 = 18 April 1894 b yest - Angelo C
          - Giovanni & Providentia Aluja
    394 = 27 = 18 Apr 1894 - Angelus
          - Joanne C & Providentia Aluja

---

[387]"U.S. World War II Draft Registration Cards, 1942," database with images, *Ancestry.com* (http://ancestry.com: accessed 16 Oct 2016), card for Angelo Cusumano, serial no. 802; citing The National Archives at St. Louis, Draft Registration Cards for Fourth Registration for Michigan, 04/27/1942 - 04/27/1942; NAI Number: 623283; Records of the Selective Service System; Record Group Number: 147.

[388]Maria Santissima delle Grazie, Terrasini, Palermo, Sicily, Italy, Marriage register, v. ? cont., 1891-1897, p. 24, Joannes C marriage 1893; *Family Search.org*, "Matrimoni 1891-1904," image 38 of 350.

[389]Maria Santissima delle Grazie, Terrasini, Palermo, Sicily, Italy, Baptismal register, v. 34, 1893-1897, record no. 70, Angelo C baptism 1894; *Family Search.org*, "Battesimi 1889-1903," image 191 of 621. AND Maria Santissima delle Grazie, Terrasini, Palermo, Sicily, Italy, Baptismal register, v. 35, 1893-1902, p. 27, Angelus C baptism 1894; *Family Search.org*, "Battesimi 1889-1903," image 394 of 621.

[390]Maria Santissima delle Grazie, Terrasini, Palermo, Sicily, Italy, Death register, v. 88, 1893-1910, p. 15, Joannes C death 1895; *Family Search.org*, "Morti 1893-1910," image 66 of 207.

death?

1894 June 18 - son Joannes died

66 = 15 = 18 June 1894 - Cusumano Joannes 2mo

      - Joannes & Providentia Aluja

The records do say Angelo (for baptism) and Joannes (for death) but they must be the same child?

1895 May 2 - son Angelo baptized[391] - died 1897[392]

  240 = #101 = 2 May 1895 - Angelo C - Giovanni & Providentia Aluja

  422 = 54 = 2 May 1895 - Angelus - Joanne C & Providentia Aluja

    death

    89 = 37 = 4 Apr 1897 - Angelus C 1y 3m

        - Joannes & Providentia Aluja

1897 Apr 8 - daughter Grazia baptized[393]

   473 = 104 = 8 Apr 1897 - Gratia - Joannes C & Providentia Aluja

1900 Nov 4 - son Angelo baptized[394]

   564 = 192 = 4 Nov 1900 - Angelus - Joannes C & Providentia Aluja

1904 Jan 10 - daughter Rosa born[395] - died 1905[396]

   181 = 62 = 12 Jan 1904 (3) - Rosa C - Joannes & Providentia Aluia

   death

   164 = 114 = 11 March 1905 (18) - Rosa C 14 m

    - Joanne & Providentia Aluja

---

[391]Maria Santissima delle Grazie, Terrasini, Palermo, Sicily, Italy, Baptismal register, v. 34, 1893-1897, record no. 101, Angelo C baptism 1895; *Family Search.org*, "Battesimi 1889-1903," image 240 of 621. AND Maria Santissima delle Grazie, Terrasini, Palermo, Sicily, Italy, Baptismal register, v. 35, 1893-1902, p. 54, Angelus C baptism 1895; *Family Search.org*, "Battesimi 1889-1903," image 422 of 621.

[392]Maria Santissima delle Grazie, Terrasini, Palermo, Sicily, Italy, Death register, v. 88, 1893-1910, p. 37, Angelus C death 1897; *Family Search.org*, "Morti 1893-1910," image 89 of 207.

[393]Maria Santissima delle Grazie, Terrasini, Palermo, Sicily, Italy, Baptismal register, v. 35, 1893-1902, p. 104, Gratia C baptism 1897; *Family Search.org*, "Battesimi 1889-1903," image 473 of 621.

[394]Maria Santissima delle Grazie, Terrasini, Palermo, Sicily, Italy, Baptismal register, v. 35, 1893-1902, p. 192, Angelus C baptism 1900; *Family Search.org*, "Battesimi 1889-1903," image 564 of 621.

[395]Maria Santissima delle Grazie, Terrasini, Palermo, Sicily, Italy, Baptismal register, v. 37, 1903-1911?, p. 62, Rosa C baptism 1904; *Family Search.org*, "Battesimi 1897-1911," image 181 of 523.

[396]Maria Santissima delle Grazie, Terrasini, Palermo, Sicily, Italy, Death register, v. 88, 1893-1910, p. 114, Rosa C death 1905; *Family Search.org*, "Morti 1893-1910," image 164 of 207.

1906 Sept 24 - daughter Rosa born[397] - died 1907[398]

   273 = 745 = 25 Sept 1906 b yest - Rosa C

     - Joannes & Providentia Aliua

     death

     178 = 127 = 68 = 18 July 1907 - C Rosa 10m

     - Joannes & Providentia Aluja

7. Salvatore 1869-1950 + Anna Saputo (1897) -> Detroit

1869 Dec 22 - born (according to Angie at Find-a-Grave)

1897 May 3 - married Anna Saputo[399]

   139 = 126 = 3 May 1897 - Salvatore C unm - Angelo & Gratia Buffa

           Anna Saputo unm - Michele & Petra Ferrante

1898 Oct 22 - son Angelo baptized[400]

     512 = 143 = 22 Oct 1898 - Angelus - Salvatore C & Anna Saputo

1906 Dec 22 - son Michael born[401]

   283 = 815 = 23 Dec 1906 b yest - Michael C

      - Salvatore C & Anna Saputo

1905 - emigrated

1910 census[402] - living next to brother Angelo

1910 Michigan Wayne Detroit wd 7 SD 1 Ed 96 sheet 5a - 311 Orleans

   36-47 Cusumano Sam 34 m 10y 1905 lab street

        Annie 32 1ch/1liv 1905

        Fronsie ? son 11 b MI [indexed Honsel]

   37-48 Cusimano Angei 35 m1 8yr 1905 lab street

---

[397]Maria Santissima delle Grazie, Terrasini, Palermo, Sicily, Italy, Baptismal register, v. 37, 1903-1911?, p. 745, Rosa C baptism 1906; *Family Search.org*, "Battesimi 1897-1911," image 273 of 523.

[398]Maria Santissima delle Grazie, Terrasini, Palermo, Sicily, Italy, Death register, v. 88, 1893-1910, p. 127, Rosa C death 1907; *Family Search.org*, "Morti 1893-1910," image 178 of 207.

[399]Maria Santissima delle Grazie, Terrasini, Palermo, Sicily, Italy, Marriage register, v. ? cont., 1891-1897, p. 126, Salvatore C marriage 1897; *Family Search.org*, "Matrimoni 1891-1904," image 139 of 350.

[400]Maria Santissima delle Grazie, Terrasini, Palermo, Sicily, Italy, Baptismal register, v. 35, 1893-1902, p. 143, Angelus C baptism 1898; *Family Search.org*, "Battesimi 1889-1903," image 512 of 621.

[401]Maria Santissima delle Grazie, Terrasini, Palermo, Sicily, Italy, Baptismal register, v. 37, 1903-1911?, p. 815, Michael C baptism 1906; *Family Search.org*, "Battesimi 1897-1911," image 283 of 523.

[402]1910 U. S. Federal census, Wayne County, Michigan, population schedule, Detroit, ward 7, enumeration district (ED) 96, sheet 5a, dwelling 36, family 47, Sam Cusumano; image, *Ancestry.com* (http://ancestry.com: accessed 6 September 2016); citing NARA microfilm publication T624, roll 682.

Rosa 30 5ch/5liv 1905
Grace dau 8 It 1905
Mary 6 / Pauline 4 / Honsely dau 2 5/12 / Josephine 3/12 -
all b MI
1910 - son Nick born
1913 - son Angelo died[403]
Angelle Gusmano - mws - d 24 June 1913 Ecorse - age about 16
accidental drowning - occ lab - b It
f Samuel b It m Anna Saputia b It
inf Samuel 174 Sherman - Mt Olivet
Detroit City Directories[404]
1918 Gussman Saml h 409 Sherman
1919/20 Gussman Saml h 409 Sherman
1920 census[405] -
1920 Michigan Wayne Detroit wd 11 - SD 145 ED 330 sh 9b - 409 Sherman
150-202 Cusumano Samuel 50 em 1909 It It It - no job
Anna 46 em 1909 It It It / Nick son 10 (indexed Mick) - b Mich
1920/21 Gusumano Saml lab h 2665 (409) Sherman - with Tony
1921/22 Cusumano Saml lab h2664 Sherman
1922/23 Cusumano Saml grindr h2645 Sherman (Philip at 2685)
1925/26 Cusamano Saml lab h??65 Sherman
1927/28 Cusimano Saml grinder r2565 Sherman
1928/29 Cusmano Sam (Annie) lab h 2665 Sherman
1930 census[406]
1930 Mi Wayne Detroit wd 11 SD22 ED82-321 sheet 4a 2665 Sherman
42-67 Cosomano Sam 60 m 35 It 1904 pa lab brass factory
Anna 53 m 19 It 1904 al

---

[403]"Michigan, Death Records, 1867-1950," database, *Ancestry.com*
(http://ancestry.com : accessed 5 Oct 2016), entry for Angelle Gusmano, 24 June
1913 (file no. 5?); Michigan Department of Community Health, Division for Vital
Records and Health Statistics, Lansing, Michigan.
[404]R. L. Polk & Co's *Detroit City Directory 1918* (Detroit, MI: R. L. Polk & Co,
1918); database with images, *Ancestry.com,* "U.S. City Directories, 1822-1995"
(http://www.ancestry.com : accessed 28 September 2016). And subsequent
directories for 1919/20-1939.
[405]1920 U. S. Federal census, Wayne County, Michigan, population schedule,
Detroit, ward 11, enumeration district (ED) 330, sheet 9b, dwelling 150, family 202,
Samuel Cusumano [indexed Cusuma]; image, *Ancestry.com* (http://ancestry.com :
accessed 6 September 2016); citing NARA microfilm publication T625, roll 810.
[406]1930 U.S. census, Wayne County, Michigan, population schedule, Detroit ward
11, enumeration district (ED)82-321, sheet 4a dwelling 42, family 67, Sam
Cosomano; image, *Ancestry.com* (http://ancestry.com : accessed 9 Nov 2016); citing
FHL microfilm 2340779; NARA microfilm T626 roll 1044.

Manno, Vito boarder 42 It 1886 pa
1930/31 Cusamano Saml (Anna) lab h2665 Sherman
1932/33 Cusamano Saml (Anna) h 2665 Sherman
1934 Cusamano Saml (Anna) h 2665 Sherman
1935 Cusamano Saml (Anna) 2665 Sherman
1939 Cusimano Saml (Annie) h2665 Sherman
1940 census[407] - (info supplied by neighbor Vita Ciaramitaro)
1940 MI Wayne Detroit wd 11 - SD1 ED84-571 sh 61a - 2665 Sherman
     107 Cusmano Sam 69 It same house
        Anna 65 It same house
     Mano Vito lodger 52 It ice cream peddler self
1950 Oct 30 - died[408]
[note - MI Death Records dates and figures do not add up]
     Sam Salvatore Cusumano - m m - b 1860 Italy - age 80
        - d 30 Oct 1950 Detroit
     f Angelo - m Grazia Buffa
Buried Mt Olivet[409]
     - Salvatore Cusumano - Dec. 22, 1869 Terrasini Favarotta - Oct. 30,
        1950 Detroit
     s/o Angelo Cusumano & Grazia Buffa - m Anna Saputo
        (d/o Michele Saputo and Pietra Ferrante)
        on May 3, 1897 in Terrasini.
     Brother of Giovanni Cusumano, Angelo Cusumano
     Mount Olivet Cemetery Plot: Section 21, Lot 1621-D, Space 1
     - Sam Cusumano
     Date of Death: Date of Interment: 11/03/1950
     Mt. Olivet Cemetery - Section 21, Lot 1621-D, Space 1

---

[407] 1940 U. S. Census, Wayne County, Michigan, population schedule, Detroit, ward 11, enumeration district (ED) 84-571, sheet 61a, household 107, Sam Cusmano; image, *Ancestry.com* (http://ancestry.com : accessed 9 Oct 2016); citing NARA microfilm publication T627, roll 1858.

[408] "Michigan Death Records, 1867-1950," database, *Ancestry.com* (http://ancestry.com : accessed 20 Sept 2016), entry for Sam Salvatore Cusumano, 30 Oct 1950, file no. 417033; citing Michigan Department of Community Health, Division for Vital Records and Health Statistics.

[409] *Findagrave.com*, database (http://findagrave.com : accessed 25 August 2016), memorial page for Salvatore Cusumano (1869-1950), Find A Grave Memorial no. 150020621, created by "Angie," citing Mt Olivet Cemetery, Detroit, Wayne, Michigan. AND Mt. Elliott Cemetery Association, database (http://www.mtelliott.com/genealogy/ : accessed 29 August 2016), Mt. Olivet Cemetery (Detroit, Wayne, Michigan), entry for Sam Cusumano (1950).

1962 - wife Anna Saputo died[410]
    Anna Cusimano
    Date of Death: Date of Interment: 11/19/1962
    Mt. Olivet Cemetery - Section 21, Lot 1621-D, Space 2

8. Angelo 1898-1913 - s/o Salvatore & Anna Saputo, gs/o Angelo & Grazia Buffa
1898 Oct 22 - baptized[411]
    512 = 143 = 22 Oct 1898 - Angelus - Salvatore C & Anna Saputo
1910 census[412] - Michigan Wayne Detroit wd 7 SD 1 Ed 96 sheet 5a - 311 Orleans
    36-47 Cusumano Sam 34 m 10y 1905 lab street
        Annie 32 1ch/1liv 1905
        Fronsie ? son 11 b MI [indexed Honsel]
1913 - died[413]
Angelle Gusmano - mws - d 24 June 1913 Ecorse - age about 16
    accidental drowning - occ lab - b It
    f Samuel b It m Anna Saputia b It
    inf Samuel 174 Sherman - Mt Olivet

8. Michael/ Nick s/o Salvatore & Anna Saputo, gs/o Angelo & Grazia Buffa
Not sure if Michael is the same person as Nick - Michael was born 1906 in Terrasini but does not appear with his parents in 1910; Nick/Mick was born 1910 in Michigan (according to the 1920 census).

---

[410]Mt. Elliott Cemetery Association, database (http://www.mtelliott.com/genealogy/ : accessed 29 August 2016), Mt. Olivet Cemetery (Detroit, Wayne, Michigan), entry for Anna Cusimano (1962).

[411]Maria Santissima delle Grazie, Terrasini, Palermo, Sicily, Italy, Baptismal register, v. 35, 1893-1902, p. 143, Angelus C baptism 1898; *Family Search.org*, "Battesimi 1889-1903," image 512 of 621.

[412]1910 U. S. Federal census, Wayne County, Michigan, population schedule, Detroit, ward 7, enumeration district (ED) 96, sheet 5a, dwelling 36, family 47, Sam Cusumano; image, *Ancestry.com* (http://ancestry.com : accessed 6 September 2016); citing NARA microfilm publication T624, roll 682.

[413]"Michigan, Death Records, 1867-1950," database, *Ancestry.com* (http://ancestry.com : accessed 5 Oct 2016), entry for Angelle Gusmano, 24 June 1913 (file no. 5?); Michigan Department of Community Health, Division for Vital Records and Health Statistics, Lansing, Michigan.

1906 Dec 22 - son Michael born[414]
    283 = 815 = 23 Dec 1906 b yest - Michael C
       - Salvatore C & Anna Saputo
1910
1920 census[415]-MichWayneDetroit wd 11-SD 145 ED 330 sh 9b
-409 Sherman
   150-202 Cusumano Samuel 50 em 1909 It It It - no job
    Anna 46 em 1909 It It It / Nick son 10 (indexed Mick) - b Mich

7. Angelo 1876-1952 + Rosa Giordano (1908) -> Detroit

1876 April 19 - born[416]
  137 = 75 = 20 April 1876 b yest - Angelus - Angelo G & Gratia Buffa
     (Anna Sapienza wife of Salvator)
1902 Nov 16 - dau Grace baptized[417]
    607 = 234 = 16 Nov 1902 - Gratia - Angelo C & Rosa Giordano
1904 - dau Mary b MI
1905 - to US
1906 - dau Pauline b MI
Detroit City Directories[418]
1906 Cusumato, Angelo lab bds 360 Riopelle
1907 - dau Angela? b MI

---

[414]Maria Santissima delle Grazie, Terrasini, Palermo, Sicily, Italy, Baptismal register, v. 37, 1903-1911?, p. 815, Michael C baptism 1906; *Family Search.org*, "Battesimi 1897-1911," image 283 of 523.

[415]1920 U. S. Federal census, Wayne County, Michigan, population schedule, Detroit, ward 11, enumeration district (ED) 330, sheet 9b, dwelling 150, family 202, Samuel Cusumano [indexed Cusuma]; image, *Ancestry.com* (http://ancestry.com: accessed 6 September 2016); citing NARA microfilm publication T625, roll 810.

[416]Maria Santissima delle Grazie, Terrasini, Palermo, Sicily, Italy, Baptismal register, v. 30, 1873-1881, p. 75, Angelus G baptism 1876; *Family Search.org*, "Battesimi 1873-1889," image 137 of 793.

[417]Maria Santissima delle Grazie, Terrasini, Palermo, Sicily, Italy, Baptismal register, v. 35, 1893-1902, p. 234, Gratia C baptism 1902; *Family Search.org*, "Battesimi 1889-1903," image 607 of 621.

[418]R. L. Polk, compiler, *Detroit City Directory for the year commencing August 1st, 1907* (Detroit, MI: R. L. Polk & Co, 1907) p nos; database with images, *Ancestry.com,* "U.S. City Directories, 1822-1995" (http://www.ancestry.com: accessed 24 September 2016). And certain subsequent directories for 1909-1939.

1908 Nov 23 - married Rosa Giordano, Detroit[419]
  256 = record #18 - Angelo C - Angelo & Gratia Buffa (20 Apr 1876)
     Rosa Giordano - Vincentio & Maria [Antonia Taormina - according to
     Angie at Find-a-Grave]
     marriage - Detroit - 23 Nov 1908
1909 Cusimono, Angelo, lab. h. 205 Orleans
1910 - dau Josephine b
1910 census[420] - living next to brother Salvatore (Sam)
1910 Michigan Wayne Detroit wd 7 SD 1 Ed 96 sheet 5a - 311 Orleans
     36-47 Cusumano Sam 34 m 10y 1905 lab street
          Annie 32 1ch/1liv 1905
          Fronsie ? son 11 b MI [indexed Honsel]
     37-48 Cusimano Angei 35 m1 8yr 1905 lab street
          Rosa 30 5ch/5liv 1905
          Grace dau 8 It 1905
          Mary 6 / Pauline 4 / Honsely dau 2 5/12 / Josephine 3/12 -
          all b MI
1912 Cusamano Angelo lab h 174 Sherman
1915 Gussamano Angelo barber h 225 Clinton?
1920 June 24 - dau Grace m John Lochiechio[421]
     John Lochiechio [Sochicchio?] 24 res Det b It peddler
        f Giovanni m Felice
     Grace Cusumano 18 res Det b It f Angelo m Rosina Giordano
     lic 1 June 1920 - marriage 24 June 1920 - P Zagni pastor
     wit Salvatore Lucavoli, Mary J Mercurio

---

[419]Maria Santissima delle Grazie, Terrasini, Palermo, Sicily, Italy, Marriage register, v. 51, 1908-1916, record no. 18, Angelo C marriage 1908-Detroit; *Family Search.org*, "Matrimoni 1905-1911," image 256 of 264.

[420]1910 U. S. Federal census, Wayne County, Michigan, population schedule, Detroit, ward 7, enumeration district (ED) 96, sheet 5a, dwelling 36, family 47, Sam Cusumano; image, *Ancestry.com* (http://ancestry.com: accessed 6 September 2016); citing NARA microfilm publication T624, roll 682.

[421]"Michigan Marriage Records, 1867-1952," database with images, *Ancestry.com* (http://ancestry.com: accessed 22 Sept 2016), entry for Grace [indexed Graceo] Cusumano, 1920 (no. 195145); citing Michigan Department of Community Health, Division for Vital Records and Health Statistics, film no. 153 (1920 Washtenaw - 1920 Wayne).

1952 Mar 13 - died[422]

Angelo Cusumano - Apr. 20, 1876 Terrasini Favarotta - Mar. 13, 1952 Detroit

Son of Angelo Cusumano and Grazia Buffa. Married Rosina Giordano (daughter of Vincenzo Giordano and Maria Antonia Taormina) on November 29, 1908 in Detroit.

Brother of Salvatore Cusumano, Giovanni Cusumano

Mount Olivet Cemetery Plot: Section 37, Tier 2, Space 412

---

[422]*Findagrave.com*, database (http://findagrave.com: accessed 25 August 2016), memorial page for Angelo Cusumano (1876-1952), Find A Grave Memorial no. 150020095, created by "Angie," citing Mt Olivet Cemetery, Detroit, Wayne, Michigan.

Detroit Cusmanos - 1st Cousins of Great Grandpa Giovanni
= Grandchildren of Giovanni & Francesca Paola Bommarito

Descendants of 6. Giuseppe 18xx + Rosaria Buffa (1858)
    7. Francesca Paola 1858
    7. Maria Pietra 1860-1931 + Salvatore Orlando (1882)
        -> St Louis
    7. Giovanni 1863-1867
    7. Grazia 1865
    7. Rosaria 1868
    7. Rosalia 1871-1904
    7. Maria 1873
    7. Giovanni 1875
    7. Grazia 1877-1935 + Giuseppe Saputo (1890) -> **Detroit**

7. Maria Pietra

1860 Dec 1 - born[423]
    301 = 141 = 2 Dec 1860 b yest - Maria Petra G
        - Joseph G & Rosalia Buffa
        (GodmotherTeresia Maninno wife of Jacobo)
    36 = #168 = 2 Dec 1860 - Pietra G -
        Giovanni G & Giuseppa Buffa
1882 June 5 - married Salvatore Orlando[424]
    82 = 49 = 5 June 1882 - Salvatore Orlando unm
        Mattheus Orlando & Matthea Orlando
    Pietra Gusmano unm - Joseph & Rosaria Buffa
The following information is from Deana Shelton's Family Tree on Ancestry (accessed 21 June 2017):
1889 Oct 29 - daughter Mattea Orlando born
    (married Joseph Moceri - died 1978)
1898 July 8 - son Matteo born Cinisi - died 1953
18xx - son Salvatore born - died 1953
1921/22 - emigrated to US

---

[423]Maria Santissima delle Grazie, Terrasini, Palermo, Sicily, Italy, Baptismal register, v. 26, 1854-1861, p. 141, Maria Petra Gusmano baptism 1860; *Family Search.org*, "Battesimi 1854-1861," image 301 of 323. AND Maria Santissima delle Grazie, Terrasini, Palermo, Sicily, Italy, Baptismal register, v. 27, 1859-1863, record no. 168, Pietra G baptism 1860; *Family Search.org*, "Battesimi 1859-1878," image 36 of 481.
[424]Maria Santissima delle Grazie, Terrasini, Palermo, Sicily, Italy, Marriage register, v. ?, 1878-1891, p. 82, Salvator Orlando marriage 1882; *Family Search.org*, "Matrimoni 1878-1891," image 49 of 238.

1930 - St Louis, Mo (wid)
1931 Nov 6 - died
     buried Calvary Cemetery, St Louis, MO

7. Grazia 1877-1935

I haven't found a baptismal record for her, only for the Grazia born 1865.
You don't suppose she shaved 12 years off her age???
1865 June 10 - Grazia, daughter of Giuseppe & Rosaria, born[425]
    211 = 63 = 11 June 1865 b yest? cond - Gratia Gusmano - Josepho &
        Rosaria Buffa
        (Godfather - Joannes G of Salvator)
1877 Dec 25 - born (based on Michigan Death Record)
1890 Jan 14 - married Giuseppe Saputo[426]
    217 = 176 = 14 Jan 1890 - Joseph Saputo unm
        - Michele & Petra Ferrante
      Gratia C unm - Joseph & Rosaria Buffa
1xxx - emigrated to US (Detroit)
1935 March 18 - died[427]
  Grace Sapato - f w m - b 25 Dec 1877 Terrasini
    - d 18 Mar 1935 Detroit - age 57
    f Giuseppe Cusumano - m Rosaria Buffa
    ---- buried Mt Olivet[428]
Mount Olivet Cemetery Plot: Section 51, Tier 39, Space 468
    Grazia "Grace" Cusumano Saputo
    Birth: Dec. 25, 1877 Terrasini Favarotta
    Death: Mar. 18, 1935 Detroit
    Lobar Pneumonia
    Daughter of Giuseppe Cusumano and Rosaria Buffa.

---

[425] Maria Santissima delle Grazie, Terrasini, Palermo, Sicily, Italy, Baptismal register, v. 28, 1862-1872, p. 63, Gratia C baptism 1865; *Family Search.org*, "Battesimi 1859-1878," image 211 of 481.

[426] Maria Santissima delle Grazie, Terrasini, Palermo, Sicily, Italy, Marriage register, v. ?, 1878-1891, p. 176, Joseph Saputo marriage 1890; *Family Search.org*, "Matrimoni 1878-1891," image 217 of 238.

[427] "Michigan, Death Records, 1867-1950," database, *Ancestry.com* (http://ancestry.com: accessed 21 September 2016), entry for Grace Saputo, 18 March 1935 (file no. 199337); Michigan Department of Community Health, Division for Vital Records and Health Statistics, Lansing, Michigan.

[428] *Findagrave.com*, database (http://findagrave.com: accessed 25 August 2016), memorial page for Grazia "Grace" Cusumano Saputo (1877-1935), Find A Grave Memorial no. #143322364, created by "Angie," citing Mt Olivet Cemetery, Detroit, Wayne, Michigan.

Married Giuseppe Saputo (son of Michele Saputo and Pietra Ferrante)
January 4, 1890.
Sister of Pietra Cusumano Orlando
Burial: Mount Olivet Cemetery Plot: Section 51, Tier 39, Space 468

Detroit Cusmanos - 1st Cousins of Great Grandpa Giovanni
= Grandchildren of Giovanni & Francesca Paola Bommarito

Descendants of 6. Filippo 1838 & Anna Orlando (1867)
- wife Anna emigrated

7. Francesca Paola 1868 + Rosolino Giliberti (1882) - *did not emigrate*

7. Giovanni 1870-1944 + Rosa Zerilli (1891) -> NY, **Detroit**

7. Giuseppe 1872-1924 + Concetta Ventimiglia (1896) -> NY **Det**

7. Catarina 1875-1941 + Giuseppe Garafalo -> NY, **Detroit**

7. Salvatore 1877-1921 + Giuseppa Calderone -> NY, **Detroit**

7. Francesco Paolo 1880-1997 + Rosalia C (1905) -> NY, **Detroit**

7. Filippo 1883-1939 + Josephine Bommarito -> NY, **Detroit**

7. Antonio 1885 + Marion Sapienza (1906 NY?)

Family of Filippo 1838-1886 & Anna Orlando (m 1867)
Wife Anna Orlando

1867 Dec 5 (I think) - married Filippo Cusmano[429]

     65 = 71 = Filippo Gusmano 29, villico, res Terr

        s/o Giovanni villaco & Fra Paola Bommarito

        Anna Orlando 20 dom, res Terr

          d/o Giuseppe & the late Caterina di Mercurio

1888 Aug 1 - godmother to son of Giuseppe & Anna La Fata C[430]

     707 = 266 = 1 Aug 1888 - Joannes Baptista

        s/o Joseph Cusumano & Anna La Fata

        (GodmotherAnna Orlando)

1905/07 - to US - first Oakfield NY, then Detroit

1910 census - with oldest son John in Oakfield NY[431]

---

[429]Palermo (Palermo), Ufficio dello stato civile, "Registro degli atti di Matrimonio [Register of Marriages], 1867" : entry #71, Filippo Gusmano; digital images, *FamilySearch.org*, "Italia, Palermo, Palermo, Stato Civile (Tribunale), 1866-1910," (https://familysearch.org/ark:/61903/3:1:3QSQ-G97B-27ZM?cc=2051639&wc=MC TM-1TG%3A351055601%2C353722501%2C353605302 : 22 May 2014), Palermo > Terrasini > image 65 of 2313; citing Tribunale di Cagliari (Cagliari Court, Cagliari). [Actually this page is from the Denunciations [Banns] section; the actual marriage is ordine #13, image 83/4. This early section is all handwritten, and is very difficult for me to read. Sorry.]

[430]Maria Santissima delle Grazie, Terrasini, Palermo, Sicily, Italy, Baptismal register, v. 31, 1882-1889, p. 266, Joannes Baptista C baptism 1888; *Family Search.org*, "Battesimi 1873-1889," image 707 of 792.

[431]1910 U. S. Federal Census, Genessee County, New York, population schedule, Oakfield Township, enumeration district (ED) 29, sheet 8a, dwelling 169, family 185, John Cusumano [indexed Cussuma]; image, *Ancestry.com* (http://ancestry.com:

1910 New York, Genessee, Oakfield SD 18 ED 29 sh8a - Webber Ave
    169-185 John Cusmano [indexed Cussuma] 40, m1 21yrs It It It - em
        1906 al - laborer gypsum mill
         Rose 41 - 5ch/4liv - It - em 1906
        Joseph 18 It em 1906 / Rose 10 It / Phillip 2 NY
        John 10/12 NY
    Polito, Tony boarder 40 wd It em 1892 al - lab gypsum mill
    Orlando, Tony boarder 26 s em 1907 al - lab gypsum mill
    Cusumano, Anna [indexed Carsumans] mother 60 wd
        8ch/8liv It em 1905
    Kalitz, Dominick 25 It em 1909 / Zelle, John 19 It em 1907
    Brumm, Massa 21 It em 1908
1920 census - with daughter Catherine Garafalo in Detroit[432]
1920 Detroit SD 145 ED 223 sheet 13b line 51- 288 Riopelle
    Cusmano, Anna 73 wid - head - 1907 grocery store
    Girafolo Catherine 44 d 1905
        Joe 38 s-in-law 1905 grocery store
        Sam 14, Philip 12, Angelo 10 all b. NY
1921/22 Detroit City Directory
    - Cusumano Anna (wid Philip) b1410 Riopelle
1930 March 29 - died Detroit[433]
    Anna Cusumano - 1501 Clinton - husband Filippo
    f w wid - b 1 July 1866 Terrasini - 63-8-9 - housework
    - d 29 March 1930 Detroit
    f Giuseppe Orlando b Terrasini - m Caterina b Terrasini
    inf Giovanni Cusumano - 2806 E Lafayette
    Mt Olivet 1 April 1930
    - buried Mt Olivet[434] - Section 51, Tier 8, Space 338
    Anna Orlando Cusumano - Jul. 1, 1856 Terrasini Favarotta - Mar. 29,
    1930 Detroit

---

accessed 4 Sept 2016); citing NARA microfilm publication T624, roll 951.

[432] 1920 U. S. Federal census, Wayne County, Michigan, population schedule, Detroit, ward 7, enumeration district (ED) 223, sheet 13b, dwelling 152, family 210, Anna Cusmano; image, *Ancestry.com* (http://ancestry.com: accessed 22 Sept 2016); citing NARA microfilm publication T625, roll 8808.

[433] "Michigan Death Records, 1867-1950," database with images, *Ancestry.com* (http://ancestry.com: accessed 20 Sept 2016), entry for Anna Cusumano, 29 March 1930, state file no. 128571, reg no. 4462; citing Michigan Department of Community Health, Division for Vital Records and Health Statistics.

[434] *Findagrave.com*, database and images (http://findagrave.com: accessed 25 August 2016), memorial page for Anna Orlando Cusumano (1866-1930), Find A Grave Memorial no. 146832535, created by "Angie," citing Mt Olivet Cemetery, Detroit, Wayne, Michigan.

Cerebral Apoplexy
Daughter of Giuseppe Orlando and Caterina DiMercurio. Married
Filippo Cusumano (son of Giovanni Cusumano and Francesca Paola
Bommarito) on April 12, 1872 in Terrasini.
Sister of Grazia Orlando Vitale

7. Giovanni 1870-1944 + Rosa Zerilli -> NY, Detroit

    8. Anna 1893

    8. Filippo 1895-1898

    8. Giuseppe 1898-1943 + Marianna di Maria (1916 MI)

        9. Rose 1917

        9. John 1919 + Ignatia Bommarito (1945)

        9. Mary 1921 + Vincenzo Lauir (1940)

        9. Annie 1922 + Salvatore Serra (1944)

        9. Paul 1924

    8. Rosa 1900 + Peter Ventimiglia (1918 MI)

        9. Victor 1920-1921

    8. Philip 1908 NY? + Helen (~1928 MI)

    8. John 1909 NY?-1969 + Louise Bommarito (1931)

        9. John 1932-1940

        9. Rose 1934

        9. Peter 1935-1938

        9. Margaret 1939

    8. Frances/Pauline 1913 MI + Sam Orlando (1929 MI)

?8. Connie 1917 MI + Harry Carolla (1937 MI)

1870 Sept 11 -born, named after paternal grandfather [435]

    321 = 168 = 12 Sept 1870 b yest - Joannes

        s/o Philippo G & Anna Orlando

1891 - married Rosa Zerilli[436]

    3 = p. 2 = 27 Nov 1891 - Joannes s/o Philippo & Anna Orlando

        Rosa Zerilli d/o Joseph & Rosa ?

---

[435]Maria Santissima delle Grazie (Chiesa Madre [Mother Church]), Terrasini,
Palermo, Sicily, Italy, Baptismal register, v. 28, 1862-1872, p. 168, Joannes
Gusmano baptism 1870; *Family Search.org*, Battesimi 1859-1878, image 321 of
481.

[436]Maria Santissima delle Grazie (Chiesa Madre [Mother Church]), Terrasini,
Palermo, Sicily, Italy, Marriage register, v. ? cont., 1891-1897, p. 2, Joannes
Gusmano marriage 1891; *Family Search.org*, "Matrimoni 1891-1904," image 3 of
350).

Not sure what this one is about[437]

??286 = 153 = 9 June 1901 - Joannes C unm - Rosalia Zerilli

1893 Feb 20 - daughter Anna, named for paternal grandmother, born[438] - godmother = aunt

163 = 117 = 20 Feb 1893 - Anna - Joanne C & Rosa Zerilli
(FP Cusumano w/o Rosolino Giliberti)

1895 Dec 5 - son Filippo born, named after paternal grandfather[439] - d. 1898

261 = #289 = 5 Dec 1895 - Filippo C
- Giovanni C & Rosa Zerilli

439=70= 5 Dec 1895 (3) - Philippus - Joannes C & Rosa Zerilli
death

114 = 52 = 14 Sept 1898 - Philippus 3 - Joannes & Rosa Zerilli

1898 Jan 29 - son Giuseppe baptized[440] - godmother = other aunt

33 = 19 = 29 Jan 1898 - Giuseppe C - Giovanni & Rosa Zerilli
(Caterina C d/o Philippo & Anna)

415 = 126 = 29 Jan 1898 (3) - Joseph
- Joannes C & Rosa Zerolli

1900 Dec 29 - daughter Rosa baptized[441]

566 = 195 = 29 Dec 1900 - Rosa - Joannes C & Rosa Zerilli

~1904/6 - emigrated - Oakfield NY

1908 - son Philip b NY

1909 - son John b NY

---

[437]Maria Santissima delle Grazie, Terrasini, Palermo, Sicily, Italy, Marriage register, v. 49 cont., 1897-1904, p. 153, Joannes C marriage 1901; *Family Search.org*, "Matrimoni 1891-1904," image 286 of 350.

[438]Maria Santissima delle Grazie, Terrasini, Palermo, Sicily, Italy, Baptismal register, v. 33?, 1889-1893, p. 117, Anna C baptism 1893; *Family Search.org*, "Battesimi 1889-1903," image 163 of 621.

[439]Maria Santissima delle Grazie, Terrasini, Palermo, Sicily, Italy, Baptismal register, v. 34, 1893-1897, record no. 289, Filippo C baptism 1895; *Family Search.org*, "Battesimi 1889-1903," image 261 of 621. AND Maria Santissima delle Grazie, Terrasini, Palermo, Sicily, Italy, Baptismal register, v. 35, 1893-1902, p. 70, Philippus C baptism 1895; *Family Search.org*, "Battesimi 1889-1903," image 439 of 621.

[440]Maria Santissima delle Grazie, Terrasini, Palermo, Sicily, Italy, Baptismal register, v. 34 continued?, 1887-1900, p.19, Giuseppe C baptism 1898; *Family Search.org*, "Battesimi 1897-1911," image 33 of 523. AND Maria Santissima delle Grazie, Terrasini, Palermo, Sicily, Italy, Baptismal register, v. 35, 1893-1902, p. 126, Joseph C baptism 1898; *Family Search.org*, "Battesimi 1889-1903," image 415 of 621.

[441]Maria Santissima delle Grazie, Terrasini, Palermo, Sicily, Italy, Baptismal register, v. 35, 1893-1902, p. 195, Rosa C baptism 1900; *Family Search.org*, "Battesimi 1889-1903," image 566 of 621.

1910 census[442] - NY, Genessee, Oakfield SD 18 ED 29 sh8a - Webber Ave
169-185 John Cusmano [indexed Cussuma] 40, m1 21yrs It It It - em 1906 al
    - laborer gypsum mill
     Rose 41 - 5ch/4liv - It - em 1906
         Joseph 18 It em 1906 / Rose 10 It / Phillip 2 NY
         John 10/12 NY
     Polito, Tony boarder 40 wd It em 1892 al - lab gypsum mill
     Orlando, Tony boarder 26 s em 1907 al - lab gypsum mill
    Cusumano, Anna [indexed Carsumans] mother 60 wd 8ch/8liv It em 1905
      Kalitz, Dominick 25 It em 1909 / Zelle, John 19 It em 1907
      Brumm, Massa 21 It em 1908

Detroit City Directories[443]

1911 Gusomano John (Det Macaroni Mfg Co) h 296 Congress e
    - with Jos & Saml
1912 Gusumano Jno (Det. Macaroni Mfg Co) and gro 176 Rivard h do (with
    Jos & Saml)
1913 Gusumano Jno (Detroit Macaroni Mfg Co) h 176 Rivard
    (with Jos & Saml)
    Gusumano Bros (Jno, Jos and Saml) gro 176 Rivard
1913 - dau Frances b MI (= Pauline?)
1914 Gusmano Jno (Gusmano Bros; Det Macaroni Mfg Co) h 176 Rivard
(with Jos & Saml)
    Gusmano Bros (Jno Jos and Saml) gro 176 Rivard
1915 Gusmano Jno & son (Jno & Jos) grocers 176 Rivard
1916 Sept 16 - son Joseph m Marianna di Maria[444]
    Giuseppe Gusumano 19 res Det b It helper
       f John m Rose Zerieli
    Marianna DiMaria 16 res Det b It – f Francesco m Maria
    lic 28 Aug 1916 - marriage 16 Sept 1916, Detroit
    - Aloysius Parodi, asst pastor -
    wit Pietro Ventimiglia, Rose Cusumano

[442] 1910 U. S. Federal Census, Genessee County, New York, population schedule, Oakfield Township, enumeration district (ED) 29, sheet 8a, dwelling 169, family 185, John Cusumano [indexed Cussuma]; image, *Ancestry.com* (http://ancestry.com: accessed 4 Sept 2016); citing NARA microfilm publication T624, roll 951.

[443] R. L. Polk, compiler, *Detroit City Directory for the year commencing August 15th, 1911* (Detroit, MI: R. L. Polk & Co, 1911); database with images, *Ancestry.com,* "U.S. City Directories, 1822-1995" (http://www.ancestry.com: accessed 24 September 2016). And subsequent directories for 1912 - 1935.

[444] "Michigan Marriages, 1868-1925," database with images, *FamilySearch* (https://familysearch.org: accessed 26 Oct 2016), Guiseppe Gusumano and Marianna Dz'Maria, 16 Sep 1916; citing Detroit, Wayne, Michigan, v 7 p 165 rn 135206, Department of Vital Records, Lansing; FHL microfilm 2,342,718.

1916 Gusmano Jno & son (Jno & Jos) grocers 176 Rivard
1917 Cusomano Jno (Garafalo Macaroni Mfg Co) h 176 Rivard
    - with Giuseppe & Philip
    Gusmano Jno gro 176 Rivard h do - with Jos
?1917 - daughter Connie born?
1918 Dec 23 - dau Rose m Peter Ventimiglio[445]
    407 - no 169727
    Pete Ventemiglio 23 res Det b It clerk f Victor m Serafina
    Rose Cusumona 17 res Det b It – f John m Rose
    lic & marriage 23 Dec 1918 - R Bradley minister
    wit Espero Brooks, Mabbie Crawford
1918 Cusumano Jno macaroni mkr r176 Rivard
    Gusmano Jno gro 176 Rivard h do - with Jos
1919/20 Gusumano Jno gro 196 Cheyne h do - with Jos
1920 census[446] - Detroit SD 145 ED 327 sh 12b line 58 - 196 Cheyne
150-267 Cusumano John head, homeowner, m, wh, 50, married, to us in
    1904, still alien, no read, no write, no speak English, b. Italy.
    proprietor store, owned/
        Rosa wife 60? 1904
    Joseph son 22 1904 yes read & write, no eng., salesman store/
        Mary his wife 19 to us 1915, read write, no Eng./
    Philip son 13 b. NY/ John son 11 b. NY/
    Frances daughter 7 b. Mi/
    Ventimiglie Peter, son in law, 22 to US 1912/ Rosa 19
        Victor 1/12 b. Mi
1920/21 Gusumano& Ventimiglia
    (Jno Gusumano & Peter Ventimiglia) grocs 756 (196) Chene
    Gusumano Jno (Gusumano & Ventimiglia) h 756 (196) Chene - with
        Jos +PV
1921/22 Gusumano & Ventimiglia
    (Jos Gusumano & Peter Ventimiglia) meats 752? Chene
    Gusumano Jno h 756 Chene - with Jos
    Cusumano Jno h2608 Laf - with Jos

---

[445]"Michigan Marriages, 1868-1925," database with images, FamilySearch
(https://familysearch.org: accessed 26 Oct 2016), Pete Ventemiglio and Rose
Cusumona, 23 Dec 1918; citing Detroit, Wayne, Michigan, v 7 p 407 rn 169727,
Department of Vital Records, Lansing; FHL microfilm 2,342,729.
[446]1920 U. S. Federal census, Wayne County, Michigan, population schedule,
Detroit, ward 11, enumeration district (ED) 327, sheet 12b, dwelling 150, family 267,
John Cusumano; image, *Ancestry.com* (http://ancestry.com: accessed 26 Oct 2016);
citing NARA microfilm publication T625, roll 810.

1922/23 Gusumano& Ventimiglia
        (Jos Gusumano & Peter Ventimiglia) groc 736 Chene
        Cusumano Jno lab h2608 Laf
        Gusumano Jno clk Gusumano & Ventimiglia r736 Chene - with Jos
1925/26 Cusumano & Ventimiglia
        (John Gusumano & Peter Ventimiglia) groc 734 Chene
        Gusumano John Gusumano & Ventimiglia r734 Chene
                John jr clk Gusumano & Ventimiglia h734 Chene
1927/28 Gusumano John (Rose) gro 756 Chene h do
                John jr clk John Gusumano r756 Chene
        Cusumano John J lab r2608 E Laf - with Philip & John
                John S (Rose) lab h2608 E Laf - with Philip & John
1928/29 Cusumano John (Rose) gro h2608 E Laf
                John jr clk r2608 E Laf - with Philip
        Gusumano John (Rose) gro 756 Cheyne h do
                - with John jr, Pauline, Philip
                John jr clk r756 Cheyne
        Gusumano Pauline r756 Cheyne - with John, John jr, Philip
1929 June 11 - dau Pauline married[447]
        Sam Orlando 22 res Det b It clerk - f Carlo m Grace Cusimano
        Pauline Gusumano 18 res Det b MI - f John m Rose Zerillo
        lic 5 June 1929 - marriage 11 June 1929 - Jesse Drake, JP
        wit Joseph, Mary, John Gusmano, Anna Russo
1930 census[448] - Michigan Wayne Detroit wd 11 SD 22 ED 82-319 sheet 1a -
2608 Lafayette
1-1 Gusmano John 59 m 12 It 1903 al milk dealer, retail milk
                Rose 59 m 20 It 1903 al
        Joe son 32 m 19 It 1905 pa retail merchant grocery store
        Mary d/law 32 m 19 Mo It It
        Rose g dau 13 / Mar g dau 9 / John g son 11 /
        Annie g dau 8 / Paul g son 6
Detroit City Directories
1930/31 Cusumano John (Rose) lab h 2608 E Laf - with Jos

---

[447]"Michigan Marriage Records, 1867-1952," database with images, *Ancestry.com*
(http://ancestry.com: accessed 19 Sept 2016), entry for Pauline Gusumano, 1929
(state file no. 82 57722, county file no. 366015); citing Michigan Department of
Community Health, Division for Vital Records and Health Statistics, film no. 248 (82
Wayne 56680-59959).
[448]1930 U.S. census, Wayne County, Michigan, population schedule, Detroit ward
11, enumeration district (ED) 82-319, sheet 1a, dwelling 1, family 1, John Gusmano;
image, *Ancestry.com* (http://ancestry.com: accessed 8 Oct 2016); citing FHL
microfilm 2340779; NARA microfilm T626 roll 1044.

1931/32 Cusumano John & Sons (John, Jos & John jr)
        milk 2608 E Laf
        John (Rose; J Cusumano & Sons) r2608 E Laf
                - with John jr, Jos
        John jr (J Cusumano & Sons) r2608 E Laf - with Jos, John
        Gusmano John clk Jos Gusmano r756 Chene - with Jos
1934 Cusmano John (Rose) h2608 E Laf
1935 Cusumano John (Rose) h2608 E Laf
1937 Nov 20 - daughter Connie m Harry Carolla[449]
        Henry Carolla 23 res Det b It truckdriver
                f James m Josephine Scardino
        Connie Cusamano 20 res Det b NY f John m Rosalee Serolli
        lic 6 Nov 1937 - marriage 20 Nov 1937
            - Fr Benedict Ferretti, RC priest - wit Paolo Furos, Rose V?
1938 Apr 29 - wife Rosa died[450]
        -St Mary's Hospital - Rosa Cusumano 756 Cheyne in US 23 y - f w m
- husb Giovanni
        b ~1879 Terrasini - ~59 - d 29 Apr 1938
        f Giuseppe Zerilli b Terrasini - m Rosa Giordano b Terrasini
        inf Joseph Cusumano 5756 Cheyne - Mt Olivet 5-3-38
        ----buried Mt Olivet[451]
        Rosa Zerilli Cusumano - 1879 Terrasini Favarotta
                - Apr. 29, 1938 Detroit
        Lobar Pneumonia
        daughter of Giuseppe Zerilli and Rosa Giordano.
        Married Giovanni Cusumano (Son of Filippo Cusumano and Anna
        Orlando) on November 28, 1891 in Terrasini.
        Half-Sister of Antonino Zerilli
1939 Gusmano John r2708 E Lafayette

---

[449]"Michigan Marriage Records, 1867-1952," database with images, *Ancestry.com*
(http://ancestry.com: accessed 4 Oct 2016), entry for Connie Cusamano, 1937 (state
file no. 194207, county file no. 512295); citing Michigan Department of Community
Health, Division for Vital Records and Health Statistics, film no. 290 (82 Wayne
194100-197369).
[450]"Michigan Death Records, 1867-1950," database with images, *Ancestry.com*
(http://ancestry.com: accessed 21 Sept 2016), entry for Rosa Cusumano, 29 Apr
1938, no. 238278, reg. no. 4674; citing Michigan Department of Community Health,
Division for Vital Records and Health Statistics.
[451]*Findagrave.com*, database and images (http://findagrave.com: accessed 25 August
2016), memorial page for Rosa Zerilli Cusumano (1879-1938), Find A Grave
Memorial no. 145862549, created by "Angie," citing Mt Olivet Cemetery, Detroit,
Wayne, Michigan.

1944 March 29 - died[452]
>Giovanni Gusumano - m w wid - b 1877 Terrasini
>>- d 29 March 1944 Detroit - age 66
>f Filippo Gusumano - m Anna Orlando

Children of Giovanni & Rosa Zerilli

8. Joseph
>s/o 7. Giovanni Cusmano & Rosa Zerilli
>g-son of 6. Filippo Gusumano & Anna Orlando
>ggs/o 5. Giovanni Cusumano + Francesca Paola Bommarito

1898 born - Italy[453]
>33 = 19 = 29 Jan 1898 - Giuseppe C - Giovanni & Rosa Zerilli
>>(Godmother - Caterina C d/o Philippo & Anna)
>415 = 126 = 29 Jan 1898 (3) - Joseph
>>- Joannes C & Rosa Zerolli

1904/1906 emigrated

1910 - with parents in NY

1916 Sept 16 - m Marianna di Maria[454] - p. 165 - no 135206
>Giuseppe Gusumano 19 res Det b It helper
>>f John m Rose Zerieli
>Marianna DiMaria 16 res Det b It – f Francesco m Maria
>lic 28 Aug 1916 - marriage 16 Sept 1916, Detroit
>>- Aloysius Parodi, asst pastor
>wit Pietro Ventimiglia, Rose Cusumano

Detroit City Directories[455]

---

[452]"Michigan, Death Records, 1867-1950," database, *Ancestry.com* (http://ancestry.com: accessed 21 September 2016), entry for Giovanni Gusumano, 19 March 1944 (file no. 320715); Michigan Department of Community Health, Division for Vital Records and Health Statistics, Lansing, Michigan.

[453]Maria Santissima delle Grazie, Terrasini, Palermo, Sicily, Italy, Baptismal register, v. 34 continued?, 1887-1900, p.19, Giuseppe C baptism 1898; *Family Search.org*, "Battesimi 1897-1911," image 33 of 523. AND Maria Santissima delle Grazie, Terrasini, Palermo, Sicily, Italy, Baptismal register, v. 35, 1893-1902, p. 126, Joseph C baptism 1898; *Family Search.org*, "Battesimi 1889-1903," image 415 of 621.

[454]"Michigan Marriages, 1868-1925," database with images, *FamilySearch* (https://familysearch.org: accessed 26 Oct 2016), Guiseppe Gusumano and Marianna Dz'Maria, 16 Sep 1916; citing Detroit, Wayne, Michigan, v 7 p 165 rn 135206, Department of Vital Records, Lansing; FHL microfilm 2,342,718.

[455]*R. L. Polk & Co's Detroit City Directory for the year commencing Sept 1, 1915* (Detroit, MI: R. L. Polk & Co, 1915) p nos; database with images, *Ancestry.com,* "U.S. City Directories, 1822-1995" (http://www.ancestry.com: accessed 24 September 2016). And subsequent directories for 1917-1939.

1915 Gusmano Jno & son (Jno & Jos) grocers 176 Rivard
        Gusmano Jos (Jno Gusmano & son) 176 Rivard
1916 Gusmano Jno & son (Jno & Jos) grocers 176 Rivard
        Gusmano Jos (Jno Gusmano & son) 176 Rivard
1917 Gusmano Jos lab b 176 Rivard - with Jno
1918 Gusmano Jos lab b176 Rivard - with Jno
1918 WWI Draft registration[456]   - ser 4258 ord 4235
Joseph Cusumano -176 Rivard- age 20 b 24 Jan 1898 - non declared alien lt
        driver Cusumano Bakery 337 Clinton
        rel - Mary Cusumano 176 Rivard
        5'4" 139# brown eyes black hair
1919/20 Gusumano Jos slsmn Jno Gusumano b 196 Cheyne - with Jno
1920 census[457] - with parents & wife - Mi Wayne Detroit SD 145 ED 327
sheet 12b - 196 Cheyne
-58 Cusumano John head, homeowner, m, wh, 50, married, to us in 1904,
        alien, no read, no write, no English, b. Italy. proprietor store, owned/
        Rosa wife 60? 1904
    Joseph son 22 - em 1904 yes read & write, no eng., salesman store/
        Mary his wife 19 to us 1915, read write, no Eng./
    Philip son 13 b. NY/ John son 11 b. NY/
    Frances daughter 7 b. Mi/
Ventimiglie Peter, son in law, 22 to us 1912/
                Rosa 19/ Victor 1/12 b. Mi
1920/21 Gusumano Jos (Gusumano & Ventimiglia) h 756 (196) Chene - with
        Jno & Peter V
1921/22 Gusumano Jos (Gusumano & Ventimiglia) h 756 Chene - with Jno
1922/23 Gusumano Jos (Gusumano & Ventimiglia) h736 Chene
        - with Jno
1930 census[458] with parents & own family- Michigan Wayne Detroit wd 11
SD 22 ED 82-319 sheet 1a - 2608 Lafayette
1-1 Gusmano John 59 m 12 It 1903 al milk dealer, retail milk

---

[456]"U.S. World War I Draft Registration Cards, 1917-1918," database with images,
Ancestry.com (http://ancestry.com: accessed 15 Oct 2016), card for Joseph
Cusumano, serial no. 4235, Draft Board 6, Wayne County, Michigan; imaged from
Family History Library microfilm.
[457]1920 U. S. Federal census, Wayne County, Michigan, population schedule,
Detroit, ward 11, enumeration district (ED) 327, sheet 12b, dwelling 150, family 267,
John Cusumano; image, *Ancestry.com* (http://ancestry.com: accessed 26 Oct 2016);
citing NARA microfilm publication T625, roll 810.
[458]1930 U.S. census, Wayne County, Michigan, population schedule, Detroit ward
11, enumeration district (ED) 82-319, sheet 1a, dwelling 1, family 1, John Gusmano;
image, *Ancestry.com* (http://ancestry.com: accessed 8 Oct 2016); citing FHL
microfilm 2340779; NARA microfilm T626 roll 1044.

Rose 59 m 20 It 1903 al

Joe son 32 m 19 It 1905 pa retail merchant grocery store

    Mary d/law 32 m 19 Mo It It

      Rose g dau 13 / Mar g dau 9 / John g son 11 /

      Annie g dau 8 / Paul g son 6

1930/31 Jos (Mary) lab h 2608 E Laf - with John

1931/32 Gusmano Jos (Mary) gro 756 Chene h do - with John?

    Cusumano Jos (Mary; J Cusumano & Sons) r2608 E Laf

      - with John, John jr

1932/33 Gusumano Joe (Mary) clk h3460 Anderdon av

1934 Gusumano Jos (Mary) h3466 Anderdon

1935 Gusmano Jos (Mary) pres Northern Distribution Co

    Gusumano Jos (Mary) mgr h3466 Anderdon

1939 Gusumano Jos (Mary) whol gro 3466 Anderdon

    - with John A, Rose T

1940 census[459] - Michigan Wayne Detroit wd 21 SD14 ED 84-1413 sheet 2a
- 3426 Anderdon
- hh 34 Gusumano Joseph 41 b It na, lived same house 1935 - business owner — shop

    Mary 40 It al

    Rosa 22 / John 21 - lab auto polish / Mary 19 / Annie 18

    Paul 16

1940 dau Mary m Vincenzo Lauir?[460]

    Mary Gusuman   abt 1920

    Vincenzo Lauir

    Mary Gusuman 20 res Det b MI f Joe m Marion Di Mario

    19 Oct 1940 - Holy Trenary (sic) Wayne

---

[459] 1940 U. S. Census, Wayne County, Michigan, population schedule, Detroit, ward 21, enumeration district (ED) 84-1413, sheet 2a, household 34, Joseph Gusumano; image, *Ancestry.com* (http://ancestry.com: accessed 27 Aug 2016); citing NARA microfilm publication T627, roll 1882.

[460] "Michigan Marriage Records, 1867-1952," database, *Ancestry.com* (http://ancestry.com: accessed 8 Oct 2016), entry for Mary Gusuman, 1940 (state file no. 236055, county file no. 555234); citing Michigan Department of Community Health, Division for Vital Records and Health Statistics, film no. 302 (82 Wayne 233530-236769).

1942 - WW2 Draft Registration[461] -   1942 Apr 27 - ser 2082
    Joseph Gusumano - 3475 Anderdon - age 44 b 24 Jan 1898 Terrasini
    contact John Gusumano samy addy son - unemployed
    5'8" 245# gray eyes gray hair ruddy complex - scar on right cheek
1943 Aug 27 - died[462]
    Joseph Gusumano - m w wid - b 24 Jan 1898 Italy - d 27 Aug 1943
            Mt Clemens, Macomb - age 45
    f Giovanni Gusumano - m Rosa Beielli (sic)
1944 Jan 23 - dau Anna m Salvatore Serra[463]
   Salvatore Serra 32 res Det b Hoboken NY - f Joseph m Santa Lupino
   Ann Gusumano 21 res Det b Det f Joseph m Marion DiMaria
        marriage 23 Jan 1944
1945 - son John m Ionatia Bommarito[464] (Ignazia?)
    John Cusumano 26 res Det b Det f Joseph m Marian DiMaria
    Ionatia Bommarito
    marriage 2 Sept 1945 - Holy Family

8. Rose
1900 Dec 29 -baptized Terrasini[465]
    566 = 195 = 29 Dec 1900 - Rosa - Joannes C & Rosa Zerilli

---

[461]"U.S. World War II Draft Registration Cards, 1942," database with images,
Ancestry.com (http://ancestry.com: accessed 16 Oct 2016), card for Joseph
Gusumano, serial no. 2082; citing The National Archives at St. Louis, Draft
Registration Cards for Fourth Registration for Michigan, 04/27/1942 - 04/27/1942;
NAI Number: 623283; Records of the Selective Service System; Record Group
Number: 147.
[462]"Michigan, Death Records, 1867-1950," database, *Ancestry.com*
(http://ancestry.com: accessed 21 September 2016), entry for Joseph Gusumano, 27
Aug 1943 (file no. 005315); Michigan Department of Community Health, Division
for Vital Records and Health Statistics, Lansing, Michigan.
[463]"Michigan Marriage Records, 1867-1952," database, *Ancestry.com*
(http://ancestry.com: accessed 4 Oct 2016), entry for Ann Gusumano, 1944 (state
file no. 303636, county file no. 622496); citing Michigan Department of Community
Health, Division for Vital Records and Health Statistics, film no. 323 (82 Wayne
302160-305469).
[464]"Michigan Marriage Records, 1867-1952," database, *Ancestry.com*
(http://ancestry.com: accessed 4 Oct 2016), entry for John Cusumano, 1945 (state
file no. 334806, county file no. 654020); citing Michigan Department of Community
Health, Division for Vital Records and Health Statistics, film no. 332 (82 Wayne
331600-334909).
[465]Maria Santissima delle Grazie, Terrasini, Palermo, Sicily, Italy, Baptismal register,
v. 35, 1893-1902, p. 195, Rosa C baptism 1900; *Family Search.org*, "Battesimi
1889-1903," image 566 of 621.

~1906 - to Oakfield NY
1910 - with parents in Oakfield NY
~1911 - to Detroit
1918 Dec 23 - m Peter Ventimiglia[466]
     407 - no 169727
     Pete Ventemiglio 23 res Det b It clerk f Victor m Serafina
     Rose Cusumona 17 res Det b It – f John m Rose
     lic & marriage 23 Dec 1918 - R Bradley minister
         wit Espero Brooks, Mabbie Crawford
1920 Jan 1 - son Victor born (died 1921)[467]
  Victor Ventimiglia - 756 Chene - b 1 Jan 1920 - d 15 Mar 1921 measles
     f Pietro Ventimiglia b It - m Rosa Cusumano b It
     inf Pietro - Mt Olivet
1920 census - with parents & husband in Detroit
Detroit City Directories[468]
1920/21 Gusumano& Ventimiglia
     (Jno Gusumano & Peter Ventimiglia) grocs 756 (196) Chene
     Gusumano Jno (Gusumano & Ventimiglia) h 756 (196) Chene - with
     Jos +PV
1921/22 Gusumano & Ventimiglia
     (Jos Gusumano & Peter Ventimiglia) meats 752? Chene
1922/23 Gusumano& Ventimiglia
     (Jos Gusumano & Peter Ventimiglia) groc 736 Chene
1925/26 Cusumano & Ventimiglia
     (John Gusumano & Peter Ventimiglia) groc 734 Chene

8. Philip s/o Giovanni Cusmano & Rosa Zerilli, g-son of Filippo
Gusumano & Anna Orlando, ggs/o Giovanni Cusumano + Francesca Paola
Bommarito
1908 born -NY

---

[466]"Michigan Marriages, 1868-1925," database with images, FamilySearch (https://familysearch.org: accessed 26 Oct 2016), Pete Ventemiglio and Rose Cusumona, 23 Dec 1918; citing Detroit, Wayne, Michigan, v 7 p 407 rn 169727, Department of Vital Records, Lansing; FHL microfilm 2,342,729.

[467]"Michigan Death Records, 1867-1950," database with images, *Ancestry.com* (http://ancestry.com: accessed 7 Oct 2016), entry for Victor Ventimeglia, 15 Mar 1921, state file no. 2292, reg no. 2568; citing Michigan Department of Community Health, Division for Vital Records and Health Statistics.

[468]R. L. Polk & Co's *Detroit City Directory 1920-21* (Detroit, MI: R. L. Polk & Co, March 1921) p nos; database with images, *Ancestry.com,* "U.S. City Directories, 1822-1995" (http://www.ancestry.com: accessed 24 September 2016). And subsequent directories 1921/22-1925/26.

1910 - with parents in NY
1920 census[469] - Detroit SD 145 ED 327 sh 12b line 58 - 196 Cheyne
Cusumano John

      head, homeowner, m, wh, 50, married, to us in 1904, still alien, no
      read, no write, no speak English, b. Italy. proprietor store, owned/ Rosa
      wife 60? 1904
      Joseph son 22 1904 yes read & write, no eng., salesman store/
           Mary his wife 19 to us 1915, read write, no Eng./
      Philip son 13 b. NY/ John son 11 b. NY/
       Frances daughter 7 b. Mi/
      Ventimiglie Peter, son in law, 22 to us 1912/ Rosa 19/
      Victor 1/12 b. Mi

Detroit City Directories[470]
1927/28 Cusumano Philip lab r2608 E Laf - with John & John J
1928/29 Cusumano Philip clk r2608 E Laf - with John
      Gusumano Philip clk r756 Cheyne - with John, John jr, Pauline
~1928 - married
1930 census[471] - Michigan Wayne Detroit wd 13 SD 22 ED 82-405 sheet 28b
- 13445 Sparling
390-31 Gusumano, Philipp 23 m 21 b NY p b Italy - clerk ret grocery
          Helen 21 m 19 Mi Pol Pol
   Coslett, Stephen b/law 29 m 29 NJ NJ NJ foreman auto parts factory
          Sallie s/law 19 m 19 Mi Pol Pol
1930/31 Gusumano Philip (Helen) driver h13445 Sparling
1931/32 Gusumano Philip (Helen) lab h13445 Sparling
1934 Gusumano Philip (Helen) slsmn h2937 Penna ave apt 6
1935 Gusumano Philip (Helen) slsmn h2937 Penna ave apt 6
1939 Gusumano Philip (Helen) milkmn h18456 Filer

---

[469]1920 U. S. Federal census, Wayne County, Michigan, population schedule,
Detroit, ward 11, enumeration district (ED) 327, sheet 12b, dwelling 150, family 267,
John Cusumano; image, *Ancestry.com* (http://ancestry.com : accessed 26 Oct 2016);
citing NARA microfilm publication T625, roll 810.
[470]*Polk's Detroit (Michigan) City Directory 1927-28, vol. LXV* (Detroit, MI: R. L.
Polk & Co, 1928?) p nos; database with images, *Ancestry.com,* "U.S. City
Directories, 1822-1995" (http://www.ancestry.com : accessed 23 Oct 2016). And
subsequent directories 1928/29-1939.
[471]1930 U.S. census, Wayne County, Michigan, population schedule, Detroit ward
13, enumeration district (ED) 82-405, sheet 28b, dwelling 390, family 31, Philipp
Gusumano; image, *Ancestry.com* (http://ancestry.com : accessed 8 Oct 2016); citing
FHL microfilm: 2340783; NARA microfilm T626 roll 1048.

8. **John** s/o Giovanni Cusmano & Rosa Zerilli, g-son of Filippo Gusumano
& Anna Orlando, ggs/o Giovanni Cusumano + Francesca Paola Bommarito
1909 born - NY
1910 - with parents in NY
1920 census[472] - Mi Wayne Detroit SD 145 ED 327 sh 12b line 58 - 196
Cheyne
Cusumano John -head, homeowner, m, wh, 50, married, to us in 1904, still
alien, no read, no write, no English, b. Italy. proprietor store, owned/ Rosa
wife 60? 1904
      Joseph son 22 1904 yes read & write, no eng., salesman store/ Mary
his wife 19 to us 1915, read write, no Eng./
      Philip son 13 b. NY/ John son 11 b. NY/
      Frances daughter 7 b. Mi/
      Ventimiglie Peter, son in law, 22 to us 1912/ Rosa 19/
      Victor 1/12 b. Mi
Detroit City Directories[473]
1925/26 Gusumano John jr clk Gusumano & Ventimiglia h734 Chene - with
    John
1927/28 Cusumano John J lab r2608 E Laf - with Philip & John
    Gusumano John jr clk John Gusumano r756 Chene - with John
1928/29 Cusumano John jr clk r2608 E Laf - with Philip & John
    Gusumano John jr clk r756 Cheyne - with John, Pauline, Philip
1931/32 Cusumano John jr (J Cusumano & Sons) r2608 E Laf
    - with Jos, John
    Gusmano John clk Jos Gusmano r756 Chene - with Jos
1931 Sept 8 - m Louise Bommarito[474]
    John Gusumano jr 22 res Det b NY groc f John m Rosa Zerrille
    Louise Bommarito 19 res Det b It
       f Peter m Margaret Giordano

---

[472] 1920 U. S. Federal census, Wayne County, Michigan, population schedule,
Detroit, ward 11, enumeration district (ED) 327, sheet 12b, dwelling 150, family 267,
John Cusumano; image, *Ancestry.com* (http://ancestry.com: accessed 26 Oct 2016);
citing NARA microfilm publication T625, roll 810.

[473] *Polk's Detroit City Directory 1925-26* (Detroit, MI: R. L. Polk & Co, 1926) p nos;
database with images, *Ancestry.com,* "U.S. City Directories, 1822-1995"
(http://www.ancestry.com: accessed 23 Oct 2016). And subsequent directories
1927/28-1939

[474] "Michigan Marriage Records, 1867-1952," database with images, *Ancestry.com*
(http://ancestry.com: accessed 17 Oct 2016), entry for John Gusumano jr, 1931
[indexed Gnsamane] (state file no. 91634, county file no. 398248); citing Michigan
Department of Community Health, Division for Vital Records and Health Statistics,
film no. 258 (82 Wayne 89320-92579).

lic 18 Aug 1931 - m 8 Sept 1931 - John F McKinlay, court of common pleas - wit - Rose Ventimiglia, Sam Orlando?

1932 Sept 22 - son John born (d 1940)

Detroit City Directories

1932/33 Gusmano John (Jennie) driver Book Clnrs & Dyers h8030 Sylvester

1934 Gusumano John (Louise) driver h8936 Sylvester apt 3

1934 - dau Rose born

1935 May 16 - son Peter born (d 1938)

1935 Cusmano John (Jennie) tailor h8936 Sylvester apt 3

1938 - son Peter died[475]

    Peter Cusumano - 3522 Belvedere - b 17 Dec 1935 Det

        - d 16 May 1938 - age 2-4-29

    f John Cusumano b NY - m Louise Bommarito b Terrasini

    inf John - Mt Olivet (Find A Grave Memorial# 146840228)

1939 Gusumano John (Jennie) driver Mondry Clnrs h3522 Belvedere

1939 - dau Margaret born

1940 - son John died[476]

    John Gusumano Jr - 3522 Belvidere - b 22 Sep 1932 Det

    - d 4 Mar 1940 - 7-5-12

    f John Gusumano b NY - m Louise Bommarito b Terrasini

    inf father - Mt Olivet

1940 census[477] - Mi Wayne Det wd 19 SD14 ED84-1223 sh63a - 3522 Belvedere

311 - Gusmano, John 30 NY same place - driver laundry

    Louise 27 It

    Rose 6 / Margaret 1 - both MI

1969 Jan - died[478]

    John Gusumano SSN: 362-09-0499

---

[475]"Michigan, Death Records, 1867-1950," database with images, *Ancestry.com* (http://ancestry.com: accessed 6 Oct 2016), entry for Peter Cusumano, 16 May 1938 (state file no. 238840, reg no. 5359); Michigan Department of Community Health, Division for Vital Records and Health Statistics, Lansing, Michigan.

[476]"Michigan Death Records, 1867-1950," database with images, *Ancestry.com* (http://ancestry.com: accessed 7 Oct 2016), entry for John Gusumano [indexed Gusumans], 9 Mar 1940, state file no. 262411, local no. 2678; citing Michigan Department of Community Health, Division for Vital Records and Health Statistics.

[477]1940 U. S. Census, Wayne County, Michigan, population schedule, Detroit, ward 19, enumeration district (ED) 84-1223, sheet 63a, household 311, John Gusmano; image, *Ancestry.com* (http://ancestry.com: accessed 26 Oct 2016); citing NARA microfilm publication T627, roll 1876.

[478]Social Security Administration, "United States Social Security Death Index," database, Ancestry.com (http://ancestry.com: accessed 27 Oct 2016), entry for John Gusumano, 1969, SS no. 362-09-0499.

Last Residence: 48224 Detroit, Wayne, Michigan, USA
b 25 Jun 1909 - d Jan 1969
SSN issued: Michigan (Before 1951)
2003 Sept 7 - wife Louise died[479]
[Louise Bommarito] SSN: 372481697
b 18 Oct 1912, Terrasini, Italy - d 7 Sep 2003
f Peter Bommarito - m Margareth Giordano
Original SSN. Signature on SSN Card: JOHN GUSUMANO II
Relationship of Signature: Signature name differs from NH's name.
Notes: Sep 1963: Name listed as LOUISE GUSUMANO
        - SS Applications & Claims
    – Louise Gusumano SSN: 372-48-1697
Last Residence: 48035 Clinton Township, Macomb, Michigan,
        b 23 Oct 1912 - d 7 Sep 2003
        SSN issued: Michigan (1963)
        - SS Death index
Both John & Louise buried Mt Olivet[480]
Gusumano, John
Date of Interment: 01/17/1969
Cemetery: Mt. Olivet Cemetery - Section 18, Lot 635, Space 1
Gusumano, Louise
Date of Interment: 09/10/2003
Cemetery: Mt. Olivet Cemetery - Section 18, Lot 635, Space 2

8. Frances/Pauline (Francesca Paola?)

~1913 - born MI
1920 census - with parents in Detroit
1929 - married Sam Orlando[481]
Sam Orlando 22 res Det b It clerk - f Carlo m Grace Cusimano

---

[479]Social Security Administration, "U.S., Social Security Applications and Claims Index, 1936-2007," database, Ancestry.com (http://ancestry.com: accessed 27 Oct 2016), entry for Louise Gusumano, 2003, SS no. 372-48-1697. And Social Security Administration, "United States Social Security Death Index," database, Ancestry.com (http://ancestry.com: accessed 27 Oct 2016), entry for Louise Gusumano, 2003, SS no. 372-48-1697.

[480]Mt. Elliott Cemetery Association, database (http://www.mtelliott.com/genealogy/ : accessed 27 Oct 2016), Mt. Olivet Cemetery (Detroit, Wayne, Michigan), entries for John (17 Jan 1969) and Louise (10 Sept 2003) Gusumano.

[481]"Michigan Marriage Records, 1867-1952," database with images, *Ancestry.com* (http://ancestry.com: accessed 19 Sept 2016), entry for Pauline Gusumano, 1929 (state file no. 82 57722, county file no. 366015); citing Michigan Department of Community Health, Division for Vital Records and Health Statistics, film no. 248 (82 Wayne 56680-59959).

Pauline Gusumano 18 res Det b MI - f John m Rose Zerillo
lic 5 June 1929 - marriage 11 June 1929 - Jesse Drake, JP
wit Joseph, Mary, John Gusmano, Anna Russo
1930 Jan 24 - son Carl born (d 1932)[482]
Carl Orlando - 740 Chene - b 24 June 1930 Det
 - d 6 Sep 1932 - age 2-11-3
f Salvatore Orlando b Palermo - m Pauline Cusumano b Det

?8. Connie
~1917 - born
1937 Nov 20 - m Harry Carolla[483]
Henry Carolla 23 res Det b It truckdriver
        f James m Josephine Scardino
Connie Cusamano 20 res Det b NY f John m Rosalee Serolli
lic 6 Nov 1937 - marriage 20 Nov 1937
- Fr Benedict Ferretti, RC priest - wit Paolo Furos, Rose V?

7. Giuseppe 1872 -1924 + Concetta Ventimiglia -> NY, **Detroit**
    8. Filippo Salvatore 1896-1981 + Josephine Maniaci
        9. Baby boy 1920-1920
        9. Constance 1922
        9. Joseph 1923-1923
        9. Antonia 1924-1925
        9. Philip 1925-1926
        9. Sarah 1927
        9. Anna 1928
        9. Joseph 1934
        9. Lena 1938
    8. Grazia Anna 1899
    8. Stefano 1902-1957 + Amber Haviland (1924)
        9. Barbara 1925 + Thomas Tortmose (1949)
        9. Joseph 1927-1997 + Shirley J Suggs
        9. Sherry 1934

---

[482]"Michigan, Death Records, 1867-1950," database with images, *Ancestry.com* (http://ancestry.com: accessed 6 Oct 2016), entry for Carl Orlando, 6 Sep 1932 (file no. 161652); Michigan Department of Community Health, Division for Vital Records and Health Statistics, Lansing, Michigan.
[483]"Michigan Marriage Records, 1867-1952," database with images, *Ancestry.com* (http://ancestry.com: accessed 4 Oct 2016), entry for Connie Cusamano, 1937 (state file no. 194207, county file no. 512295); citing Michigan Department of Community Health, Division for Vital Records and Health Statistics, film no. 290 (82 Wayne 194100-197369).

9. James 1938
8. Anna 1905-1910
8. Anna 1910 + Salvatore Buffa (1926)
9. John 1928
9. Joe 1931
9. Catherine 1932
8. Ida/Gina 1912 + Thomas Serra (1928)
8. Grazia 1914-1914
8. Frances 1915-1915
8. Maria 1915-1915
8. Frances 1918 + Joe Militello (1941)
8. Giuseppe 1921-1921

He apparently went back & forth to Sicily - or his wife did.
1872 Oct 19 - born[484]
363 = 204= 19 Oct 1872 - Joseph G s/o Philippus & Anna Orlando
(Godmother Philippa Consiglio, unm of Salvatore)
1896 June 8 - married Concetta Ventimiglia[485]
116 = 104 = 8 June 1896 - Joseph C unm - Philippo & Anna Orlando
Concepta Ventimiglia - Stephano & Caterina Moceri
1896 Nov 17 - son Filippo Salvatore baptized[486]
463 = 94 = 17 Nov 1896 - Philippus Salvator
- Joseph C & Concepta Ventimiglia
1920 - son Philip m Josephine Maniaci
(Children: Constance, Sarah, Anna, Joseph, Lena)
1979 - wife Josephine died in Los Angeles County, CA
1981 Nov 15 - died - in Michigan,
but apparently buried in LA County

---

[484]Maria Santissima delle Grazie (Chiesa Madre [Mother Church]), Terrasini, Palermo, Sicily, Italy, Baptismal register, v. 28, 1862-1872, p. 204, Joseph Gusmano baptism 1872; *Family Search.org*, Battesimi 1859-1878, image 363 of 481.

[485]Maria Santissima delle Grazie (Chiesa Madre [Mother Church]), Terrasini, Palermo, Sicily, Italy, Marriage register, v. ? cont., 1891-1897, p. 104, Joseph Gusmano marriage 1896; *FamilySearch.org*, "Matirmoni 1891-1904," image 116 of 350.

[486]Maria Santissima delle Grazie, Terrasini, Palermo, Sicily, Italy, Baptismal register, v. 35, 1893-1902, p. 94, Philippus Salvator C baptism 1896; *Family Search.org*, "Battesimi 1889-1903," image 463 of 621.

1899 Nov 12 - daughter Grazia Anna baptized[487]
        95 = 225 = 12 Nov 1899 - Grazia Anna C
                - Giuseppe & Concetta Ventimiglia
        540 = 168 = 12 Nov 1899 - Gratia Anna
                - Joseph C & Concepta Ventimiglia
? 1900 - to Oakfield, NY? Wife Concetta there 1900, 1909?
1902 Sept 8 - son Stefano baptized[488]
        602 = 228 = 8 Sept 1902 - Stephano -
        Joseph C & Concepta Ventimiglia
                (Godfather Rosolino Giliberti)
1905 - daughter Anna born (died 1910)
        death[489]
        202 = 150 = 15 July 1910 - C Anna 5
        - Joseph & Concetta Ventimiglia
Detroit City Directories[490]
1907 Cusmano Jos bds 154 Larned e (with Saml)
~1910 - dau Annie born
1911 Gusomano Jos (Det Macaroni Mfg Co) bds 296 Congress e - with John
        & Saml
1912 Cusimano Jos clk Saml Cusimano bds 271 Clinton (with Saml)
        Gusumano Jos (Det. Macaroni Mfg Co) bds 176 Rivard
        (with Jno & Saml)

---

[487]Maria Santissima delle Grazie, Terrasini, Palermo, Sicily, Italy, Baptismal register,
v. 34 continued?, 1887-1900, p. 225, Grazia Anna C baptism 1899; *Family
Search.org*, "Battesimi 1897-1911," image 95 of 523. AND Maria Santissima delle
Grazie, Terrasini, Palermo, Sicily, Italy, Baptismal register, v. 35, 1893-1902, p.
168, Gratia Anna C baptism 1899; *Family Search.org*, "Battesimi 1889-1903," image
540 of 621.

[488]Maria Santissima delle Grazie, Terrasini, Palermo, Sicily, Italy, Baptismal register,
v. 35, 1893-1902, p. 228, Stephano C baptism 1902; *Family Search.org*, "Battesimi
1889-1903," image 602 of 621.

[489]Maria Santissima delle Grazie, Terrasini, Palermo, Sicily, Italy, Death register, v.
88, 1893-1910, p. 150, Anna C death 1910; *Family Search.org*, "Morti 1893-1910,"
image 202 of 207.

[490]R. L. Polk, compiler, *Detroit City Directory for the year commencing August 1st,
1907* (Detroit, MI: R. L. Polk & Co, 1907) p nos; database with images,
Ancestry.com, "U.S. City Directories, 1822-1995" (http://www.ancestry.com:
accessed 24 September 2016). And subsequent directories for 1911-1922/23.

1912 - wife and children Stephen & Annie emigrate[491]

    Sant'Anna - Palermo-NY arr 6 June 1912

    line 26 Ventimiglia Concetta 33 housewife Terrasini at home father
Ventimiglia Stefano -   to Detroit MI - in US before? Yes 1900-1909?
Oakfield NY - to husb Gusmano, Giuseppe 140? Riopelle St Det b Palermo,
Terrasini

    line 27 Gusmano Stefano 9

    line 28 Gusmano Anna 2

~1912 - dau Ida born   (= Gina?)

1913 Coseman Jos lab h 377 Riopelle?

    Gusmano Jos (Gusmano Bros) bds 176 Rivard

    (with Jno & Saml)

    Gusumano Jos (Detroit Macaroni Mfg Co) 176 Rivard

    (with Jno & Saml)

1914 Gusmano Jos (Gusmano Bros; Det Macaroni Mfg Co)

    bds 176 Rivard (with Jno & Saml)

1914 - dau Grazia Cusmano born & died[492]

    - 226 Fort wd 3 - d 14 Apr 1914 stillborn

    f Giuseppe b It, m Concetta Ventraglia b It

    inf Bagnasco - Mt Olivet

1915 - dau Francis Cusamano born & died[493]

    - 187 Rivard - b 5 Feb 1915 - d 3 Mar - age 26d

    f Joe Cusamano b It - m unk

    inf John P Burke - Mt Olivet

1915 - dau Maria Cusmano born & died[494]

    - 187 Rivard wd 5 -

    b 16 Dec 1915 - d 20 Dec 1915 (premature - 7mos)

---

[491]*Statue of Liberty - Ellis Island Foundation*, database with images
(http://www.ellisisland.org : accessed 3 September 2016), "Ship Manifest: Manifest
for *Sant'Anna*," entry for Concetta Ventimiglia, age 33, arrived 6 June 1912. Also
Stefano Gusmano, age 9 and Anna Gusmano, age 2.

[492]"Michigan, Death Records, 1867-1950," database with images, *Ancestry.com*
(http://ancestry.com : accessed 5 Oct 2016), entry for Grazia Cusmano, 14 Apr 1914
(file no. 2923); Michigan Department of Community Health, Division for Vital
Records and Health Statistics, Lansing, Michigan.

[493]"Michigan Death Records, 1867-1950," database with images, *Ancestry.com*
(http://ancestry.com : accessed 6 Oct 2016), entry for Francis Cussman, 3 Mar 1915,
state file no. 1720; citing Michigan Department of Community Health, Division for
Vital Records and Health Statistics.

[494]"Michigan, Death Records, 1867-1950," database with images, *Ancestry.com*
(http://ancestry.com : accessed 5 Oct 2016), entry for Maria Cusmano, 20 Dec 1915
(file no. 9345); Michigan Department of Community Health, Division for Vital
Records and Health Statistics, Lansing, Michigan.

f Joseph b It - m Concetta Ventimiglia b It

inf Joseph - Mt Olivet

?1917 Cusomano Guiseppe

(Garafalo Macaroni Mfg Co) r 301 Monroe - with Jno & Philip

~1918 - dau Frances born

1918 Cusimano Jos lab h 678 Monroe

1918 WWI Draft Registration[495] - 1918 Sept 12 - ser 3020 ord 4099

Joe Cusmano - 678 Monroe - age 45 b July don't know day 1873 - non declared alien

maccaroni maker - emp himself - 625 Lafayette

rel Concetta

med ht med build light brown eyes black hair

1920 census[496] - Mi Wayne Det wd 11 SD 145 ED 327 sheet1a line 14 678 Monroe -

3-5 Gusnamo Joseph 55 It 1912 street laborer

Mary 40, Philip 28, Stephen 17, Annie 9 all It all to US 1912 -

Stephen, Philip - vegetable peddlers

Gina 7, Frances f 1 8/12 both b. Mich

3-6 Giardano Samuel 24 It 1911 al - lab street

Rosa 26 It 1911 / Jack 7 / Stephen 2 6/12 / August 5/12

3-7 Valenti Angelo 38 It 1912 al - lab factory

Jennie 30 1912 It

1920/21 Cusimono Jos lab 2628 (678) Monroe

1921 - son Guiseppe Cusumano born & died[497]

Guiseppe Cusumano- 2628 Monroe- b 24 Aug 1921 Det

- d 5 Sep 1921 premature - 12 d

f Guiseppe Cusumano b It - m Concetta Ventinuglia b It

inf Giuseppe - Mt Olivet

1921/22 Cusmano Jos h2628 Monroe

1922/23 Cusimano Jos lab h2628 Monroe

---

[495]"U.S. World War I Draft Registration Cards, 1917-1918," database with images, *Ancestry.com* (http://ancestry.com: accessed 15 Oct 2016), card for Joe Cusmano, serial no. 3020, Draft Board 8, Wayne County, Michigan; imaged from Family History Library microfilm.

[496]1920 U. S. Federal census, Wayne County, Michigan, population schedule, Detroit, ward 11, enumeration district (ED) 327, sheet 1ba, dwelling 3, family 5, Joseph Gusmano [indexed Cusnamo]; image, *Ancestry.com* (http://ancestry.com: accessed 26 Oct 2016); citing NARA microfilm publication T625, roll 810.

[497]"Michigan, Death Records, 1867-1950," database with images, *Ancestry.com* (http://ancestry.com: accessed 6 Oct 2016), entry for Giuseppe Cusumano, 5 Sep 1921 (state file no. 582 7238, reg no. 8178); Michigan Department of Community Health, Division for Vital Records and Health Statistics, Lansing, Michigan.

1924 - died[498]

Guiseppe Cusumano - 2612 Monroe - m w m - wife Concetta Ventemiglia
   b 15 Nov 1872 Terrasini - 51-2-14 - peddler - d 29 Jan 1924
   f Filippo Cusumano b Terrasini - m Anna Orlando b Terrasini
   inf Concetta Ventemiglia 3612 Monroe - Mt Olivet 2-1-24
   - buried Mt Olivet[499]

   Giuseppe Cusumano - Nov. 19, 1873 Terrasini Favarotta - Jan. 29,
1924 Detroit
   Burial: Mount Olivet Cemetery Plot: Sec 12

wife Concetta

Detroit City Directories[500]

1925/26 Cusmano Concetta (wid Jos) r 2412 Monroe (2612?)
   - with Philip
1928/29 Cusimano Mary (wid Jos) r2612 Monroe
   - with Philip & Stephen
1930 census[501] - Mi Wayne Detroit wd 11 - SD22 ED82-319 sheet 19a -
2612 Monroe ave
238-2 Weeden Richard / Callie
   - 3 Cusinano Concetta 52 wd m14 It 1905 al
         Frances dau 11 MI
   -3a -   Stephen head 27 m21 It 1905 al huckster fruit & veg
         Amber 26 m20 Mi
         Barbara 5 / Joseph 3 b MI
   -4 Buffa Sam 22 m19 It 1919 al peddler fruit
      Anna 19 m16 It 1915 al
      John 1 6/12 Mi
   -5 Cusimano, Philipp head 35 m23 It 1905 al huckster fruit & veg

---

[498]"Michigan Death Records, 1867-1950," database with images, *Ancestry.com*
(http://ancestry.com : accessed 21 Sept 2016), entry for Giuseppe (indexed
Guiseppe) Cusumano, 29 Jan 1924, no. 58235591, reg. no. 1171; citing Michigan
Department of Community Health, Division for Vital Records and Health Statistics
[499]*Findagrave.com*, database and images (http://findagrave.com : accessed 25 August
2016), memorial page Giuseppe Cusumano, Mt. Olivet Cemetery, Detroit, Wayne,
Michigan, Find A Grave Memorial no. 137266850, created by Renee.
[500]Polk's *Detroit City Directory 1925-26* (Detroit, MI: R. L. Polk & Co, 1926) p nos;
database with images, *Ancestry.com*, "U.S. City Directories, 1822-1995"
(http://www.ancestry.com : accessed 23 Oct 2016). And subsequent directories
1928/29-1939.
[501]1930 U.S. census, Wayne County, Michigan, population schedule, Detroit ward
11, enumeration district (ED) 82-319, sheet 19 a, dwelling 238, family 5, Philipp
Cusimano; image, *Ancestry.com* (http://ancestry.com : accessed 30 Sept 2016); citing
FHL microfilm 2340779; NARA microfilm T626 roll 1044. Also family 3 Concetta
Cusinano and family 3a Stephen Cusinano.

        Josephine 30 m20 It 1919 al
        Constance 8 Mi / Sarah 3 Mi / Anna 1 3/12
    -6 Lentini Joe 49 m20 It 1911 al lab street construction
        Rose 44 m15 It 1902 al
        Joe 16 / Sam 14 - b Mi
1934 Cusmano Constance (wid Jos) h2085 Sherman
1935 Cusmano Constance (wid Jos) h2685 Sherman
1939 Cusmano Constance (wid Jos) h2685 Sherman - with Frances
1940 census[502] - Mi Wayne Detroit wd 11 SD1 ED84-571 sh 6b
2685 Sherman - 102 Cusmano Concetta 59 wd It al same house
 -extra info - age at 1st marriage 16 - # of children 20??
        Frances dau 21 s Mi new worker
    Buffa Sam s/law 21 It pa same house fruit peddler own
        Anna dau 29 It al same house
        John gson 11 / Joe gson 9 / Caterina gdau 8 - all b MI
1968 Dec 8 - Concetta died - buried Mt Olivet[503]
        Concetta Cusumano - Jan. 8, 1878 - Dec. 12, 1968
            Date of Interment: 12/16/1968
        Burial: Mount Olivet Cemetery Plot: Sec 12, space 2

Children of 7. Giuseppe & Concetta Ventimiglia

8. Filippo Salvatore 1896-1981 + Josephine Maniaci
1896 Nov 17 - baptized[504]
        463 = 94 = 17 Nov 1896 - Philippus Salvator
        - Joseph C & Concepta Ventimiglia
1905 - emigrated

---

[502] 1940 U. S. Census, Wayne County, Michigan, population schedule, Detroit, ward 11, enumeration district (ED) 84-571, sheet 6b, household 102, Concetta Cusman [indexed Cusamano]; image, *Ancestry.com* (http://ancestry.com: accessed 9 Oct 2016); citing NARA microfilm publication T627, roll 1858.

[503] *Findagrave.com*, database and images (http://findagrave.com: accessed 25 August 2016), memorial page for Concetta Cusumano, Mt. Olivet Cemetery, Detroit, Wayne, Michigan, Find A Grave Memorial no. 137299364, created by Renee.

[504] Maria Santissima delle Grazie, Terrasini, Palermo, Sicily, Italy, Baptismal register, v. 35, 1893-1902, p. 94, Philippus Salvator C baptism 1896; *Family Search.org*, "Battesimi 1889-1903," image 463 of 621.

1910 census[505] - New York, Genessee, Oakfield SD 18 ED 29 sh 11a -
Garibaldi St - 207-240 Vintemelia, Joseph head 26 It em 1903 al - lab
gypsum mill
      Cusman, Phillip nephew 13 It 1905
1917 - WWI Draft Registration[506] - 1917 June 5 - no 239
      Phillip Cusumano - 678 Monroe - age 21
       b 15 Nov 1896 Terrasini alien
      f b Terrasini - employer Joe Cusumano 678 Monroe
      nearest rel Concetta Cusumano 678 Monroe
      med ht med build brown eyes black hair
1920 - with parents in Detroit
1920 Jan 24 m Josephine Maniaci[507]
      Philip Cusimano 22 res Det b It merchant
         f Joseph m C Ventimiglia
      Josephine Maniaci 20 f Isadore m Lena Monella
      lic 24 Oct 1919 - marriage 24 [26?] Jan 1920
      P Zagni clergyman -   wit Faro & Grace Tocca
1920 Dec 21 - baby boy born & died[508]
Baby Cusumano - Male - 421 Sherman - d 21 Dec 1920 stillborn
      f Filippo Cusumano b Terrasini
      - m Guisepa Maniaci b Terrasini
      inf Filippo - Mt Olivet
Detroit City Directory
1920/21 Cusimano Philip pdlr 2685 (421) Sherman
1922 - dau Constance born

---

[505] 1910 U. S. Federal Census, Genessee County, New York, population schedule, Oakfield Township, enumeration district (ED) 29, sheet 11a, dwelling 208, family 241, Tony Cusmano; image, *Ancestry.com* (http://ancestry.com : accessed 4 Sept 2016); citing NARA microfilm publication T624, roll 951.

[506] "U.S. World War I Draft Registration Cards, 1917-1918," database with images, *Ancestry.com* (http://ancestry.com : accessed 15 Oct 2016), card for Phillip Cusumano, serial no. 239, Draft Board 13, Wayne County, Michigan; imaged from Family History Library microfilm.

[507] "Michigan Marriage Records, 1867-1952," database with images, *Ancestry.com* (http://ancestry.com : accessed 23 Sept 2016), entry for Philip Cusimano, 1920 (no. 183671); citing Michigan Department of Community Health, Division for Vital Records and Health Statistics, film no. 153 (1920 Washtenaw - 1920 Wayne).

[508] "Michigan, Death Records, 1867-1950," database with images, *Ancestry.com* (http://ancestry.com : accessed 6 Oct 2016), entry for Baby Cusumano, 21 Dec 1920 (file no. 14756 [index says 14545]); Michigan Department of Community Health, Division for Vital Records and Health Statistics, Lansing, Michigan.

1921/22 Cusimano Philip fruit h2635 Sherman

1922/23 Cusumano Philip pdlr h2685 Sherman (Saml at 2645)

1923 July 9 - son Joseph b - died 26 October 1923[510]

> Giuseppe Cusumano - 2612 Monroe - b 9 July 1923 Det - d 26 Oct
> 1923 - 3m 17d - malnutrition
> f Filippo Cusumano b It - m Guseppe Maniaci b It
> inf Filippo - Mt Olivet Find A Grave Memorial# 146775339

1924 Aug 28 - dau Antonina b (died 21 Mar 1925)[511]

> Antonina Cusumano - 2612 Monroe - b 28 Aug 1924 Det
> - d 21 Mar 1925 - age 6-21 - overfeeding
> f Filippo Cusumano b It - m Giuseppa Maniaci b It
> inf Filippo - Mt Olivet Find A Grave Memorial# 146773624

1925/26 Cusmano Philip pdlr h2412 Monroe - with Concetta

1925 Dec 15 - son Philip b (died 11 Apr 1926)[512]

> Philip Cusimano 2612 Monroe - b 15 Dec 1925 Det
> - d 11 Apr 1926 - 0-3-26
> f Philip Cusimano b Terrasini
> - m Josephine Maniaci b Terrasini
> inf Philip - Mt Olivet

1927 - dau Sarah b

1928 - dau Anna b

1928/29 Cusimano Philip (Josephine) pdlr r2612 Monroe
> - with Mary, Stephen

---

[509]*Polk's Detroit City Directory 1921-22, vol LIX* (Detroit, MI: R. L. Polk & Co, 1922) p nos; database with images, *Ancestry.com,* "U.S. City Directories, 1822-1995" (http://www.ancestry.com: accessed 23 Oct 2016). And subsequent directories 1922/23-1939.

[510]"Michigan, Death Records, 1867-1950," database with images, *Ancestry.com* (http://ancestry.com: accessed 6 Oct 2016), entry for Giusseppe Cusumano, 26 Agu 1923 (state file no. 582 32330, reg no. 12071); Michigan Department of Community Health, Division for Vital Records and Health Statistics, Lansing, Michigan.

[511]"Michigan, Death Records, 1867-1950," database with images, *Ancestry.com* (http://ancestry.com: accessed 6 Oct 2016), entry for Antonina Cusumano, 21 Mar 1925 (state file no. 582 50522, reg no. 3413); Michigan Department of Community Health, Division for Vital Records and Health Statistics, Lansing, Michigan.

[512]"Michigan Death Records, 1867-1950," database with images, *Ancestry.com* (http://ancestry.com: accessed 7 Oct 2016), entry for Philip Cusimano, 11 Apr 1926, state file no. 582 66481, reg no. 5812; citing Michigan Department of Community Health, Division for Vital Records and Health Statistics.

1930 census[513] - Mi Wayne Detroit wd 11 - SD22 ED82-319 sheet 19a -
2612 Monroe ave
238 -5 Cusimano, Philipp head 35 m23 It 1905 al huckster fruit & veg
     Josephine 30 m20 It 1919 al
     Constance 8 Mi / Sarah 3 Mi / Anna 1 3/12
1934 - son Joseph b
1938 - dau Lena b
1939 Cusmano Philip (Josepine) pdlr h4921 Holcomb
1940 census[514] - Mi Wayne Det wd 19 SD14 ED84-1237 sh 9a - 4921
Holcomb
166 Gusimano, Philip 43 It same place dealer fruits
     Josephine 40 It
     Constance 17 / Sarah 13 / Anna 12 / Joseph 6 / Lena 2
1942 - WWII Draft Registration[515] - 1942 Apr 27 - ser 4088
     Philip Gusmano - 4921 Holcomb - age 45
     b 15 Nov 1896 Terrasini
     contact Concetta Gusmano 2685 Sherman
     emp Ford Rouge
     5'6" 185# brown eyes black hair ruddy complex
1942-79 - moved to California
1979 - wife Josephine died in Los Angeles County, CA[516]
     Josephine Cusmano - Jun. 1, 1899 - Jul. 17, 1979
          Josephine's birth and death dates and death location were found
          in the California Death Records Index. She shares a headstone
          with Philip Cusmano.
     Burial: Queen of Heaven Cemetery

---

[513] 1930 U.S. census, Wayne County, Michigan, population schedule, Detroit ward 11, enumeration district (ED) 82-319, sheet 19 a, dwelling 238, family 5, Philipp Cusimano; image, *Ancestry.com* (http://ancestry.com : accessed 30 Sept 2016); citing FHL microfilm: 2340779; NARA microfilm T626 roll 1044. Also family 3 Concetta Cusinano, family 3a Stephen Cusinano and family 4 Anna Buffa.

[514] 1940 U. S. Census, Wayne County, Michigan, population schedule, Detroit, ward 19, enumeration district (ED) 84-1237, sheet 9a, household 166, Philip Gusimano; image, *Ancestry.com* (http://ancestry.com : accessed 26 Oct 2016); citing NARA microfilm publication T627, roll 1877.

[515] "U.S. World War II Draft Registration Cards, 1942," database with images, *Ancestry.com* (http://ancestry.com : accessed 16 Oct 2016), card for Philip Gusmano, serial no. 4088; citing The National Archives at St. Louis, Draft Registration Cards for Fourth Registration for Michigan, 04/27/1942 - 04/27/1942; NAI Number: 623283; Records of the Selective Service System; Record Group Number: 147.

[516] *Findagrave.com*, database and images (http://findagrave.com : accessed 28 Oct 2016), memorial page for Josephine Cusmano (1899-1979), Find A Grave Memorial no. 125080611, created by Ann O.

- Rowland Heights, LA County, CA
Plot: Section C, Tier 33, Grave 56
1981 Oct 3- died[517] - in Michigan, but apparently buried in LA County.
Philip Cusmano 15 Nov 1896 - 3 Oct 1981
Male   Warren, Macomb, Michigan
---Philip Cusmano SSN: 385-12-7868
Last Residence: 91355 Valencia, Los Angeles, California, USA
b 15 Nov 1896 - d Oct 1981
SSN issued: Michigan (Before 1951) - ssi death index
----buried Queen of Heaven Cemetery, LA county, CA[518]
Philip's birth and death dates and death location were found in the Social Security Death Index. He shares a headstone with Josephine Cusmano.
Burial: Queen of Heaven Cemetery-
 Rowland Heights, Los Angeles County
Plot: Section C, Tier 33, Grave 56

8. Stefano 1902

1902 Sept 8 - baptized[519]
602 = 228 = 8 Sept 1902 - Stephano
- Joseph C & Concepta Ventimiglia
(Godfather - Rosolino Giliberti)
1912 - emigrated, with mother & sister Anna[520]
Sant'Anna - Palermo-NY arr 6 June 1912
line 26 Ventimiglia Concetta 33 housewife Terrasini
at home father Ventimiglia Stefano - going to Detroit MI

---

[517]"Michigan Death Index, 1971-1996," database, *Ancestry.com* (http://ancestry.com: accessed 13 Oct 2016), entry forPhilip, 3 Oct 1981, no. 4245; citing Michigan Department of Vital and Health Records, *Michigan Death Index*, Lansing, MI, USA. AND Social Security Administration, "United States Social Security Death Index," database, Ancestry.com (http://ancestry.com: accessed 28 Oct 2016), entry for Philip Cusmano, 1981, SS no. 385-12-7868.

[518]*Findagrave.com*, database and images (http://findagrave.com: accessed 28 Oct 2016), memorial page for Philip Cusmano (1896-1981), Find A Grave Memorial no. 125080610, created by Ann O.

[519]Maria Santissima delle Grazie, Terrasini, Palermo, Sicily, Italy, Baptismal register, v. 35, 1893-1902, p. 228, Stephano C baptism 1902; *Family Search.org*, "Battesimi 1889-1903," image 602 of 621.

[520]*Statue of Liberty - Ellis Island Foundation*, database with images (http://www.ellisisland.org: accessed 3 September 2016), "Ship Manifest: Manifest for *Sant'Anna*," entry for Concetta Ventimiglia, age 33, arrived 6 June 1912. Also Stefano Gusmano, age 9 and Anna Gusmano, age 2.

- in US before? Yes 1900-1909? Oakfield NY - to husb Gusmano, Giuseppe
140? Riopelle St Det b Palermo, Terrasini
  line 27 Gusmano Stefano 9
  line 28 Gusmano Anna 2
1920 - with parents in Detroit
1924 - m Amber Haviland[521]
  Stephen Gusmano - Amber Haviland - 1924
  Macomb Co - no 11400 - lic 27 June 1924 - no info about marriage
  Stephen Gusmano 21 res Det b It wholesale f Joe Gusmano m Mary
  Resnamelia
  Amber Haviland 20 res Mt Clemens b Bay City f Thomas Haviland m
  Lillian Merkel
1925 - dau Barbara born
Detroit City Directories[522]
?1925/26 Gusmano Steph pdlr r2176 Baldwin
1927 - son Joseph born
1928/29 Cusimano Steph (Amber) pdlr h2612 Monroe
  - with Philip, Mary
1930 census[523] - Mi Wayne Detroit wd 11 - SD22 ED82-319 sheet 19a -
2612 Monroe ave
282 - 3 Cusinano Concetta 52 wd m14 It 1905 al
    Frances dau 11 MI
 -3a - Stephen head 27 m21 It 1905 al huckster fruit & veg
    Amber 26 m20 Mi
    Barbara 5 / Joseph 3 b MI
Detroit City Directories
1930/31 Cusimano Steph (Amber) pdlr h 12281 Camden
1931/32 Cusimano Steph (Amber) slsmn h12281 Camden
1932/33 Cusimano Steph (Amber) pdlr h12281 Camden
1934 - dau Sherry born

---

[521]"Michigan Marriages, 1868-1925," database with images, FamilySearch
(https://familysearch.org/ark:/61903/1:1:NQQK-MW5 : 4 December 2014), Stephen
Gusmono and Amber Haviland, 27 Jun 1924; citing Macomb, Michigan, item 6 p rn
11400, Department of Vital Records, Lansing; FHL microfilm 2,342,763.
[522]Polk's *Detroit City Directory 1925-26* (Detroit, MI: R. L. Polk & Co, 1926) p nos;
database with images, *Ancestry.com,* "U.S. City Directories, 1822-1995"
(http://www.ancestry.com : accessed 23 Oct 2016). And subsequent directories
1928/29-1939.
[523]1930 U.S. census, Wayne County, Michigan, population schedule, Detroit ward
11, enumeration district (ED) 82-319, sheet 19 a, dwelling 238, family 3a, Stephen
Cusimano; image, *Ancestry.com* (http://ancestry.com : accessed 30 Sept 2016); citing
FHL microfilm: 2340779; NARA microfilm T626 roll 1044. Also family 3 Concetta
Cusinano, family 4 Anna Buffa and family 5 Philip Cusimano.

1934 Cusimano Steph (Amber) pdlr h12281 Camden
1935 Cusimano Steph (Amber) pdlr h12281 Camden
1938 - son James born
1939 Cusemano Step (Amber) fruit h12281 Camden
1940 census[524] - Mi Wayne Detroit wd 21 SD14 ED84-1504 sheet 9b - 12281 Camden
235 Cusimano Stephen 37 It pa same house fruit dealer fruit market
    Amber 36 Mi
    Barbara 15 / Joseph 13 / Sherry 6 / James 2 - all b MI
1949 - dau Barbara m Thomas Tortmose[525]
    5 Nov 1949 St Clair Shores, Monroe
    Thomas Tortomose
    Barbara Lee Marchetta Cusimano 24 res Grosse Pointe Woods b Det -
    f Stephen m Amber Haviland
    marriage 5 Nov 1949 - St Clair Shores - to Thomas Tortomose
1957 Sept - died[526]
    Stephen Cusimano SSN: 363-36-6227
    b 5 Sep 1902 - d Sep 1957
    SSN issued: Michigan (1952-1953)
1961 Nov 6 - son Joseph m Shirley J Suggs
    (according to their shared gravestone)
1977 - wife Amber died[527]
    Amber Cusimano / [Amber Winsky] / [Amber Densmore] SSN: 382202044
    b 7 Mar 1904, Bay City (Caro) MI - d Apr 1977
    f Thomas Densmore - m Lillian Mekkel - Type of Claim: Original SSN.
    Jul 1942: Name listed as AMBER CUSIMANO;
    Feb 1958: Name listed as AMBER WINSKY;

---

[524] 1940 U. S. Census, Wayne County, Michigan, population schedule, Detroit, ward 21, enumeration district (ED) 84-1504, sheet 9b, household 235, Stephen Cusimano; image, *Ancestry.com* (http://ancestry.com: accessed 9 Oct 2016); citing NARA microfilm publication T627, roll 1885.

[525] "Michigan Marriage Records, 1867-1952," database, *Ancestry.com* (http://ancestry.com: accessed 23 Sept 2016), entry for Barbara Lee Marchetta Cusimano, 1949 (state file no. 448967, county file no. 770257); citing Michigan Department of Community Health, Division for Vital Records and Health Statistics, film no. 367 (82 Wayne 446740-450049).

[526] Social Security Administration, "United States Social Security Death Index," database, Ancestry.com (http://ancestry.com: accessed 28 Oct 2016), entry for Stephen Cusimano, 1957, SS no.363-36-6227.

[527] Social Security Administration, "United States Social Security Death Index," database, Ancestry.com (http://ancestry.com: accessed 28 Oct 2016), entry for Amber Cusimano, 1977, SS no. 382-20-2044.

May 1972: Name listed as AMBER T WINSKY
Her mother married Thomas Densmore in 1902; they were together for
the 1910 census, but filed for divorce in 1916 (granted in 1918).
Lillian Merkel Densmore m James B Haviland in 1918.
1997 - son Joseph died[528]
Joseph Stephen Cusimano / [Joseph S Cusimano]/[Joseph Cusimano]
SSN: 370300893
b 7 Mar 1927, Detroit - d 30 May 1997
f Steve Cusimano m Amber Havealand
Type of Claim: Original SSN.
Notes: Jan 1948: Name listed as JOSEPH STEPHEN CUSIMANO;
 31 Aug 1987: Name listed as JOSEPH S CUSIMANO;
10 Jun 1997: Name listed as JOSEPH CUSIMANO
– buried Parkhill Cemetery, Paris, Mecosta Co, MI[529]
Joseph S Cusimano - Mar. 7, 1927 - May 30, 1997

8. Anna 1910 + Salvatore Buffa

~1910 - born
1912 - to US[530]
Sant'Anna - Palermo-NY arr 6 June 1912
line 26 Ventimiglia Concetta 33 housewife Terrasini at home father
Ventimiglia Stefano - to Detroit MI - in US before? Yes 1900-1909?
Oakfield NY - to husb Gusmano, Giuseppe 140? Riopelle St Det b Palermo,
Terrasini
line 27 Gusmano Stefano 9
line 28 Gusmano Anna 2
1920 - with parents in Detroit
1926 Nov 12 - married Salvatore Buffa[531]

---

[528]Social Security Administration, "U.S., Social Security Applications and Claims Index, 1936-2007," database, Ancestry.com (http://ancestry.com: accessed 27 Oct 2016), entry for Joseph Stephen Cusimano, 1997, SS no. 370-30-0893.

[529]*Findagrave.com*, database and images (http://findagrave.com: accessed 28 Oct 2016), memorial page for Joseph S Cusimano (1927-1997), Find A Grave Memorial no. 94990649, created by Cathy Taylor.

[530]*Statue of Liberty - Ellis Island Foundation*, database with images (http://www.ellisisland.org : accessed 3 September 2016), "Ship Manifest: Manifest for *Sant'Anna*," entry for Concetta Ventimiglia, age 33, arrived 6 June 1912. Also Stefano Gusmano, age 9 and Anna Gusmano, age 2.

[531]"Michigan Marriage Records, 1867-1952," database with images, *Ancestry.com* (http://ancestry.com: accessed 22 Sept 2016), entry for Annie Cusumano, 1926 (state file no. 82 15107, county file no. 320393); citing Michigan Department of Community Health, Division for Vital Records and Health Statistics, film no. 235 (82 Wayne 14050-17299).

Salvatore Buffa 21 res Det b It peddler f John m Maria
Annie Cusumano 18 res Det b It f Joseph m Concetta
lic 9 Oct 1926 - marriage 12 Nov 1926 - ? Gordon, JP
wit Joseph & Philip Gusumano

1930 census[532] - Mi Wayne Detroit wd 11 - SD22 ED82-319 sheet 19a - 2612 Monroe ave

238-2 Weeden Richard / Callie
- 3 Cusinano Concetta 52 wd m14 It 1905 al
   Frances dau 11 MI
-3a - Stephen head 27 m21 It 1905 al huckster fruit & veg
   Amber 26 m20 Mi
   Barbara 5 / Joseph 3 b MI
-4 Buffa Sam 22 m19 It 1919 al peddler fruit
  Anna 19 m16 It 1915 al
  John 1 6/12 Mi
-5 Cusimano, Philipp head 35 m23 It 1905 al huckster fruit & veg
  Josephine 30 m20 It 1919 al
  Constance 8 Mi / Sarah 3 Mi / Anna 1 3/12
-6 Lentini Joe 49 m20 It 1911 al lab street construction
  Rose 44 m15 It 1902 al
  Joe 16 / Sam 14 - b Mi

1940 census[533] - Mi Wayne Detroit wd 11 SD1 ED84-571 sh 6b - 2685 Sherman

102 Cusmano Concetta 59 wd It al same house -extra - age at 1st marriage 16 - # of children 20??
  Frances dau 21 s Mi new worker
 Buffa Sam s/law 21 It pa same house fruit peddler own
  Anna dau 29 It al same house
  John gson 11 / Joe gson 9 / Caterina gdau 8 - all b MI

8. Ida/Gina 1912

~1912 - born MI
1920 - with parents in Detroit

---

[532] 1930 U.S. census, Wayne County, Michigan, population schedule, Detroit ward 11, enumeration district (ED) 82-319, sheet 19 a, dwelling 238, family 5, Philipp Cusimano; image, *Ancestry.com* (http://ancestry.com: accessed 30 Sept 2016); citing FHL microfilm 2340779; NARA microfilm T626 roll 1044. Also family 3 Concetta Cusinano and family 3a Stephen Cusinano.

[533] 1940 U. S. Census, Wayne County, Michigan, population schedule, Detroit, ward 11, enumeration district (ED) 84-571, sheet 6b, household 102, Concetta Cusman [indexed Cusamano]; image, *Ancestry.com* (http://ancestry.com: accessed 9 Oct 2016); citing NARA microfilm publication T627, roll 1858.

1928 Apr 28 - married Thomas Serra[534]
    certificate - Thomas Serra 20 res Det b MI auto worker
        f Joseph m Vincenza
    Ida Cusmano 17 res Det b Mi f Joseph m Concetta
    lic 13 Mar 1928 - marriage 28 Apr 1928
     Cogitan? Captan? Serra - Gaetana Cusmano
        - Rev Anthony L – Catholic priest
    wit Salvatore Buffa, Anna Buffa

8. Frances 1918

~1918 - born MI
1920 - with parents in Detroit
1930 census[535] - Mi Wayne Detroit wd 11 - SD22 ED82-319 sheet 19a -
2612 Monroe ave
238-2 Weeden Richard / Callie
   - 3 Cusinano Concetta 52 wd m14 It 1905 al
         Frances dau 11 MI
   -3a -   Stephen head 27 m21 It 1905 al huckster fruit & veg
         Amber 26 m20 Mi
         Barbara 5 / Joseph 3 b MI
  -4 Buffa Sam 22 m19 It 1919 al peddler fruit
     Anna 19 m16 It 1915 al
     John 1 6/12 Mi
  -5 Cusimano, Philipp head 35 m23 It 1905 al huckster fruit & veg
     Josephine 30 m20 It 1919 al
     Constance 8 Mi / Sarah 3 Mi / Anna 1 3/12
  -6 Lentini Joe 49 m20 It 1911 al lab street construction
     Rose 44 m15 It 1902 al
     Joe 16 / Sam 14 - b Mi

---

[534]"Michigan Marriage Records, 1867-1952," database, *Ancestry.com*
(http://ancestry.com: accessed 19 Sept 2016), entry for Ida Cusmano, 1928 (state
file no. 82 38281, county file no. 343778); citing Michigan Department of
Community Health, Division for Vital Records and Health Statistics, film no. 242 (82
Wayne 37020-40299).

[535]1930 U.S. census, Wayne County, Michigan, population schedule, Detroit ward
11, enumeration district (ED) 82-319, sheet 19 a, dwelling 238, family 5, Philipp
Cusimano; image, *Ancestry.com* (http://ancestry.com: accessed 30 Sept 2016); citing
FHL microfilm 2340779; NARA microfilm T626 roll 1044. Also family 3 Concetta
Cusinano and family 3a Stephen Cusinano.

1941 Dec 27 - married Joe Militello[536]

> Joe Militello
> Frances Cusmano 23 res Det b MI f Joseph m Concetta
> marriage 27 Dec 1941 - Holy Family, Detroit

7. Catarina 1875-1941 + Giuseppe Garafalo -> NY, **Detroit**

> 8. Sam 1906
> 8. Philip 1908
> 8. Angelo 1910
> 8. John 1911 NY - 1912 Detroit

1875 June 29 - born, named after maternal grandmother[537]

> 113=50=30 June 1875 - Catherina b yest
> > - Philippo G & Anna Orlando
>
> (Godmother Rosalia X wife of Joannes La Fata)

1xxx - married Giuseppe Garafalo

1905 - emigrated to Oakfield, NY with husband[538]

> SS Sicilia - Palermo (16 Mar) - NY (31 Mar)
> Garofalo, Giuseppe 23 m m workman Terrasini
> > - to b/law Gusmano, Salvatore, 242 x, Oakfield, NY
> > > Gusumano, Caterine 30 wife Terrasini ditto

1906 - son Sam born, NY

1908 - son Philip born, NY

19xx - son Angelo born, NY

1911 - son John born, NY (died 1912, Detroit)[539]

> John Garofalo 217 Fort wd 5 - b 24 Sep 1911 NY
> > - d 13 June 1912 Det - 0-8-18
>
> f Joseph Garofalo b It - m Catherine Cusamano b It

---

[536]"Michigan Marriage Records, 1867-1952," database, *Ancestry.com* (http://ancestry.com : accessed 4 Oct 2016), entry for Frances Cusmano, 1941 (state file no. 259928, county file no. 574290); citing Michigan Department of Community Health, Division for Vital Records and Health Statistics, film no. 310 (82 Wayne 259760-263039).

[537]Maria Santissima delle Grazie (Chiesa Madre [Mother Church]), Terrasini, Palermo, Sicily, Italy, Baptismal register, v. 30, 1873-1881, p. 51, Catherina Gusmano baptism 1875; FamilySearch.org, "Battesimi 1873-1889," image 113 of 793.

[538]*Statue of Liberty - Ellis Island Foundation*, database with images (http://www.ellisisland.org : accessed 3 September 2016), "Ship Manifest: Manifest for *Sicilia*," handwritten on form, entry for Giuseppe Garafalo, age 23, and Caterine Gusumano, age 30, arrived 31 March 1905.

[539]"Michigan Death Records, 1867-1950," database with images, *Ancestry.com* (http://ancestry.com : accessed 7 Oct 2016), entry for John Garofalo, 13 June 1912, file no. 2973; citing Michigan Department of Community Health, Division for Vital Records and Health Statistics.

1917 Detroit City Directory[540]
>   1917 Cusomano Guiseppe
>   (Garafalo Macaroni Mfg Co) r 301 Monroe - with Jno & Philip

1920 census[541] - Detroit SD 145 ED 223 sheet 13b line 51- 288 Riopelle
>   Cusmano, Anna 73 wid - head - 1907 grocery store
>   Girafolo Catherine 44 dau 1905, Joe 38 s-in-law 1905 grocery store
>   Sam 14, Philip 12, Angelo 10 all b. NY

1922 Detroit City Directory
>   Garaffolo, Giuseppe gro 1501 Clinton
>   (street section - just below crossing for Riopelle)

1930 census[542] - Detroit - SD 21 ED 82-179 sh 15a - 1505 Clinton
>   -41 Garofalo, Joe 48 m 18 It It It grocer
>   Catherine wife 55 m 28 Ot
>   Sam 23 NY bondsman / Angelo 20 NY

1940 census[543] - Detroit - SD 1 ED 84-302 sh 41 - 1501 Clinton

65 - Garofalo, Joseph 59 It al same place in 1935 - beer salesman, beer store
>   Catherina wife 66 It
>   Sam 35 It - beer salesman / Bell 25 Va

1941 Aug 19 - died, Detroit[544]
>   Catherine Garofalo - 1874, Italy - Aug. 19, 1941
>   Year of birth estimated from multiple censuses.
>   Date of death is date of burial.
>   Her maiden name may be Cusmano, as her mother Anna Cusmano was
>   living with the family in the 1920 census.
>   Burial: Mount Olivet Cemetery - Section 59, Lot 653, Space 4

---

[540]R. L. Polk & Co's *Detroit City Directory 1917* (Detroit, MI: R. L. Polk & Co, 1917) p 740; database with images, *Ancestry.com,* "U.S. City Directories, 1822-1995" (http://www.ancestry.com: accessed 24 September 2016).

[541]1920 U. S. Federal census, Wayne County, Michigan, population schedule, Detroit, ward 7, enumeration district (ED) 223, sheet 13b, dwelling 152, family 210, Anna Cusmano; image, *Ancestry.com* (http://ancestry.com: accessed 22 Sept 2016); citing NARA microfilm publication T625, roll 8808.

[542]1930 U.S. census, Wayne County, Michigan, population schedule, Detroit wd 7, enumeration district (ED) 82-179, sheet 15a, dwelling 169, family 41, Joe Garofalo; image, *Ancestry.com* (http://ancestry.com: accessed 11 March 2018); NARA microfilm publication T626, no roll no. given..

[543]1940 U. S. Census, Wayne County, Michigan, population schedule, Detroit, ward 7, enumeration district (ED) 84-302, sheet 4a, household 65, Joseph Garofalo; image, *Ancestry.com* (http://ancestry.com: accessed 11 March 2018); citing NARA microfilm publication T627, roll 1850.

[544]*Findagrave.com,* database and images (http://findagrave.com: accessed 25 August 2016), memorial page for Catherine Garofalo, Mt. Olivet Cemetery, Detroit, Wayne, Michigan, Find A Grave Memorial no. 126072926, created by Stephen Cantrell.

7. Salvatore 1877 - 1921 (in the Italian Navy)

8. Philip 1902 NY + Lillian Hoffman (1925), Rose Barcarella (1931),
Eleanor Beauvais (1942)
8. Marino 1908 NY
8. Annie 1909 NY
8. John 1911 NY-1971 + Mary Formicola 1933-1936 div
9 Josephine 1934
+ Dorothy J Palen/Listivan
9. Sam 1935
9. Marion 1939
9. Anna 1940-1940
+ Eleanor Grillo
8. Mary 1911 MI - 1913
8. Mike 1915-1967 + Annie Lobarzhek
9. Sam 1934-1935
8. Joseph 1916-1984 + Lillian (~1938)
9. Sam 1939
9. Rudolph 1940
8. Jack 1918-2003 + Mary Magdalene Tucker (1941)

1877 Nov 1 - born[545]
168 = 106 = 3 Nov 1877 - Salvator
- Philippi G & Anna Orlando (b 3 days ago?)
~1902 - married Giuseppa Calderone
1902 - son Philip b NY
1908 - son Marino b NY
1909 - dau Annie b NY
1910/12 - emigrated
1910 census[546] - NY, Genessee, Oakfield Twp, SD18 ED29, Sheet 10 a
194-220 Fasolda, Joseph 28
Casmano, Sam boarder 25 married 7yrs It em 1910 al
- lab gypsum mill
1911 - son John b NY

---

[545]Maria Santissima delle Grazie, Terrasini, Palermo, Sicily, Italy, Baptismal register,
v. 30, 1873-1881, p. 106, Salvator C baptism 1877; *Family Search.org*, "Battesimi
1873-1889," image 168 of 793.
[546]1910 U. S. Federal Census, Genessee County, New York, population schedule,
Oakfield Township, enumeration district (ED) 29, sheet 10a, dwelling 194, family
220, Sam Casmano; image, *Ancestry.com* (http://ancestry.com: accessed 27 Aug
2016); citing NARA microfilm publication T624, roll 951.

Detroit City Directories[547]

1911 Gusomano Saml (Det Macaroni Mfg Co) bds 296 Congress e - with
    John & Jos

1911 - dau Mary b MI (d 1913)[548]

Mary Gusumano 176 Rivard - b 20 Oct 1911 - d 20 Mar 1913 - 1-5-0
    f Sam Gusumano b It - m Josephine Caldarone b It
    inf Sam - Mt Olivet

1912 Gusumano Saml (Det. Macaroni Mfg Co) bds 176 Rivard
    (with Jno & Jos)

1913 Gusmano Saml (Gusmano Bros) bds 176 Rivard
    (with Jno & Jos)
    Gusumano Saml (Detroit Macaroni Mfg Co) 176 Rivard
    (with Jno & Jos)

1914 Gusmano Saml (Gusmano Bros; Det Macaroni Mfg Co)
    bds 176 Rivard (with Jno & Jos)

1915 - son Mike b MI

1915 Gusimano Saml lab h 626 Congress e

1916 Gusimano Saml mach b 626 Congress

1917 - son Joseph b MI

1918 - WWI Draft Registration[549] - 1918 Sept 12 - ser 3994 ord 3680
    Salvatore Gusmano - 626 Congress - age 40 b 1 Nov 1877 - non
declared alien
    molder Ford
    rel Josie wife
    med ht, stout, brown eyes & hair

1919 - son Jack b MI

1919/20 Cusmano, Saml - lab. h. 626 Congress E

547R. L. Polk, compiler, *Detroit City Directory for the year commencing August 15th, 1911* (Detroit, MI: R. L. Polk & Co, 1911) p nos; database with images, *Ancestry.com,* "U.S. City Directories, 1822-1995" (http://www.ancestry.com: accessed 24 September 2016). And subsequent directories 1912-1922/23.

548"Michigan Death Records, 1867-1950," database with images, *Ancestry.com* (http://ancestry.com: accessed 7 Oct 2016), entry for Mary Gusumano, 20 Mar 1913, file no. 2191; citing Michigan Department of Community Health, Division for Vital Records and Health Statistics.

549"U.S. World War I Draft Registration Cards, 1917-1918," database with images, *Ancestry.com* (http://ancestry.com: accessed 15 Oct 2016), card for Salvatore Gusmano, serial no. 3994, Draft Board 13, Wayne County, Michigan; imaged from Family History Library microfilm.

1920 census[550] - Detroit SD 145 ED 327 sheet 22 wd 11 line 85
 - 626 E. Congress -   Cusumano, Sam 42 1912 machinist factory
          Josephine 41 1912
          Philip 18 b. NY (sic), Marina son 12 NY
           Annie 11, John 9 NY
          Mike 5, Joseph 3, Jack 1 b. Mich
          Bong Hong 87 1903 China - prop laundry
1922/23 Cusmano Saml autowkr h2634 Congress
1923 Oct 27 - died Detroit[551]
Grace Hospital - Salvatore Cusumano aka Gusumano
        - 2636 Congress m w m - wife Giuseppa Caldarone
        b 2 Nov 1877 Italy - 45-11-21 - lab - d 27 Oct 1923
        f Filippo Cusumano b Italy - m Anna Orlando b Italy
        inf Giovanni Cusumano 2636 Congress - Mt Olivet 10-29-23
        ----buried Mt Olivet[552]
        Salvatore Cusumano
        Birth: Nov. 2, 1877 Terrasini Favarotta
        Death: Oct. 27, 1923 Detroit
        Typhoid Fever, Broncho Pneumonia
        Son of Filippo Cusumano and Anna Orlando. Husband of Giuseppa
        Caldarone.
        Brother of Filippo Cusumano, Caterina Cusumano Garofalo, Giuseppe
        Cusumano, Burial: Mount Olivet Cemetery

Children of 7. Salvatore & Giuseppa Calderone

8. Philip 1902 NY
1902 born - NY

---

[550] 1920 U. S. Federal census, Wayne County, Michigan, population schedule, Detroit, ward 11, enumeration district (ED) 328, sheet 22 b, dwelling 28, family 23, Sam Cusonano; image, *Ancestry.com* (http://ancestry.com : accessed 6 September 2016); citing NARA microfilm publication T625, roll 810.
[551] "Michigan Death Records, 1867-1950," database with images, *Ancestry.com* (http://ancestry.com : accessed 21 Sept 2016), entry for Salvatore Cusumano, 27 Oct 1923, no. 58232368, reg. no. 12114; citing Michigan Department of Community Health, Division for Vital Records and Health Statistics
[552] *Findagrave.com*, database and images (http://findagrave.com : accessed 25 August 2016), memorial page for Salvatore Cusumano, Mt. Olivet Cemetery, Detroit, Wayne, Michigan, Find A Grave Memorial no. 148083993, created by "Angie."

1920 census[553] - Mi Wayne Detroit SD 145 ED 327 sheet 22 wd 11 line 85 -
626 E. Congress - Cusumano, Sam 42 1912 machinist factory
        Josephine 41 1912
     Philip 18 b. NY (sic), Marina son 12 NY, Annie 11, John 9 NY
        Mike 5, Joseph 3, Jack 1 b. Mich
        Bong Hong 87 1903 China - prop laundry
1925 - married Lillian Hoffman[554]
     Philip Gusmano 23 res Det b It instructor
     f Salvatore m Josephine Calderone
     Lillian Hoffman 25 res Det b MI cigar maker
     f Lawrence m Agnes Miller - m 1x
     lic 31 Oct 1925 - marriage 7 Nov 1925 - Arthur E Gordon, justice
     - wit Lottie, Louis Serba
1930
1931 - married Rose Bacarella[555]
     Philip Gusmano 28 res Det b It boxer
     f Salvatore, m Josephine Calderone m 1x
     Rose Bacarella 20 res Det b MI - f Joseph, m Frances Mangiapane
     lic 26 May 1931 - marriage 23 July 1931
     name? Judge common pleas - wit Gene & Rose Capella
1934 - wife Rose died[556]
     Rose Gusmano fwm - husband Philip - 9810 Edgewood, Det
     b 22 Mar 1911 Det - d 25 May 1934 - 23-2-13
     (Leland Sanitarium [TB], Ypsi, Washtenaw Co - in for 4 mo 7 d)
     f Joseph Bacarella b It - m Frances Manchpine b It
     inf Leland Sanitarium

---

[553] 1920 U. S. Federal census, Wayne County, Michigan, population schedule, Detroit, ward 11, enumeration district (ED) 328, sheet 22 b, dwelling 28, family 23, Sam Cusonano; image, *Ancestry.com* (http://ancestry.com: accessed 6 September 2016); citing NARA microfilm publication T625, roll 810.

[554] "Michigan Marriage Records, 1867-1952," database with images, *Ancestry.com* (http://ancestry.com: accessed 22 Sept 2016), entry for Philip Gusmano, 1925 (file no. 301430); citing Michigan Department of Community Health, Division for Vital Records and Health Statistics, film no. 186 (1925 Wayne).

[555] "Michigan Marriage Records, 1867-1952," database, *Ancestry.com* (http://ancestry.com: accessed 19 Sept 2016), entry for Philip Gusmano, 1931 (state file no. 86778, county file no. 394351); citing Michigan Department of Community Health, Division for Vital Records and Health Statistics, film no. 257 (82 Wayne 86040-89319).

[556] "Michigan Death Records, 1867-1950," database with images, *Ancestry.com* (http://ancestry.com: accessed 7 Oct 2016), entry for Rose Gusmano, 25 May 1934, file no. 81-4073; citing Michigan Department of Community Health, Division for Vital Records and Health Statistics.

1940
1942 - married Eleanor Beauvais[557]
      Phil Gusmano 39 res Det b Italy f Sam m Josephine Calderone
      Eleanor Beauvais 32 res Det b Mi f Alexander m Georgianna Roger

8. Marino 1908 NY

1908 NY
1920 census[558] - Mi Wayne Detroit SD 145 ED 327 sheet 22 wd 11 line 85 -
626 E. Congress - Cusumano, Sam 42 1912 machinist factory
      Josephine 41 1912
      Philip 18 b. NY (sic), Marina son 12 NY, Annie 11, John 9 NY
            Mike 5, Joseph 3, Jack 1 b. Mich
            Bong Hong 87 1903 China - prop laundry
?1928/29 Cusumano Mario mech r1974 Sherman - with Michl
I think this is Mario/Mike + Betty Orlando s/o Salvatore & Grace Palazzolo

8. Annie 1909 NY

1920 census[559] - Mi Wayne Detroit SD 145 ED 327 sheet 22 wd 11 line 85 -
626 E. Congress - Cusumano, Sam 42 1912 machinist factory
      Josephine 41 1912
      Philip 18 b. NY (sic), Marina son 12 NY, Annie 11, John 9 NY
            Mike 5, Joseph 3, Jack 1 b. Mich
            Bong Hong 87 1903 China - prop laundry

8. John 1911 NY

1911 NY

---

[557]"Michigan Marriage Records, 1867-1952," database, *Ancestry.com*
(http://ancestry.com : accessed 22 Sept 2016), entry for Phil Gusmano, 1942 (state
file no. 273954, county file 592229); citing Michigan Department of Community
Health, Division for Vital Records and Health Statistics, film no. 314 (82 Wayne
272800-276099).
[558]1920 U. S. Federal census, Wayne County, Michigan, population schedule,
Detroit, ward 11, enumeration district (ED) 328, sheet 22 b, dwelling 28, family 23,
Sam Cusonano; image, *Ancestry.com* (http://ancestry.com : accessed 6 September
2016); citing NARA microfilm publication T625, roll 810.
[559]1920 U. S. Federal census, Wayne County, Michigan, population schedule,
Detroit, ward 11, enumeration district (ED) 328, sheet 22 b, dwelling 28, family 23,
Sam Cusonano; image, *Ancestry.com* (http://ancestry.com : accessed 6 September
2016); citing NARA microfilm publication T625, roll 810.

1920 census[560] - Mi Wayne Detroit SD 145 ED 327 sheet 22 wd 11 line 85 -
626 E. Congress - Cusumano, Sam 42 1912 machinist factory
 Josephine 41 1912
 Philip 18 b. NY (sic), Marina son 12 NY, Annie 11, John 9 NY
  Mike 5, Joseph 3, Jack 1 b. Mich
  Bong Hong 87 1903 China - prop laundry
1933 married Mary Formicola[561]
 John Gusmano 23 res Detroit b NY driver f Sam m Josephine
Calderone
 Mary Formicola 18 res Det b MI f Joseph m Catherina Bruno
 lic 18 Mar 1933 - marriage 22 April 1933 - Holy Family
 - Fr Benedict Feretti RC priest - wit James Polisi, Rose Cusumano
1934 - dau Josephine born (= Jay from 1940?)
1936 - divorce[562] - state file #62918 - docket no. 253-881
 John Gusmano - m 22 Apr 1933, Wayne Co - spouse Mary
 papers filed 26 Mar 1936, decree granted 21 Sept 1936 decree
absolute, alimony granted
 1 child, Josephine, age 2
1936 - ex-wife married Mike Saputo[563]
 Mike Saputo 31 res Det b It lab f Joseph m Virginia Vitale
 Mary Cusmano 21 res Det b MI
 f Joseph Formicola m Catherine Burno - m1x, div
 lic 15 Oct 1936 - marriage 24 Oct 1936
 - wit Jack & Virginia Palazzoli - Charles Retbiner judge

All from here on is speculation

---

[560]1920 U. S. Federal census, Wayne County, Michigan, population schedule,
Detroit, ward 11, enumeration district (ED) 328, sheet 22 b, dwelling 28, family 23,
Sam Cusonano; image, *Ancestry.com* (http://ancestry.com: accessed 6 September
2016); citing NARA microfilm publication T625, roll 810.
[561]"Michigan Marriage Records, 1867-1952," database with images, *Ancestry.com*
(http://ancestry.com: accessed 22 Sept 2016), entry for John Gusmano, 1933 (state
file no. 106946, county file no. 417756); citing Michigan Department of Community
Health, Division for Vital Records and Health Statistics, film no. 263 (82 Wayne
105600-108899).
[562]"Michigan, Divorce Records, 1897-1952," database with images, *Ancestry.com*
(http://ancestry.com: accessed 29 Oct 2016), entry for John Gusmano, 1936 (state
file no. 62918, docket no. 253-881); citing Michigan Department of Community
Health, Division for Vital Records and Health Statistics, Lansing, Michigan.
[563]"Michigan Marriage Records, 1867-1952," database with images, *Ancestry.com*
(http://ancestry.com: accessed 4 Oct 2016), entry for Mary Gusmano, 1936 (state file
no. 169453, county file no. 486728); citing Michigan Department of Community
Health, Division for Vital Records and Health Statistics, film no. 282 (82 Wayne
167751-171079).

???19xx (1932?) - married Dorothy Palen/Listivan

1935 - son Sam born

1939 - son Marion born

1940 - dau Anna born & died[564]

Baby Anna Gusmano 768 Navahoe - b 2 Jan 1940 - d 4 Jan 1940 - age 2d
> f John b Oakfield NY, m Dorothy Listivan b Albany NY
>
> inf Anna Gusmano 768 Navahoe - Mt Olivet

Detroit City Directory 1939[565]
> 1939 Gusmano John (Dorothy A) assmblr h768 Navahoe

1940 census[566] - Michigan Wayne Detroit wd 21 SD14 ED84-1362 sheet 4a -
768 Navahoe - hh64
> Cusmano John 31 m8 NY utility man auto mfg - same place
> > Dorothy 29 m8 NY
> >
> > Jay dau 6 / Sam 5 / Marion son 1 - all MI

1945 - wife Dorothy died[567] - Eloise, Wayne, MI
> Dorothy Gusmano b 28 Nov 1911 NY
>
> - d 16 June 1945 Eloise, Wayne Co - age 33
>
> f Walter Palen - m Anna   [husband John Gusmano b NY]

19xx - married Eleanor Grillo
> *The only source I have for this is a couple of online family trees.*

1971 Aug 3 - died[568]

– John Gusmano SSN: 375-05-3861

---

[564]"Michigan Death Records, 1867-1950," database with images, *Ancestry.com*
(http://ancestry.com: accessed 5 Oct 2016), entry for Anna Gusmano, 4 Jan 1940,
state no. 259942, local 125; citing Michigan Department of Community Health,
Division for Vital Records and Health Statistics.

[565][Polk's Detroit (Wayne County, Michigan) City Directory 1939] [I do not actually
have the bib info], p. 688; "U.S. City Directories, 1822-1995," database with images,
Ancestry.com (http://www.ancestry.com: accessed 23 Oct 2016).

[566]1940 U. S. Census, Wayne County, Michigan, population schedule, Detroit, ward
21, enumeration district (ED) 84-1362, sheet 4a, household 64, John Cusmano;
image, *Ancestry.com* (http://ancestry.com: accessed 9 Oct 2016); citing NARA
microfilm publication T627, roll 1880.

[567]"Michigan Death Records, 1867-1950," database, *Ancestry.com*
(http://ancestry.com: accessed 5 Oct 2016), entry for Dorothy Gusmano, 16 June
1945, no. 02682; citing Michigan Department of Community Health, Division for
Vital Records and Health Statistics.

[568]"Michigan, Death Index, 1971-1996," *Ancestry.com* (http://ancestry.com: accessed
5 Oct 2016), entry for John Gusmano, 3 Aug 1971; citing Michigan Department of
Vital and Health Records, *Michigan Death Index*, Lansing, MI. And Social Security
Administration, "U.S., Social Security Death Index, 1935-2014," database,
Ancestry.com (http://ancestry.com: accessed 29 Oct 2016), entry for John Gusmano,
1971, SS no. 375-05-3861.

Last Residence: 48043 Mount Clemens, Macomb, Michigan, USA
        b 1 Mar 1910 - d Aug 1971
    SSN issued: Michigan (Before 1951)
– Buried Resurrection Cemetery[569]
    John Gusmano   Date of Death: AUGUST 3, 1971
    Resurrection Cemetery - Section 21, Lot 636, Space 3

2009 - wife Eleanor died, buried Resurrection Cemetery
    Eleanor Gusmano   Date of Death: FEBRUARY 9, 2009
    Resurrection Cemetery Section 21, Lot 636, Space 4

8. Mike 1915

1914 Mar 1 - born MI
    (the exact date comes from the Cusmano Family Tree - pcusmano1 -
on Ancestry - accessed 29 Oct 2016)
1920 census[570] - Mi Wayne Detroit SD 145 ED 327 sheet 22 wd 11 line 85 -
626 E. Congress - Cusumano, Sam 42 1912 machinist factory
    Josephine 41 1912
    Philip 18 b. NY (sic), Marina son 12 NY, Annie 11, John 9 NY
        Mike 5, Joseph 3, Jack 1 b. Mich
        Bong Hong 87 1903 China - prop laundry
1930
19xx - married Annie Lobarzhek
Detroit City Directories[571]
1934 Cusmano Mike (Anna) diemaker h1033 Canton - with Josephine
1934 - son Sam b (d 1935)[572]
Sam Cusmano 3343 Hendricks - b 2 Feb 1934 - d 39 Mar 1935 - age 1-1-27
    f Mike b Detroit - m Anne Lobarzhek b Det

---

[569]Mt. Elliott Cemetery Association, database (http://www.mtelliott.com/genealogy/ :
accessed 29 August 2016), Resurrection Cemetery, Clinton Twp., Macomb Co.,
entries for John (3 August 1971) and Eleanor (9 Feb 2009) Gusmano.
[570]1920 U. S. Federal census, Wayne County, Michigan, population schedule,
Detroit, ward 11, enumeration district (ED) 328, sheet 22 b, dwelling 28, family 23,
Sam Cusonano; image, *Ancestry.com* (http://ancestry.com : accessed 6 September
2016); citing NARA microfilm publication T625, roll 810.
[571]*Polk's Detroit (Wayne County, Michigan) City Directory 1934 vol. LXXI* (Detroit,
MI: R. L. Polk & Co, 1934) p. 521,794; database with images, Ancestry.com
(http://www.ancestry.com : accessed 11 Oct 2016). And subsequent directory for
1935.
[572]"Michigan Death Records, 1867-1950," database with images, *Ancestry.com*
(http://ancestry.com : accessed 6 Oct 2016), entry for Sam Cusmano, 29 March 1935,
state file no. 194786, reg no. 3842; citing Michigan Department of Community
Health, Division for Vital Records and Health Statistics.

inf father - Mt Olivet

1935 Cusmano Michl (Anna) autowkr h3343 Hendricks apt 2

1940 census[573] - Mi Wayne Detroit wd 21 SD14 ED84-1486 sheet 216b -
5080 Alter Rd - 52 Cusmano Jacob head 22s MI same place lab foundry
 Michael brother 25m MI same place assembler automobile
manufacture / Annie sister/law 25m MI same place
 Josephine mother 62 wd It same place
 - 53 Cusmano Joseph head 23 m Mi same place
  assembler automobile hardware
  Jillian? [indexed William] wife 22 Mi same place
  Samuel 1 / Rudolph 5/12

1967 Sept - died - buried Mt Olivet[574]
 Mike Cusmano - Date of Interment: 09/26/1967
 Mt. Olivet Cemetery - Section Q, Lot 1581, Space 1

1994 - wife Anne died - buried Mt Olivet
 Ann Cusmano -Date of Interment: 08/01/1994
 Mt. Olivet Cemetery - Section Q, Lot 1581, Space 2

8. Joseph 1917

1916 Apr 26 - born MI
 (the exact date - and the middle name Nicholas - comes from the
 Cusmano Family Tree - pcusmano1 - on Ancestry - accessed 29 Oct
 2016)

1920 census[575] - Mi Wayne Detroit SD 145 ED 327 sheet 22 wd 11 line 85 -
626 E. Congress - Cusumano, Sam 42 1912 machinist factory
 Josephine 41 1912
 Philip 18 b. NY (sic), Marina son 12 NY, Annie 11, John 9 NY
  Mike 5, Joseph 3, Jack 1 b. Mich
  Bong Hong 87 1903 China - prop laundry

1930

---

[573] 1940 U. S. Census, Wayne County, Michigan, population schedule, Detroit, ward 21, enumeration district (ED) 84-1486, sheet 216b, household 52, Jacob Cusmano and household 53 Joseph Cusmano [indexed Cusmans]; image, *Ancestry.com* (http://ancestry.com: accessed 9 Oct 2016); citing NARA microfilm publication T627, roll 1884.

[574] Mt. Elliott Cemetery Association, database (http://www.mtelliott.com/genealogy/ : accessed 29 August 2016), Mt Olivet Cemetery (Detroit, Wayne, MI), entries for Mike (Sept 1967) and Anne (1994) Cusmano.

[575] 1920 U. S. Federal census, Wayne County, Michigan, population schedule, Detroit, ward 11, enumeration district (ED) 328, sheet 22 b, dwelling 28, family 23, Sam Cusonano; image, *Ancestry.com* (http://ancestry.com: accessed 6 September 2016); citing NARA microfilm publication T625, roll 810.

Detroit City Directories[576]

1935 Cusmano Jos autowkr r1033 Canton - with Josephine

~1938 - married Lillian

1939 Cusmano Jos N (Lillian) autowkr h5080 Alter - with Jas, Josephine

1940 census[577] - Mi Wayne Detroit wd 21 SD14 ED84-1486 sheet 216b - 5080 Alter Rd

52 Cusmano Jacob head 22s MI same place lab foundry

     Michael brother 25m MI same place assembler automobile manufacture / Annie sister/law 25m MI same place

     Josephine mother 62 wd It same place

53 Cusmano Joseph head 23 m Mi same place assembler automobile hardward

     Jillian? [indexed William] wife 22 Mi same place

     Samuel 1 / Rudolph 5/12

     ?1984 Feb 13 - died

1984 died?

     Joseph N. Cusmano

     Date of Death: December 6, 1984 Date of Interment: 12/10/1984

     Resurrection Cemetery Section 4, Lot 590, Space 5

2004 - wife Lillian died

     Lillian Cusmano

     Date of Death: March 22, 2004 Date of Interment: 03/25/2004

     Resurrection Cemetery Section 4, Lot 590, Space 6

Both are buried in Resurrection Cemetery[578]

8. Jack 1919

1918 July 11- MI

     (the exact date - and the middle name Noel - comes from the Cusmano Family Tree - pcusmano1 - on Ancestry - accessed 29 Oct 2016)

---

[576]*Polk's Detroit (Wayne County, Michigan) City Directory 1935 vol LXXII* (Detroit, MI: R. L. Polk & Co, 1935); database with images, Ancestry.com (http://www.ancestry.com: accessed 11 Oct 2016). And subsequent directory for 1939.

[577]1940 U. S. Census, Wayne County, Michigan, population schedule, Detroit, ward 21, enumeration district (ED) 84-1486, sheet 216b, household 52, Jacob Cusmano and household 53 Joseph Cusmano [indexed Cusmans]; image, *Ancestry.com* (http://ancestry.com: accessed 9 Oct 2016); citing NARA microfilm publication T627, roll 1884.

[578]Mt. Elliott Cemetery Association, database (http://www.mtelliott.com/genealogy/ : accessed 29 August 2016), Resurrection Cemetery (Clinton Twp, Macomb, MI), entries for Joseph (13 Feb 1984) and Lillian (22 March 2004) Cusmano.

1920 census[579] - Mi Wayne Detroit SD 145 ED 327 sheet 22 wd 11 line 85 -
626 E. Congress - Cusumano, Sam 42 1912 machinist factory
       Josephine 41 1912
       Philip 18 b. NY (sic), Marina son 12 NY, Annie 11, John 9 NY
              Mike 5, Joseph 3, Jack 1 b. Mich
              Bong Hong 87 1903 China - prop laundry
1930
1939 Detroit City Directory[580]
       1939 Cusmano Jack autowkr r5680 Alter - with Jos N, Josephine
1940 census[581] - Mi Wayne Detroit wd 21 SD14 ED84-1486 sheet 216b -
5080 Alter Rd
52 Cusmano Jacob head 22s MI same place lab foundry
       -Michael brother 25m MI same place assembler automobile
manufacture / Annie sister/law 25m MI same place
       Josephine mother 62 wd It same place
53 Cusmano Joseph head 23 m Mi same place assembler automobile
hardware
       Jillian? [indexed William] wife 22 Mi same place
       Samuel 1 / Rudolph 5/12
1941 Aug 13 - m Mary Magdalene Tucker[582]
       Jack Cusmano 23 res Det b MI f Salvatore m Josephine Caldarone
       marriage 13 Aug 1941 - Bass Line, Macomb to Mary Magdalene Tucker

---

[579] 1920 U. S. Federal census, Wayne County, Michigan, population schedule,
Detroit, ward 11, enumeration district (ED) 328, sheet 22 b, dwelling 28, family 23,
Sam Cusonano; image, *Ancestry.com* (http://ancestry.com: accessed 6 September
2016); citing NARA microfilm publication T625, roll 810.

[580] [Polk's Detroit (Wayne County, Michigan) City Directory 1939] [I do not actually
have the bib info], p. 417; "U.S. City Directories, 1822-1995," database with images,
Ancestry.com (http://www.ancestry.com: accessed 23 Oct 2016).

[581] 1940 U. S. Census, Wayne County, Michigan, population schedule, Detroit, ward
21, enumeration district (ED) 84-1486, sheet 216b, household 52, Jacob Cusmano
and household 53 Joseph Cusmano [indexed Cusmans]; image, *Ancestry.com*
(http://ancestry.com: accessed 9 Oct 2016); citing NARA microfilm publication
T627, roll 1884.

[582] "Michigan Marriage Records, 1867-1952," database, *Ancestry.com*
(http://ancestry.com: accessed 23 Sept 2016), entry for Jack Cusmano, 1941 (state
file no. 252061, county file no. 570604); citing Michigan Department of Community
Health, Division for Vital Records and Health Statistics, film no. 307 (82 Wayne
249900-253199).

2003 Feb 13 - died - buried Resurrection Cemetery[583]
        Jack N. Cusmano
        Date of Death: February 13, 2003 Date of Interment: 02/18/2003
        Resurrection Cemetery Section 29, Lot 811, Space 3
2013 Oct - wife Mary died - buried Resurrection Cemetery
        Cusmano, Mary M.   Date of Interment: 10/18/2013
        Resurrection Cemetery Section 29, Lot 811, Space 4

7. Francesco Paolo 1880

This is Paul who married Rosalia, Grandpa Jack's sister.
        8. Anna 1907 NY - 1982 MI + Vincenzo Bommarito
                9. Peter 1923
                9. Margaret 1931
        8. Lena 1909 NY-1992 MI + Anthony Cusenza (1926)
                9. Leona ~1927 + – Sambone
                9. Leonard (Tony) 1929
            + Joseph C Cortese
                9. William
                9. Mary
        8. Philip 1914 MI - 1989 MI + Frances Manzo (1940)
        8. John 1915-2007 + Ruth Koelsch (1940)
                9. Paul
                9. Rose
        8. Frances 1916-1916
        8. Joe 1917-1918
        8. Joe 1919-1920
        8. Frances 1920-2002 + Peter Zbercot
                9. Veronica
                9. John
        8. Mary 1922-1999 + James Wayne
                9. Anthony
            + – Drew
        8. Lorenza 1925-26
1880 Oct 29 born, Terrasini, son of Filippo and Anna Orlando Gusumano[584]
        257 = 184 = 30 Oct 1880 b yest - Francesco Paolo
                - Philippo G & Anna Orlando

---

[583]Mt. Elliott Cemetery Association, database (http://www.mtelliott.com/genealogy/ :
accessed 29 August 2016), Resurrection Cemetery (Clinton Twp, Macomb, MI),
entries for Jack N (13 Feb 2003) and Mary M (2013) Cusmano.
[584]Municipio di Terrasini, Provincia di Palermo, certificato di nascita no. 218 (1880),
Francesco Paolo Gusmano; Terrasini Ufficio Stato Civile..

1899 Feb 27 - received a Foglio di Ricognizione (I think an ID card)[585]
   "per le persone della gente di mare di seconda categorico" - reg no.
   16968 - pescatore
190x Jan 1 - Napoli - received a Certificato di Buona Condotta[586]
   not sure what this was - it seemed to be an unlimited leave, signed by
   the captain of the vessel. (He was, according to Dan Mallory, in the
   Italian Navy.)[587]
1905 - married Rosalia G[588]
   46 = 19 = 15 March 1905 - Francesco Paolo G
      - Filippo & Anna Orlando
      Rosalia G - Joannes & Antonina M
1905 - emigrated to US[589]

   I haven't found the ship on which he sailed, but Dan found this
document - it's some sort of pre-emigration form: "Domande alle quali
deve rispondere l'emigrante prima di ricevere il biglietto d'imbarco per
New York." I think it means "questions which the emigrant needs to
answer before getting a ticket to NY" - and there is a NB which says
that they will have to answer these same questions in the same way
when the arrive in the US: false statements are subject to fine or
imprisonment. [note - I didn't write down all the questions - some of
them were stupid, like are you a polygamist and so forth.]

   Gusumano, Fr Paolo 24 male married mariner Italian citizen
born Terrasini, Palermo, going to Oakfield Box ——, ticket paid for by
self, going to brother Gusumano, Salvatore, Oakfield Box 297, good
health, not a criminal or a polygamist.

---

[585]Capitianeria di Porto, Palermo, Foglio di Ricognizione; Mallory Family Collection,
privately owned by Daniel Mallory, email private; scanned image sent to Lee
Bothwell, 29 Aug 2016.
[586]Certificato di Buona Condotta, Mallory Family Collection, privately owned by
Daniel Mallory, email private; scanned image sent to Lee Bothwell, 29 Aug 2016.
[587] Daniel Mallory, "John Joseph Cusmano,"Mallory Family Collection, privately
owned by Daniel Mallory, email private; scanned image sent to Lee Bothwell, 29
Aug 2016.
[588]Maria Santissima delle Grazie (Chiesa Madre [Mother Church]), Terrasini,
Palermo, Sicily, Italy, Marriage register, v. X, 1904-1909, p.19, Francesco Paolo
Gusmano marriage 1905; *Family Search.org*, "Matrimoni 1905-1911," image 46 of
264).
[589]Mallory, "John Joseph Cusmano."

1905 Sept 2 -Rosalia arrived on the *Neapolitan Prince* (Palermo to NY)[590]
Cusumano, Rosalia 19 f married - from Terrasini - going to my
husband Cusumano, Paolo, Box 342 Oakfield, NY
The rest of the information I gathered about them and their children is in
Section II, part 8a Rosalia - p. 99.

7. Filippo 1883-1939
+ Josephine Bommarito -> NY, **Detroit**
8. Philip 1905 NY + Lena Rina (1929)
9. Philip 1930
9. John 1931
8. Joseph 1906 NY-1946 MI
8. Angelo 1907 NY-1960 MI + Dorothy Celuk (1940)
+ Mary
+ Grazia Bommarito
8. Rosie 1914-1930
8. Anna 1916-1916
8. John 1918
8. Anna 1921
8. Sam 1924-1926

1883 April 20 - baptized[591]
421 = 45 = 20 Apr 1883 - Philippus - Philippo C & Anna Orlando
1902 - emigrated
19xx m Josephine Bommarito
1905 - son Philip b NY
1906 - son Joseph b NY
1907 - son Angelo b NY
1910 - m Mary
1910 census[592] - NY, Genessee, Oakfield Twp, SD18 ED29, Sheet 10 b -
Garibaldi St -

---

[590]Manifest, *Neapolitan Prince*, 2 September 1905, p.51, line 17, Rosalia Cusumano,
age 19; images, "New York Passenger Lists, 1820-1957," *Ancestry.com*
(http://ancestry.com: accessed 27 August 2016).
[591]Maria Santissima delle Grazie, Terrasini, Palermo, Sicily, Italy, Baptismal register,
v. 31, 1882-1889, p. 45, Philippus G baptism 1883; *Family Search.org*, "Battesimi
1873-1889," image 421 of 792.
[592]1910 U. S. Federal Census, Genessee County, New York, population schedule,
Oakfield Township, enumeration district (ED) 29, sheet 10b, dwelling 206, family
239, Philip Cusmano; image, *Ancestry.com* (http://ancestry.com: accessed 27 Aug
2016); citing NARA microfilm publication T624, roll 951.

206-239 Cusmano, Phillip head 26 It em 1902al - lab gypsum mill
(next page 11a)   Mary 18 m1 0yrs It em 1903
                Philip jr 5 NY / Joseph 4 / Angelo 3
19xx - m Grazia Bommarito
1914 - dau Rosie b
Detroit City Directories[593]
1914 Cusmono Philip lab h 185 Rivard
1916 - dau Anna b&d[594]
 Anna Cusumano - 189 Rivard - b 14 Mar 1916 MI
        - d 22 Oct 1916 - age 7m 10d
        f Filippo Cusumano, b It - m Nuzia Bommarito b Terrasini
        inf Filippo - Mt Olivet
        1917 Cusomano Philip (Garafalo Macaroni Mfg Co) b 176 Rivard -
        with Jno & Jos
        Gusmano Philip h 189 Rivard
1918 - son John b
1918 WWI Draft Registration[595] - Sept 12 - ser 4284 ord 1225
        Phillip Cusumano - 189 Rivard - age 34 b 15 June 1884
         - non declared alien It
        macaroni mfg owner 259 Lafayette
        rel - Grace 189 Rivard
        5'8" med build brown eyes black hair
Detroit City Directories
1919/20 Cusumano, Philip - hlpr b. 582 Macomb
1920 census[596] - Michigan Wayne Detroit wd 11 SD 145 ED 329 sheet 13a -
582 Macomb

---

[593]R. L. Polk & Co's *Detroit City Directory for the year commencing Sept 1, 1914*
(Detroit, MI: R. L. Polk & Co, 1914) p 775; database with images, *Ancestry.com,*
"U.S. City Directories, 1822-1995" (http://www.ancestry.com: accessed 24
September 2016). Also several subsequent directories for 1917, 1919/20, through
1935.
[594]"Michigan, Death Records, 1867-1950," database with images, *Ancestry.com*
(http://ancestry.com: accessed 6 Oct 2016), entry for Anna Cusumano, 22 Oct 1916
(file no. 9926); Michigan Department of Community Health, Division for Vital
Records and Health Statistics, Lansing, Michigan.
[595]"U.S. World War I Draft Registration Cards, 1917-1918," database with images,
Ancestry.com (http://ancestry.com: accessed 15 Oct 2016), card for Phillip
Cusumano, serial no. 4284, Draft Board 6, Wayne County, Michigan; imaged from
Family History Library microfilm.
[596]1920 U. S. Federal census, Wayne County, Michigan, population schedule,
Detroit, ward 11, enumeration district (ED) 329, sheet 13a, dwelling 209, family 296,
Philippe Gausmano; image, *Ancestry.com* (http://ancestry.com: accessed 27 Aug
2016); citing NARA microfilm publication T625, roll 810.

209-296 Gausmano, Philipe 36 1903 al It box maker box factory
        Grace 26 1904 It
        Philip 17 NY box maker, box factory / Joseph 15 NY / Angelo
        14 MI / Rosie 6 Mi / John 1 9/12
1921 - dau Anna born
Detroit City Directories
1921/22 Cusmano Philip lab h2700 Macomb
1924 - son Sam b (d 1926)[597]
  Sam Cusumano - 2700 Macomb - b 2 Oct 1924 Det
        - d 10 Apr 1926 - age 1-6-8
        f Filippo Cusumano b Terrasini - m Grazia Bommarito b Palermo
        inf Filippo - Mt Olivet
        (Section 54, Tier 32, Space 744
         - Find A Grave Memorial# 146842033)
1925/26 Cusamana Philip lab h3700 Macomb
1928/29 Cusmano Philip (Grace) lab h2700 Macomb
1930 - dau Rose died[598]
        Rosa Cusumano - 2700 Macomb - fws - b 29 May 1914 Det
        - d 30 Sep 1930 - 16-4-1
        f Filippo Cusumano b Terrasini - m Grazia Bommarito b Terrasini
        inf Filippo - Mt Olivet
        (Section 51, Tier 7, Space 644
         - find-a grave Memorial# 146775196)
Detroit City Directories
1930/31 Cusmano Philip (Grace) r2700 Macomb
1931/32 Cusmano Philip P (Grace) lab h2700 Macomb
1932/33 Cusmano Philip P (Grace) lab h2700 Macomb
1934 Cusmano Philip P (Grace) h2700 Macomb
1935 Cusmano Philip P (Grace) h2700 Macomb
1939 - died Detroit[599]
        ---Philip Cusmano - Deaconess Hospital

---

[597]"Michigan, Death Records, 1867-1950," database with images, *Ancestry.com* (http://ancestry.com: accessed 6 Oct 2016), entry for Sam Cusumano, 10 Apr 1926 (state file no. 582 66432, reg no 5763); Michigan Department of Community Health, Division for Vital Records and Health Statistics, Lansing, Michigan.
[598]"Michigan, Death Records, 1867-1950," database with images, *Ancestry.com* (http://ancestry.com: accessed 6 Oct 2016), entry for Rosa Cusumano, 30 Sep 1930 (state file no. 135710, reg no. 12297); Michigan Department of Community Health, Division for Vital Records and Health Statistics, Lansing, Michigan.
[599]"Michigan Death Records, 1867-1950," database with images, *Ancestry.com* (http://ancestry.com: accessed 20 Sept 2016), entry for Philip Cusmano, 25 Aug 1939, state file no. 255104, reg. no. 9365; citing Michigan Department of Community Health, Division for Vital Records and Health Statistics.

2148 E Fort - in US 32 y - w m m - wife Grazia
b abt 1883 Terrasini - age abt 56 retired - d 25 Aug 1939 Detroit
f Filippo b Terrasini - m Anna Orlando b Terrasini
inf Angelo Cusmano 8004 Townsend
Mt Olivet 28 Aug 1939
- buried Mt Olivet[600]
Filippo "Phillip" Cusmano - 1883 Terrasini Favarotta
- Aug. 25, 1939 Detroit - Coronary Thrombosis
Son of Filippo Cusmano (AKA Cusumano) and Anna Orlando.
Brother of Caterina Cusumano Garofalo, Salvatore Cusumano,
Giuseppe Cusumano
Burial: Mount Olivet Cemetery Plot: Section 60, Tier 6, Space 311
Wife Grace
1940 census[601] - Mi Wayne Detroit wd 11 SD1 ED84-564 sh 9b 2684
Macomb
154 Cusmano Joe head 32s NY same house body assembler auto factory
    Grace mother 47 wd It same place
    John brother 22s MI same place motor assembler auto factory
    Anna sister 19s MI

Children of Filippo & Josephine/Grazia Bommarito

8. Philip 1905 NY

1905 born - NY
1910 - with parents in NY
1920 census[602] - Mi Wayne Detroit SD 145 ED 329 sheet 13a wd 11 - 582
Macomb
    209-296 Gausmano, Philipe 36 1903 al It box maker box factory
        Grace 26 1904 It

---

[600]*Findagrave.com*, database and images (http://findagrave.com: accessed 25 August
2016), memorial page for Filippo "Phillip" Cusmano, Mt. Olivet Cemetery, Detroit,
Wayne, Michigan, Find A Grave Memorial no. 143428498, created by "Angie."
[601]1940 U. S. Census, Wayne County, Michigan, population schedule, Detroit, ward
11, enumeration district (ED) 84-564, sheet 9b, household 154, Joe Cusmino; image,
Ancestry.com (http://ancestry.com: accessed 9 Oct 2016); citing NARA microfilm
publication T627, roll 1858.
[602]1920 U. S. Federal census, Wayne County, Michigan, population schedule,
Detroit, ward 11, enueration district (ED) 329, sheet 13a, dwelling 209, family 296,
Philippe Gausmano; image, *Ancestry.com* (http://ancestry.com: accessed 27 Aug
2016); citing NARA microfilm publication T625, roll 810.

Philip 17 NY box maker, box factory / Joseph 15 NY / Angelo
14 MI / Rosie 6 Mi / John 1 9/12

1928 Sept 29 - m Lena Rini[603]
      Mr Philip Cusmano   29 Sep 1928   Detroit, Wayne
      blotty, diffy to read cert - Philip Gusumano res Det b NY f Philip m
Grace Bommarito
       Lina Rina? (Antonina) - f John m Rose
      wit Michael Grillo, Rosa --- -marriage 29 Sept 1928 -
      Rev Anthony R – catholic priest
1930 - son Philip born
1930 census[604]- Michigan Wayne Detroit wd 13 SD 22 ED 82-375 sheet 5b -
3745 Lafayette - 78-32 Rini, John 48m21 It 1899 al salesman fruit
          Rose 46 m19 It 1899 al
            Anna 20 Mi / John jr 18 / Nicholas 14 / Joseph 9 / Mary5
      Gusmano Philip sr s/law 25 m23 NY salesman fruits & veg
            Lena dau 22 m20 MI
            Philip jr grandson 9/12 MI
Detroit City Directories[605]
1930/31 Gusmano Philip (Lena) pdlr h3745 E Laf
1931 - son John born
1931/32 Gusmano Philip (Lena) driver h3745 E Laf
1934 Gusimino Philip (Rena) h3745 E Laf
1935 Gusmano Philip (Lena) h3745 E Laf
1939 Gusmano Philip (Lena) driver E&BBCo3745 E Lafayette
1940 census[606] - Mi Wayne Det wd 13 SD1 ED84-676 sh4b
- 3745 E Lafayette - 12 - Rini John 59 It same house (all)

---

[603]"Michigan Marriage Records, 1867-1952," database, *Ancestry.com*
(http://ancestry.com: accessed 19 Sept 2016), entry for Philip Cusmano, 1928 (state
file no. 82-47274, county file no. 354429); citing Michigan Department of
Community Health, Division for Vital Records and Health Statistics, film no. 245 (82
Wayne 46850-50159).
[604]1930 U.S. census, Wayne County, Michigan, population schedule, Detroit ward
13, enumeration district (ED) 82-375, sheet 5b, dwelling 78, family 32, Phillip
Gusmano; image, *Ancestry.com* (http://ancestry.com: accessed 8 Oct 2016); citing
FHL microfilm: 2340781; NARA microfilm T626 roll 1046.
[605]R. L. Polk, compiler, *Detroit City Directory, 1930-31* (Detroit, MI: R. L. Polk &
Co, 1930) p. 885; database with images, Ancestry.com (http://www.ancestry.com:
accessed 17 September 2016). And subsequent directories for 1931/32-1939.
[606]1940 U. S. Census, Wayne County, Michigan, population schedule, Detroit, ward
13, enumeration district (ED) 84-676, sheet 4b, household 12, Philip Gusmano;
image, *Ancestry.com* (http://ancestry.com: accessed 26 Oct 2016); citing NARA
microfilm publication T627, roll 1861.

Rose 57 It

Anna 30 Mi teacher / Nick 23 MI stock carrier auto plant /

Joseph 20 porter / Mary 15

Gusmano, Philip s/law 35 NY truck driver, brewery

Lena 32 MI / Philip jr 10 / John 9

8. Joseph 1906 NY

1906 born - NY

1910 - with parents in NY

1920 census[607] - Mi Wayne Detroit - SD 145 ED 329 sheet 13a wd 11 - 582 Macomb

> 209-296 Gausmano, Philipe 36 1903 al It box maker box factory
> > Grace 26 1904 It
> > Philip 17 NY box maker, box factory / Joseph 15 NY / Angelo
> > 14 MI / Rosie 6 Mi / John 1 9/12

1940 census[608] - Mi Wayne Detroit wd 11 SD1 ED84-564 sh 9b

2684 Macomb

154 Cusmano Joe head 32s NY same house body assembler auto factory

> Grace mother 47 wd It same place

> John brother 22s MI same place motor assembler auto factory

> > Anna sister 19s MI

1946 June 12- died[609]

> Joseph Cusmano - m s - b 1906 Oakfield NY - age 40 -
> > d 12 June 1946 Eloise, Wayne Mi
> f Philip Cusmano - m Josephine Bommarito

8. Angelo 1907 NY

1907 born - NY

1910 - with parents in NY

---

[607]1920 U. S. Federal census, Wayne County, Michigan, population schedule, Detroit, ward 11, enueration district (ED) 329, sheet 13a, dwelling 209, family 296, Philippe Gausmano; image, *Ancestry.com* (http://ancestry.com: accessed 27 Aug 2016); citing NARA microfilm publication T625, roll 810.

[608]1940 U. S. Census, Wayne County, Michigan, population schedule, Detroit, ward 11, enumeration district (ED) 84-564, sheet 9b, household 154, Joe Cusmino; image, *Ancestry.com* (http://ancestry.com: accessed 9 Oct 2016); citing NARA microfilm publication T627, roll 1858.

[609]"Michigan Death Records, 1867-1950," database, *Ancestry.com* (http://ancestry.com: accessed 20 Sept 2016), entry for Joseph Cusmano, 12 June 1946, no. 022325; citing Michigan Department of Community Health, Division for Vital Records and Health Statistics.

1920 census[610] - Mi Wayne Detroit - SD 145 ED 329 sheet 13a wd 11 - 582
Macomb
209-296 Gausmano, Philipe 36 1903 al It box maker box factory
          Grace 26 1904 It
          Philip 17 NY box maker, box factory / Joseph 15 NY / Angelo
          14 MI / Rosie 6 Mi / John 1 9/12
1939 - father died - informant = Angelo Cusmano 8004 Townsend
1940 March 26 - m Dorothy S Celuk[611]
      index Angelo Cusmano b ~1908 NY age 32
          f Philip m Grace Bommarito
      Dorothy S Celuk 31 f George m Celia Kuzowski
      m 26 March 1940 Detroit
1960 Feb - died[612] - buried Mt Olivet[613]
      - - Angelo Cusmano SSN: 363-09-4987
      b 5 Aug 1906 - d Feb 1960
      SSN issued: Michigan (Before 1951)
      ---- Angelo Cusmano Date of Interment: 02/05/1960
      Mt. Olivet Cemetery Section 10, Lot 516, Space 7
1996 - wife Dorothy died[614] - buried Mt Olivet[615]
      - - Sophie Doroty Celuk [Dorothy S Cusmano] SSN: 378101663
      b 9 Jul 1907, Wyandotte, Michigan - d 6 Apr 1996
      f George Celuk - m Ceilia Kusinkawski

---

[610]1920 U. S. Federal census, Wayne County, Michigan, population schedule, Detroit, ward 11, enueration district (ED) 329, sheet 13a, dwelling 209, family 296, Philippe Gausmano; image, *Ancestry.com* (http://ancestry.com: accessed 27 Aug 2016); citing NARA microfilm publication T625, roll 810.

[611]"Michigan Marriage Records, 1867-1952," database, *Ancestry.com* (http://ancestry.com: accessed 19 Sept 2016), entry for Angelo Cusmano, 1940 (state file no. 236994, county file no. 526420); citing Michigan Department of Community Health, Division for Vital Records and Health Statistics, film no. 303 (82 Wayne 236770-240059).

[612]Social Security Administration, "United States Social Security Death Index," database, Ancestry.com (http://ancestry.com: accessed 29 Oct 2016), entry for Angelo Cusmano, 1980, SS no. 363-09-4987.

[613]Mt. Elliott Cemetery Association, database (http://www.mtelliott.com/genealogy/ : accessed 29 August 2016), Mt. Olivet Cemetery (Detroit, Wayne, Michigan), entry for Angelo Cusmano (Feb 1960).

[614]Social Security Administration, "United States Social Security Death Index," database, Ancestry.com (http://ancestry.com: accessed 29 Oct 2016), entry for Dorothy Cusmano, 1996, SS no. 378-10-1663.

[615]Mt. Elliott Cemetery Association, database (http://www.mtelliott.com/genealogy/ : accessed 29 August 2016), Mt. Olivet Cemetery (Detroit, Wayne, Michigan), entry for Dorothy Cusmano (Apr 1996).

Type of Claim: Original SSN.
Notes: Jan 1937: Name listed as SOPHIE DOROTY CELUK;
19 Jul 1989: Name listed as DOROTHY S CUSMANO
— Dorothy S. Cusmano - 4 Jul 1904 - 6 Apr 1996
Residence: Hamtramck, Wayne, Michigan
 Place of Death: Hamtramck, Wayne, MI
- - - - Dorothy Cusmano Date of Interment: 04/09/1996
Mt. Olivet Cemetery Section 10, Lot 516, Space 8

8. John 1918

1918 born
1920 - with parents in Detroit
1930
1940 - with mother & siblings in Detroit

8. Anna 1921

1921 - born
1930
1940 - with mother & siblings in Detroit
1941 Aug 23 - m Sam Granata[616]

Sam Granata
Ann Cusmano age 20 res Det b MI f Philip m Grace Bommarito
marriage 23 Aug 1941 - Detroit

7. Antonio 1885 + Marion Sapienza (1906 NY?)

8. Anna 1907 NY
    1910 - with parents in NY
    1920 - with parents in Detroit
    1930
    1940 -
8. Philip 1910 NY + Jennie
    1910 - with parents in NY
    1920 - with parents in Detroit

---

[616]"Michigan Marriage Records, 1867-1952," database, *Ancestry.com*
(http://ancestry.com : accessed 4 Oct 2016), entry for Ann Cusmano, 1941 (state file
no. 252627, county file no. 571388); citing Michigan Department of Community
Health, Division for Vital Records and Health Statistics, film no. 307 (82 Wayne
249900-253199).

1930

~1939 - married Jennie

       7. Anthony P 1940 NY

1940 - in NY

8. Dominic 1911 NY + Rose

    1920 - with parents in MI

    1930

    ~1940 - married Rose

    1940 - in NY

8. Rose 1915 NY

    1920 - with parents in MI

8. Josephine 1918 MI

    1920 - with parents in MI

1885 June 13 - born[617]

  525 = 138 = 14 June 1885 b yest - Antoninus - Philippo G & Anna Orlando

  44 = #138 = 14 June 1885 b yest - Antonio G - Filippo G & Anna Orlando

1900/03 - emigrated

19xx - married Marion (Mary Sapienza)

1907 - dau Anna born

1910 - son Philip born

1910 census[618] - New York, Genessee, Oakfield SD 18 ED 29 sh 11a - Garibaldi St

    207-240 Vintemelia, Joseph head 26 It em 1903 al - lab gypsum mill

        Cusman, Phillip nephew 13 It 1905

    208-241 Cusmano, Tony 25 m1 4yrs It em 1900 - lab gypsum mill

        Mary wife 23 2ch/2liv It em 1899

        Anna 3 NY / Philip 2/12 NY

1911 - son Dominic born

1915 - dau Rose b NY

191x - moved to Detroit

---

[617]Maria Santissima delle Grazie, Terrasini, Palermo, Sicily, Italy, Baptismal register, v. 31, 1882-1889, p. 138, Antonius G baptism 1885; *Family Search.org*, "Battesimi 1873-1889," image 525 of 792. AND Maria Santissima delle Grazie, Terrasini, Palermo, Sicily, Italy, Baptismal register, v. 32, 1884-1889, record no. 138, Antonio G baptism 1885; *Family Search.org*, "Battesimi 1884-1887," image 44 of 103.

[618]1910 U. S. Federal Census, Genessee County, New York, population schedule, Oakfield Township, enumeration district (ED) 29, sheet 11a, dwelling 208, family 241, Tony Cusmano; image, *Ancestry.com* (http://ancestry.com : accessed 4 Sept 2016); citing NARA microfilm publication T624, roll 951.

Detroit City Directories[619]
1916 Cusmano Anthony lab h 297 Clinton
1917 Cusomano Anthony lab h 293 Clinton
1917 June 15 - WWI Draft Registration[620] - no 434 - stamp 1232
Antonio Cusumano - 293 Clinton - age 30 b 11 Nov 1886 Terrasini - alien
    occupation concrete - Jefferson Mills co
    dependents wife and 4 children (claims exemption)
    ht tall build med brown eyes black hair
1918 Casumano Anthony lab h293 Clinton
1918 - dau Josephine b MI
1920 census[621] - Detroit SD 1 ED 223 sheet 13a - wd 7 line 44 Cusmano
Tony - 293 Clinton
    151-209 Cusmano, Tony 33 1903, Marion 30 1905 - lab plaster mill
        Ann 14, Philip 11, Dominic 9, Rose 5 all b. NY
        Josephine 2 b. Mich
Detroit City Directories
1920/21 Gusumano Tony lab b 2665 (409) Sherman - with Saml
1921/22 Cusimano Anthony plstr h2683 Sherman
1921 - dau Anna m Tony Lentini[622]
    Tony Lentina 26 res Det b It salesman
    f Liberato m Magdalen Pasqual?
    Anna Cusmano 16 res Det b NY f Tony m Maria Sapienza
    lic 22 Sep - marriage 22 Sept 1921 - L Eugene Sharp, justice
    wit Gene Grande, Casare Pellerito
19xx - moved back to NY

---

[619]R. L. Polk & Co's *Detroit City Directory for the year commencing Sept 1, 1916*
(Detroit, MI: R. L. Polk & Co, 1916) p. 922; database with images, *Ancestry.com,*
"U.S. City Directories, 1822-1995" (http://www.ancestry.com: accessed 24
September 2016). Also selected subsequent directories to 1921/22
[620]"U.S. World War I Draft Registration Cards, 1917-1918," database with images,
Ancestry.com (http://ancestry.com: accessed 15 Oct 2016), card for Antonio
Cusumano, serial no. 434, Draft Board 8, Wayne County, Michigan; imaged from
Family History Library microfilm.
[621]1920 U. S. Federal census, Wayne County, Michigan, population schedule,
Detroit, ward 7, enumeration district (ED) 223, sheet 13a, dwelling 151, family 209,
Tony Cusmano; image, *Ancestry.com* (http://ancestry.com: accessed 27 Aug 2016);
citing NARA microfilm publication T625, roll 808.
[622]"Michigan Marriage Records, 1867-1952," database with images, *Ancestry.com*
(http://ancestry.com: accessed 23 Sept 2016), entry for Anna Cusmano, 1921 (no.
219586); citing Michigan Department of Community Health, Division for Vital
Records.

1925 New York State Census[623] - Oakfield, Genesee p 18 (Garibaldi)
>   Cusmano, Tony w m 40 Italy 20 yrs in US al lab canning factory
>   Marian 38 Italy 21 yrs in US al
>   (p. 19) Phil 16 / Dominick 14 / Rose 10 / Josephine 7
1930 census[624] - NY Genesee Oakfield SD8 Ed 19-32, sheet 15 a - South St
157-372 Lentine Tony 34 m 25 It something in gypsum mill
>   Anna 23 m 14 NY
>   Madeline 6 / Albert 6 [? Index says 5 - diffy to read] / Anthony 3
>   Phillip and Jack 1 2/12 - all b NY
358-373 Cusmans, Tony mw 45 m age 21 It - em 1914 al lab canning factory
>   Mary 43 m 19 It em 1914
>   Philip 21 / Dominic 19 / Rose 15 / Josephine 13
>   Fontana, Steve
1940 census[625] - NY Genesee Oakfield SD39 ED19-32 sh 11b - S. Oak St -
household 210 - Cusmano, Dominic 28 NY - lab canning factory
>   Rose 29 NY
household 206 - Cusmano, Anthony 54 Italy papers applied for
>   - laborer canning factory
>   Marion 53 wife Italy / Josephine 22 Mich - lab, canning factory
household 207 - Cusmano, Philip 30 NY - lab canning factory
>   Jennie 29 wife Argentina, South America
>   Anthony P 8/12 NY
1953 Jan 7 - life claim to SS[626] (for retirement or disability)
>   Tony Cusmano b 16 Mar 1887, Italy
>   Claim Date: 7 Jan 1953 - Life Claim
>   03 Dec 1976: Name listed as TONY CUSMANO

---

[623] 1925 New York state census, Genesee county, population schedule, Oakfield, p. 18, for Tony Cusmano household; image, Ancestry.com (http://ancestry.com: accessed 22 Sept 2016); citing New York State Archives, state poplulation schedules, 1925.

[624] 1930 U.S. census, Genesee County, New York, population schedule, Oakfield, enumeration district (ED) 19-32, sheet 15a, dwelling 358, family 373, Tony Cusmano [indexed Cacenaur]; image, *Ancestry.com* (http://ancestry.com: accessed 8 Oct 2016); citing FHL microfilm 2341175; NARA microfilm T626 roll 1440. Also family 372 Tony Lentine [indexed Lentrue].

[625] 1940 U. S. Federal Census, Genessee County, New York, population schedule, Oakfield Township, enumeration district (ED) 19-42, sheet 11a, household(s) 201, 206, 207, Dominick, Anthony, Philip Cusmano; image Ancestry.com (http://ancestry.com: accessed 8 September 2016); citing NARA microfilm publication T627, roll 2539.

[626] Social Security Administration, "U.S., Social Security Applications and Claims Index, 1936-2007," database, Ancestry.com (http://ancestry.com: accessed 30 Oct 2016), entry for Tony Cusmano, 1953, life claim [no SS# given].

Children of Antonio & Mary Sapienza

8. Anna

1907 - born

1910 - with parents in NY

1920 - with parents in Detroit

1921 - married Tony Lentine[627]

    Tony Lentina 26 res Det b It salesman

    f Liberato m Magdalen Pasqual?

    Anna Cusmano 16 res Det b NY f Tony m Maria Sapienza

    lic 22 Sep - marriage 22 Sept 1921 - L Eugene Sharp, justice

    wit Gene Grande, Casare Pellerito

192x - moved back to NY

1930 census[628] - NY Genesee Oakfield SD8 Ed 19-32, sheet 15 a - South St

157-372 Lentine Tony 34 m 25 It something in gypsum mill

    Anna 23 m 14 NY

    Madeline 6 / Albert 6 [? Index says 5 - diffy to read] / Anthony 3

        Phillip and Jack 1 2/12 - all b NY

358-373 Cusmans, Tony mw 45 m age 21 It - em 1914 al lab canning factory

    Mary 43 m 19 It em 1914

    Philip 21 / Dominic 19 / Rose 15 / Josephine 13

    Fontana, Steve

193x - moved back to MI

1940 census[629] - MI Wayne Detroit wd 13 - SD1 ED84-676 sh 8a

 - 3385 E Fort

124 Lentine, Anthony 46 It - same place in 1935 - tire decorator, tire factory

    Anna 32 NY / Madeline 16 / Albert 15 / Anthony jr 13 / Jack 11 /

    Phillip 11 - all b NY /   Mary 1 MI

---

[627]"Michigan Marriage Records, 1867-1952," database with images, *Ancestry.com* (http://ancestry.com: accessed 23 Sept 2016), entry for Anna Cusmano, 1921 (no. 219586); citing Michigan Department of Community Health, Division for Vital Records.

[628]1930 U.S. census, Genesee County, New York, population schedule, Oakfield, enumeration district (ED) 19-32, sheet 15a, dwelling 358, family 373, Tony Cusmano [indexed Cacenaur]; image, *Ancestry.com* (http://ancestry.com: accessed 8 Oct 2016); citing FHL microfilm 2341175; NARA microfilm T626 roll 1440. Also family 372 Tony Lentine [indexed Lentrue].

[629]1940 U. S. Federal Census, Wayne County, Michigan, population schedule, Detroit, ward 13, enumeration district (ED) 84-676, sheet 8a, household 124, Anthony Lentine; image Ancestry.com (http://ancestry.com: accessed 8 September 2016); citing NARA microfilm publication T627, roll 1876. (Also family 125, Salvatore Serra [indexed Sarra].)

1987 - died (living at St Clair Shores)

8. Philip s/o Tony & Marion gs/o Filippo Gusumano & Anna Orlando,
ggs/o Giovanni Cusumano & Francesca Paola Bommarito
1910 born - NY
1910 - with parents in NY
1920 - with parents in Detroit
19xx married Jennie LNU
1940 - son Anthony P born NY
1940 census[630] - NY Genessee Oakfield SD39 ED19-32 sheet 11b - South
Oak St - household 207 - Cusmano, Philip 30 NY - lab canning factory
          Jennie 29 wife Argentina, South America
          Anthony P 8/12 NY

8. Dominic s/o Tony & Marion gs/o Filippo Gusumano & Anna Orlando,
ggs/o Giovanni Cusumano & Francesca Paola Bommarito
1911 born - NY
1920 - with parents in MI
19xx - married Rose
Detroit City Directories[631]
?1930/31 Cusmano Dominic (Rose) lab h 2729 E Laf
1940 census[632] - NY Genessee Oakfield SD39 ED19-32 sheet 11b
- South Oak St
household 201 - Cusmano, Dominic 28 NY - lab canning factory
          Rose 29 NY

---

[630]1940 U. S. Federal Census, Genessee County, New York, population schedule,
Oakfield Township, enumeration district (ED) 19-42, sheet 11a, household 207,
Philip Cusmano; image Ancestry.com (http://ancestry.com: accessed 8 September
2016); citing NARA microfilm publication T627, roll 2539.
[631]R. L. Polk, compiler, *Detroit City Directory, 1930-31* (Detroit, MI: R. L. Polk &
Co, 1930) p. 617; database with images, Ancestry.com (http://www.ancestry.com:
accessed 17 September 2016).
[632]1940 U. S. Federal Census, Genessee County, New York, population schedule,
Oakfield Township, enumeration district (ED) 19-42, sheet 11a, household(s) 201,
206, 207, Dominick, Anthony, Philip Cusmano; image Ancestry.com
(http://ancestry.com: accessed 8 September 2016); citing NARA microfilm
publication T627, roll 2539.

Descendants of the OTHER Giovanni

Alternate Giovanni, 1841- + Ignatia Napolitano

This is the second Giovanni to be born to Giovanni and Francesca Paola Bommarito. It is possible that he is actually our Great Grandfather, if we assume our GG was a bigamist, and everyone in Terrasini - priests, relatives, friends - was ok with that. I don't think that is terribly likely, so it is easier to assume that for some reason Giovanni and Francesca Paola gave two sons the same name. Giovanni-the-father had a another son (Angelo) who also named two of his sons Giovanni.

I have no information about him except what is in the church records, and I have no idea what he did for a living or when he died. After the birth of Marianna in 1888, he disappears from the records, so possibly he moved to another city, or possibly he emigrated. Three of his children did emigrate, and ended up in Detroit.

1836-1840 - born, Terrasini, Palermo, Sicily - son of Giovanni & Francesca Paola Bommarito

    1836 May 6 - baptized Maria Santissima delle Grazie, Terrasini[633]

        328 = 3 = 6 May 1836 (3) - Joannes G

            - Joannes G & Francesca Paola Bommarito

    1840 Aug 2 - baptized Maria Santissima delle Grazie, Terrasini[634]

        403 = 74 = 2 Aug 1840 b today - Joannes

            - Joanne G & Francesca Paola Bommarito

    1841 born - based on marriage license (married 1867, age 26)[635]

1867 May 12 - married Ignazia (Agnes) Napolitano[636]

    194 = 57 = 12 May 1867 - Joannes G -

        s/o Joannes & Francesca Paola Bommarito

        Ignatia Napolitano

---

[633]Maria Santissima delle Grazie (Chiesa Madre [Mother Church]), Terrasini, Palermo, Sicily, Italy, Baptismal register, 1835-1869, v. 20, p. 3, Joannes Gusmano baptism 1836; *Family Search.org*, "Battesimi 1818-1869," image 328 of 485.

[634]Maria Santissima delle Grazie (Chiesa Madre [Mother Church]), Terrasini, Palermo, Sicily, Italy, Baptismal register, v. 20, 1835-1869, p. 74, Joannes Gusmano baptism 1840; *FamilySearch.org,* "Battesimi 1818-1869," image 403 of 485.

[635]Palermo (Palermo), Ufficio dello stato civile, "Registro degli atti di Matrimonio [Register of Marriages], 1867" : entry #14, Giovanni Gusmano; digital images, *FamilySearch.org*, "Italia, Palermo, Palermo, Stato Civile (Tribunale), 1866-1910," (https://familysearch.org/ark:/61903/3:1:3QSQ-G97B-27ZM?cc=2051639&wc=MC TM-1TG%3A351055601%2C353722501%2C353605302 : 22 May 2014), Palermo > Terrasini > image 44 of 2313; citing Tribunale di Cagliari (Cagliari Court, Cagliari).

[636]Maria Santissima delle Grazie (Chiesa Madre [Mother Church]), Terrasini, Palermo, Sicily, Italy, Marriage register, v. 45, 1862-1878, p. 57, Joannes Gusmano marriage 1867; *Family Search.org*, "Matrimoni 1814-1878," image 194 of 453.

44 = 14 = Giovanni Gusmano 26, Terrasini
        s/o Giovanni & Fra Paola Bommarito
    Ignatia Napolitano 23 Terr
        d/o Filippo & Rosalia Consiglio [637]
1868 Feb 20 - son Giovanni born, named after paternal grandfather[638]
    baptized Maria Santissima delle Grazie, Terrasini
    264 = 114 = 21 Feb 1868 b yest conditional baptism - Joannes G s/o
        Joane G & Ignatia Napolitano
        (Godfather Salvator Orlando)
1869 April 29 - son Philip born, named after maternal grandfather[639]
    baptized Maria Santissima delle Grazie, Terrasini
    298 = 146 = 30 Apr 1869 b yest - Philippus G
        s/o Joannes & Ignatia Napolitano
        (Godfather Antonius Napolitano)
1869 - son Giovanni died[640]
    131 = 89 = 10 Aug 1869 - Joannes G
        - Joannes & Ignatia Napolitano
1871 Jan 23 - daughter Francesca Paola born, named after paternal
grandmother[641] - baptized Santa Rosalia Favarotta, Terrasini
    93 = 89 = 24 Jan 1871 b yest - Francesca Paola
        - Joannes G & Ignatia Napolitano
    (Godmother Rosaria Randazzo, wife of Salvatore Gusmano)

---

[637]Palermo (Palermo), Ufficio dello stato civile, "Registro degli atti di Matrimonio [Register of Marriages], 1867" : entry #14, Giovanni Gusmano.
[638]Maria Santissima delle Grazie (Chiesa Madre [Mother Church]), Terrasini, Palermo, Sicily, Italy, Baptismal register, v. 28, 1862-1872, p. 114, Joannes Gusmano baptism 1868; *Family Search.org*, " Battesimi 1859-1878," image 264 of 481).
[639]Maria Santissima delle Grazie (Chiesa Madre [Mother Church]), Terrasini, Palermo, Sicily, Italy, Baptismal register, v. 28, 1862-1872, p. 146, Philippus Gusmano baptism 1869; *FamilySearch.org*, "Battesimi 1859-1878," image 298 of 481.
[640]Maria Santissima delle Grazie (Chiesa Madre [Mother Church]), Terrasini, Palermo, Sicily, Italy, Death register, v. ?, 1860-1870, p. 89, Joannes Gusmano death 1869; *Family Search.org*, "Morti 1860-67," image 131 of 159.
[641]Santa Rosalia Favarotta (daughter church), Terrasini, Palermo, Sicily, Italy, Baptismal register v. 25, 1854-1871, p. 89, Francesca Paola Gusmano baptism 1871; *Family Search.org*, "Battesimi 1854-1861," image 93 of 323.

1872 Oct - daughter Rosaria born, named after maternal grandmother[642]
    baptized Maria Santissima delle Grazie, Terrasini
    363 = 204 = 18 Oct 1872 b yest - Rosaria G
        d/o Joannes & Ignatia Napolitano
        (Godfather Vincentius Misuraca)
1874 Nov 11- daughter Grazia born[643]
    baptized Maria Santissima delle Grazie, Terrasini
    102 = 39 = 12 Nov 1874 b yest - Gratia
        - Joannes G & Ignatia Napolitano
        (Godmother Gratia Bommarito, unm d/o Mario)
1876 March 13 - dau Rosaria died[644]
    214 = 93 = 13 March 1876 - Rosaria G, 3
        - Joannes & Ignatia Napolitano
1877 March 8 - son Giovanni born[645]
    baptized Maria Santissima delle Grazie, Terrasini
    155 = 93 = 9 March 1877 b yest - Joannes G
        - Joannes & Ignatia Napolitano
    (Godparents Petrus Bommarito & Antonia Finazzo his wife)
1878 Oct 27 - daughter Rosaria born[646]
    baptized Maria Santissima delle Grazie, Terrasini
    190 = 128 = 28 Oct 1878 - b yest Rosaria
        - Joanne G & Ignatia Napolitano
        (Godmother Anna Orlando, wife of Philip)

---

[642]Maria Santissima delle Grazie (Chiesa Madre [Mother Church]), Terrasini, Palermo, Sicily, Italy, Baptismal register, v. 28, 1862-1872, p. 204, Rosaria Gusmano baptism 1872; *FamilySearch.org*, "Battesimi 1859-1878," image 363 of 481.

[643]Maria Santissima delle Grazie (Chiesa Madre [Mother Church]), Terrasini, Palermo, Sicily, Italy, Baptismal register, v. 30, 1873-1881, p. 39, Gratia Gusmano baptism 1874; *Family Search.org*, "Battesimi 1873-1889," image 102 of 792.

[644]Santa Rosalia Favarotta (daughter church), Terrasini, Palermo, Sicily, Italy, Death register v. 82, 1818-1878, p. 93, Rosaria G death 1876; *Family Search.org*, "Morti 1818-1859," image 214 of 562.

[645]Maria Santissima delle Grazie (Chiesa Madre [Mother Church]), Terrasini, Palermo, Sicily, Italy, Baptismal register, v. 30, 1873-1881, p. 93, Joannes Gusmano baptism 1877; *FamilySearch.org*, "Battesimi 1873-1889," image 155 of 792.

[646]Maria Santissima delle Grazie (Chiesa Madre [Mother Church]), Terrasini, Palermo, Sicily, Italy, Baptismal register, v. 30, 1873-1881, p. 128, Rosaria Gusmano baptism 1878; *FamilySearch.org*, "Battesimi 1873-1889," image 190 of 792.

1880 Dec 11 - son Rosario born[647]
        baptized Maria Santissima delle Grazie, Terrasini
        261 = 188 = 12 Dec 1880 b yest - Rosario
                - Joannes G & Ignatia Napolitano
                (Godfather Antonius La Fata of Joannes)
1881? - daughter Sarah born???? (Death cert, Detroit)[648]
        1950 May 7 - died, Detroit
        Sarra Amore - f w m - b 1881 Italy
        - d 7 May 1950 Detroit - age 69
        f John Cusamano - m Agnes Napolitano
1883 Feb 6 - twins Maria Anna and Catharina born[649]
        baptized Maria Santissima delle Grazie, Terrasini
        414 = 40 = 7 Feb 1883 b yest - Catharina
                - Joanne C & Ignatia Napolitano
                (Joseph Napolitano & Josepha Cammarata his wife)
        414 = 40 = 7 Feb 1883 b yest - Maria Anna
                - d/o Joannes & Ignatia Napolitano
                (Vitus Bommarito, son of Vitus)
1883 Feb 16 - Marianna died[650]
        208 = 144 = 16 Feb 1883 - Marianna G 1m
                - Joannes & Ignatia Napolitano

---

[647]Maria Santissima delle Grazie (Chiesa Madre [Mother Church]), Terrasini, Palermo, Sicily, Italy, Baptismal register, v. 30, 1873-1881, p. 188, Rosario Gusmano baptism 1880; *FamilySearch.org*, "Battesimi 1873-1889," image 261 of 792.

[648]"Michigan, Death Records, 1867-1950," database, *Ancestry.com* (http://ancestry.com: accessed 21 September 2016), entry for Sarra Amore, 7 May 1950 (file no. 409760); Michigan Department of Community Health, Division for Vital Records and Health Statistics, Lansing, Michigan.

[649]Maria Santissima delle Grazie (Chiesa Madre [Mother Church]), Terrasini, Palermo, Sicily, Italy, Baptismal register, v. 31, 1882-1889, p. 40, Catharina & Maria Anna Gusmano baptism 1883; *Family Search.org*, "Battesimi 1873-1889," image 414 of 792.

[650]Maria Santissima delle Grazie, Terrasini, Palermo, Sicily, Italy, Death register, v. 86, 1871-1887, p. 144, Marianna G death 1883; *Family Search.org*, "Morti 1871-1892," image 208 of 476.

1884 Dec 26 - son Giovanni born[651]

    baptized Maria Santissima delle Grazie, Terrasini
    504 = 120 = 120 = 27 Dec 1884 b yest - Joannes
        - Joanne G & Ignatia Napolitano
        (Vincentius Bommarito, son of Antonius)
    24 = # 364 = 27 Dec 1884 b yest - Giovanni C
        - Giovanni C & Ignazia Napolitano

1888 Feb 17 - daughter Marianna born[652]

    baptized Maria Santissima delle Grazie, Terrasini
    682 = 248 = 18 Feb 1888 b yest - Marianna
     d/o Joannes Cusumano & Ignatia Napolitano
        (Victorius La Fata)
    44 = 120 = #57 = 18 Feb 1888 - Maria Anna G
    - Giovanni & Ignatia Napolitano

Nothing further known about him.

1905/08 - son Giovanni emigrated to US

1910 - daughter Marianna emigrated to US

1913 - daughter Marianna m Giacomo (James) Fici in Detroit

1916 - son Giovanni (John) m Catherine Matranga, Detroit

1944 - daughter Marianna Fici d Detroit

1945 - son Giovanni (John) d Detroit

1950 - daughter Sarah? d Detroit

---

[651]Maria Santissima delle Grazie (Chiesa Madre [Mother Church]), Terrasini, Palermo, Sicily, Italy, Baptismal register, v. 31, 1882-1889, p. 120, Joannes Gusmano baptism 1884; *FamilySearch.org*, "Battesimi 1873-1889," image 504 of 792. AND Maria Santissima delle Grazie, Terrasini, Palermo, Sicily, Italy, Baptismal register, v. 32, 1884-1889, record no. 364, Giovanni C baptism 1884; *Family Search.org*, "Battesimi 1884-1887," image 24 of 103.

[652]Maria Santissima delle Grazie (Chiesa Madre [Mother Church]), Terrasini, Palermo, Sicily, Italy, Baptismal register, v. 31, 1882-1889, p. 248, Marianna Gusmano baptism 1888; *FamilySearch.org*, "Battesimi 1873-1889," image 682 of 792. AND Maria Santissima delle Grazie, Terrasini, Palermo, Sicily, Italy, Baptismal register, v. 32 continued?, 1887-1889, p. 120, record no. 57, Maria Anna G baptism 1888; *Family Search.org*, "Battesimi 1887-1889," image 44 of 90.

Children of 6.Giovanni & Ignatia Napolitano

7. Giovanni 1868-1869

7. Filippo 1869

7. Francesca Paola 1871

7. Rosaria 1872-1876

7. Grazia 1874

7. Giovanni 1877

7. Rosaria 1878

7. Rosario 1880

7. Sarah 1881 - to Detroit - only record is the death record

  1950 May 7 - died, Detroit[653]

  Sarra Amore - f w m - b 1881 Italy

  - d 7 May 1950 Detroit - age 69

  f John Cusamano - m Agnes Napolitano

7. Maria Anna 1883-1883

7. Catharina 1883

7. Giovanni 1884 - to Detroit

7. Marianna 1888 - to Detroit

7. Giovanni

1884 Dec 26 - born[654]

  baptized Maria Santissima delle Grazie, Terrasini 504 = 120 = 120 =

27 Dec 1884 b yest - Joannes

   - Joanne G & Ignatia Napolitano

    (Vincentius Bommarito, son of Antonius)

  24 = # 364 = 27 Dec 1884 b yest - Giovanni C

   - Giovanni C & Ignazia Napolitano

  Mi Death records say: 1886 Dec 24 born, Italy

1xxx - emigrated to US

---

[653]"Michigan, Death Records, 1867-1950," database, *Ancestry.com* (http://ancestry.com: accessed 21 September 2016), entry for Sarra Amore, 7 May 1950 (file no. 409760); Michigan Department of Community Health, Division for Vital Records and Health Statistics, Lansing, Michigan.

[654]Maria Santissima delle Grazie (Chiesa Madre [Mother Church]), Terrasini, Palermo, Sicily, Italy, Baptismal register, v. 31, 1882-1889, p. 120, Joannes Gusmano baptism 1884; *FamilySearch.org*, "Battesimi 1873-1889," image 504 of 792.AND Maria Santissima delle Grazie, Terrasini, Palermo, Sicily, Italy, Baptismal register, v. 32, 1884-1889, record no. 364, Giovanni C baptism 1884; *Family Search.org*, "Battesimi 1884-1887," image 24 of 103.

1916 married Caterina (Catherine/Katherine) Matranga[655]
     lic 23 Aug 1916 - Giovanni Cusmano 28 res Det b Ita lab
          f Giovanni m -gnatzia
          Caterina Matranga 18 res Det b Ita f Joseph m -sephina
          marriage 7 Oct 1916 Detroit - John Boschi pastor
          wit Josephine Catalona, Joe Oliva
Detroit City Directories[656]
1917 Cusmano Jno - lab h420 Fort e
1918 Sept 12 - WW I Draft Registration[657]- ser 1110 (1119?) ord 1722
     John Gusmano - 420 Fort - age 34 b 25 Dec 1884
        - non declared alien It
        lathe hand Ford - Highland Park
        wife Catherina Gusmano
        med ht, stout, brown eyes & hair
Detroit City Directories
1918 Cusmano Jno lab h420 Fort e
1919/20 Cusmano Jno - lab. b. 420 Fort E
1919 Aug 26 - dau Agnes born
     (according to Stacey Matranga Family Tree
        - ancestry - accessed 4 Oct 2016)
1920 census, Michigan, Wayne, Detroit SD 145 ED 272 sheet 1b - wd 9 -
420 E Fort[658]
     12-19 Cusmanu, John 34 1908 pa It factory ford motor
        Katherine 28 1901 al
        Agnes 3/12 Mi   T 625-806
Detroit City Directories
1920/21 Cusmano Jno shoemkr 1974 (420) Fort

---

[655]"Michigan Marriage Records, 1867-1952," database, *Ancestry.com* (http://ancestry.com: accessed 19 Sept 2016), entry for Giovanni Cusmano, 1916 (file no. 134987); citing Michigan Department of Community Health, Division for Vital Records and Health Statistics, film no. 131 (1916 Wayne).

[656]R. L. Polk & Co's *Detroit City Directory 1917* (Detroit, MI: R. L. Polk & Co, 1917) p. 739; database with images, *Ancestry.com,* "U.S. City Directories, 1822-1995" (http://www.ancestry.com: accessed 24 September 2016). Also several subsequent directories to 1939.

[657]"U.S. World War I Draft Registration Cards, 1917-1918," database with images, *Ancestry.com* (http://ancestry.com: accessed 15 Oct 2016), card for John Gusmano, serial no. 1110, Draft Board 10, Wayne County, Michigan; imaged from Family History Library microfilm.

[658]1920 U.S. census, Wayne County, Michigan, population schedule, Detroit ward 9, enumeration district (ED)272, sheet 1b dwelling 12, family 19, John Cusmanu; image, *Ancestry.com* (http://ancestry.com: accessed 28 Sept 2016); citing NARA microfilm publication T625, roll 806.

1921/22 Cusmano Jno lab 1974 Fort e
1925/26 Cusmano John lab h2913 Townsend
1927/28 Cusmano John(Kath) lab h2913 Townsend
1928/29 Cusmano John (Kath) autowkr h2943 Townsend
1930 census Mi Wayne Detroit wd 17 SD22 ED82-562 sheet 8a - 2943 Townsend[659]

     106-73 Cusmano John 41 m 27 It 1905 Papers
     - machine operator auto factory
         Katherine 31 m 17 It 1900 al
         Agnes 10 Mi

Detroit City Directories

1930/31 Cusmano John (Cath) lab h2943 Townsend
1931/32 Cusmano John (Cath) mach h2943 Townsend
~1931 - daughter Catherine born
1932/33 Cusmano John (Cath) mach h2943 Townsend
1934 Cusmano John (Kath) asmblr h2943 Townsend
1935 Cusmano John (Cath) lab h2943 Townsend
1939 Cusmano John (Kath) lab h2943 Townsend
1940 census Mi Wayne Det wd 17 SD14 ED84-1077 sh 4a - 2943 Townsnd[660]
107 Cusmano, John 48 It same house punch press operator, auto. corp
         Catherine 41 It / Agnes 20 MI / Josephine 8 MI
1940 Sept 28 - daughter Agnes married Henry Phillips[661]
     Agnes Cusmano age 20 b MI f John m Catherine Matranga
         Henry Phillips age 23 b MI f Henry m Marie de Wilde
         married 28 Sept 1940 - Detroit, Wayne, MI

---

[659] 1930 U.S. census, Wayne County, Michigan, population schedule, Detroit ward 17, enumeration district (ED)82-562, sheet 8a dwelling 106, family 73, John Cusmano; image, *Ancestry.com* (http://ancestry.com: accessed 28 Sept 2016); citing FHL microfilm 2340790; NARA microfilm T626, roll 1055.

[660] 1940 U. S. Census, Wayne County, Michigan, population schedule, Detroit, ward 17, enumeration district (ED) 84-1077, sheet 4a, household 107, John Cusmano [I don't know how it was indexed - I had to browse]; image, *Ancestry.com* (http://ancestry.com: accessed 5 Nov 2016); citing NARA microfilm publication T627, roll 1872.

[661] "Michigan Marriage Records, 1867-1952," database, *Ancestry.com* (http://ancestry.com: accessed 4 October 2016), entry for Agnes Cusmano, 1940 (state file no. 233125, county file no. 548853); citing Michigan Department of Community Health, Division for Vital Records and Health Statistics, film no. 301 (82 Wayne 230250-233529).

1942 Apr 27 - WWII Draft Registration[662] - ser 540
      Giovanni Cusumano - 2943 Townsend - age 57
          b 25 Dec 1884 Terrasini
          contact Joe Bologna 2944 Baldwin   emp Ford Rouge
          5'5" brown eyes brown hair light complex
1945 Aug 17 - died, Detroit[663]
      John Cusmano - m m - b 24 Dec 1886 Italy - age 58
          - d 17 Aug 1945 Detroit
        f John - m Agnes Napolitano
    -Buried Mt Olivet[664]
          John Cusmano Date of Interment: 08/21/1945
              Cemetery: Mt. Olivet Cemetery
            Location: Section 18, Lot 91-G, Space 1
1950 June 7 - widow Catherine m Anthony Palmer[665]
    Anthony Palmer
    Catherine Cusmano 50 res Det b Balestrate It
        f Joseph Matranga m Josephine Abate

---

[662]"U.S. World War II Draft Registration Cards, 1942," database with images, *Ancestry.com* (http://ancestry.com : accessed 16 Oct 2016), card for Giovanni Cusmano, serial no. 540; citing The National Archives at St. Louis, Draft Registration Cards for Fourth Registration for Michigan, 04/27/1942 - 04/27/1942; NAI Number: 623283; Records of the Selective Service System; Record Group Number: 147.

[663]"Michigan Death Records, 1867-1950," database, *Ancestry.com* (http://ancestry.com : accessed 20 Sept 2016), entry for John Cusmano, 17 Aug 1945, no. 340029; citing Michigan Department of Community Health, Division for Vital Records and Health Statistics.

[664]Mt. Elliott Cemetery Association, database, (http://www.mtelliott.com/genealogy/ : accessed 31 August 2016), Mt. Olivet Cemetery (Detroit, Wayne, Michigan), entry for John Cusmano (21 August 1945).

[665]"Michigan Marriage Records, 1867-1952," database, *Ancestry.com* (http://ancestry.com : accessed 4 Oct 2016), entry for Catherine Cusmano, 1950 (state file no. 458844, county file no. 781665); citing Michigan Department of Community Health, Division for Vital Records and Health Statistics, film no. 370 (82 Wayne 456660-459999).

1950 July 1 - daughter Josephine m Ollie Mastronardi[666]
    Ollie Mastronardi
    Josephine Cusmano 19 res Det b Det
    f John m Catherine Matranga
    marriage 1 July 1950

7. Marianna 1888

1888 Feb 17 - born[667] -
baptized Maria Santissima delle Grazie, Terrasini
    682 = 248 = 18 Feb 1888 b yest - Marianna
            Joannes Cusumano & Ignatia Napolitano
                (Victorius La Fata)
    44 = 120 = #57 = 18 Feb 1888 - Maria Anna G
            - Giovanni & Ignatia Napolitano
            Michigan death records say 1888 Feb 26 - born Italy
            (father John, mother Agnes Napolitano)
1910 - to US
1913 Dec 22- married Giacomo Fici[668]
(Register entry) 101449 - Dec 22, 1913
        - Giacomo Fici 25 res Detroit b Italy
                - father Luigi, mother Giuseppa Bondega
        Marianna Cusumano [Ammano] 23 res Detroit b Italy - father
                Giovanni, mother Agnozia [transcribed Syrozia] Napolitano

---

[666]"Michigan Marriage Records, 1867-1952," database, *Ancestry.com*
(http://ancestry.com: accessed 4 Oct 2016), entry for Josephine Cusmano, 1950
(state file no. 462187, county file no. 783773); citing Michigan Department of
Community Health, Division for Vital Records and Health Statistics, film no. 371 (82
Wayne 460000-463299).

[667]Maria Santissima delle Grazie (Chiesa Madre [Mother Church]), Terrasini,
Palermo, Sicily, Italy, Baptismal register, v. 31, 1882-1889, p. 248, Marianna
Gusmano baptism 1888; *FamilySearch.org*, "Battesimi 1873-1889," image 682 of
792. AND Maria Santissima delle Grazie, Terrasini, Palermo, Sicily, Italy, Baptismal
register, v. 32 continued?, 1887-1889, p. 120, record no. 57, Maria Anna G baptism
1888; *Family Search.org*, "Battesimi 1887-1889," image 44 of 90.

[668]"Michigan Marriage Records, 1867-1952," database, *Ancestry.com*
(http://ancestry.com: accessed 19 Sept 2016), entry for Giocomo Fici, 1914 (no.
101449); citing Michigan Department of Community Health, Division for Vital
Records and Health Statistics, film no. 121 (1914 Wayne). AND "Michigan,
Marriage Records, 1867-1953," database with images, Ancestry.com
(http://ancestry.com: accessed 25 Aug 2016), register image, Marianna Cusumano
[indexed Marianna Ammano], Dec 1913, no. 101449; citing Michigan Department of
Community Health, Division for Vital Records and Health Statistics, film 117 (113
Wayne - 1914 Branch).

[index entries: Marianna Rimmario   abt 1889 10 Jan 1914   Detroit
Giocomo Fici - also indexed as Ammano
     - 1914 film says see 1913 - this info is from both entries
lic 22 Dec 1913 - Giocomo Fici 2 It f Luigi m Giuseppa Bonaza
     Mariana Cusumano 25 f Giovanni m Ignazia Napolitan
     marriage 10 Jan 1914 - John Boschi pastor
     wit Frank Caruso, Sam Napolitano
1930 census Mi Wayne Det wd 19 SE 22 ED 82-690 sheet 2b - 8751
Bessemer Ave[669]
42-20 Fici, James mw 45 m age 26 Italy -> em 1912
     - papers applied for - lab street contractor
    Maria 44 m 23 Italy -> em 1910
    Louis son 15 / John 13 / Josephine 12 / Nancy 10 /
    Agnes 8 / Sam 4 ½ - all b MI
1944 Sept 22 - died[670]
file no. 327393- Marianna Ficci f m born Feb 1888 Italy - d 22 Sep 1944
Detroit - age 56 - father John Cusumano - mother Agnes Napolitano file no.
327393   - buried Mt Olivet Section 18, Lot 69-B, Space 2

---

[669] 1930 U.S. census, Wayne County, Michigan, population schedule, Detroit ward 19, enumeration district (ED) 82-690, sheet 2b, dwelling 42, family 20, James Fici; image, *Ancestry.com* (http://ancestry.com: accessed 2 Sept 2016); citing FHL microfilm: 2340795; NARA microfilm publication T626.

[670] "Michigan Death Records,1867-1950," database, *Ancestry.com* (http://ancestry.com: accessed 2 Sept 2016), entry for Marianna Ficci, file no. 327393; citing Michigan Department of Community Health, Division for Vital Records and Health Statistics. Also "Michigan Death Certificates, 1921-1952," *Family Search*, Marianna Ficci.

Family Trees

I haven't created an index for this project (yet) so this is by way of being a substitute. I have condensed it somewhat, often including only the lines that passed through or ended up in Detroit.

Names in bold type are the names people were known by or used most often.

The date in parentheses after the woman's name is the marriage date.

First cousins of Great Grandpa Giovanni

(grandchildren of Giovanni & Francesca Paola Bommarito)
1. Antonio/Andrea ~1562 & Girolama?
0. Lorenzo 1582 & Antonia/Antonella d'Amato
1. Salvatore 1616 -1665   + Margarita di Paci (1652)
2. Angelo (Mr) ~1664-1722 + Francesca Cracciolo (1689-died 1732)
3. Giovanni 1694-1761 + Anna Maria Purpura (1732)
4. Carlo **Francesco Paolo** 1752-1821 + Gaetana Palazzolo (1781)
5. **Giovanni** Vito 1795-1871 + Francesca Paola Bommarito

Descendants of the other Giovanni

www.ingramcontent.com/pod-product-compliance
Lightning Source LLC
Chambersburg PA
CBHW061626250726
48659CB00004B/1098